Living with Precariousness

Living with Precariousness

Edited by
Christina Lee and Susan Leong

BLOOMSBURY ACADEMIC
LONDON • NEW YORK • OXFORD • NEW DELHI • SYDNEY

BLOOMSBURY ACADEMIC
Bloomsbury Publishing Plc, 50 Bedford Square, London, WC1B 3DP, UK
Bloomsbury Publishing Inc, 1359 Broadway, New York, NY 10018, USA
Bloomsbury Publishing Ireland, 29 Earlsfort Terrace, Dublin 2, D02 AY28, Ireland

BLOOMSBURY, BLOOMSBURY ACADEMIC and the Diana logo
are trademarks of Bloomsbury Publishing Plc

First published in Great Britain 2023
Paperback edition published 2026

Series design by Adriana Brioso
Cover image © G.M.B. Akash/Panos Pictures

A catalogue record for this book is available from the British Library.

Library of Congress Cataloging-in-Publication Data
Names: Lee, Christina, 1976- editor. | Leong, Susan (Susan Mee Mee), editor.
Title: Living with precariousness/edited by Christina Lee and Susan Leong.
Description: London; New York: Bloomsbury Academic, 2023. |
Includes bibliographical references and index.
Identifiers: LCCN 2022054979 (print) | LCCN 2022054980 (ebook) | ISBN 9780755639298
(hardback) | ISBN 9780755639335 (paperback) | ISBN 9780755639304 (epub) |
ISBN 9780755639311 (pdf) | ISBN 9780755639328
Subjects: LCSH: Economic security–Social aspects. | Precarious employment–Social
aspects. | Human security–Social aspects.
Classification: LCC HC59.3.L58 2023 (print) | LCC HC59.3 (ebook) |
DDC 339.4/6–dc23/eng/20221119
LC record available at https://lccn.loc.gov/2022054979
LC ebook record available at https://lccn.loc.gov/2022054980

ISBN: HB: 978-0-7556-3929-8
         PB: 978-0-7556-3933-5
         ePDF: 978-0-7556-3931-1
         eBook: 978-0-7556-3930-4

Typeset by Integra Software Services Pvt. Ltd.

For product safety related questions contact productsafety@bloomsbury.com.

To find out more about our authors and books visit www.bloomsbury.com
and sign up for our newsletters.

To Eng Guan and Gerk Hong Lee
And in memory of Chia Yew Kay, beloved mentor and foster father

Contents

Figures

Contributors

Caterina Albano is Reader in Visual Culture and Science at Central Saint Martins, University of the Arts London, UK. She lectures, publishes and curates in the fields of art, cultural history and cultural theory. Caterina is the author of *Out of Breath: Vulnerability of Air in Contemporary Art* (2022), *Memory, Forgetting and the Moving Image* (2016) and *Fear and Art in the Contemporary World* (2012).

Salem Askari is a research assistant at the Centre for Human Rights Education, Curtin University, Australia. Since arriving in Australia in 2013, he has been a passionate advocate for refugees and people seeking asylum in Western Australia. In 2021, Salem won the Judges' Choice Award in the Western Australian Multicultural Awards for his leading role in the Western Australian Refugee and People Seeking Asylum Network.

Kevin Bales, CMG, is Professor of Contemporary Slavery and Research Director at the Rights Lab at the University of Nottingham, UK. In 2001, he co-founded the NGO Free the Slaves, a group that has liberated thousands of slaves worldwide. Kevin's most recent book, *Blood and Earth: Modern Slavery, Ecocide, and the Secret to Saving the World* (2016), explores the deadly link between slavery and environmental destruction.

Ben Beitler is a doctoral candidate in the Department of French at the University of California, Berkeley, USA. He studies representations of environmental struggle in francophone film and literature, with a special interest in conflicts of expertise. His work has appeared in *Paragraph* and *Continuum: Journal of Media and Cultural Studies*.

Anna Branford is a careers educator at RMIT University, Australia. She is an internationally published children's author whose books include the *Violet Mackerel* series, and whose research has been published in the *Australian Journal of Anthropology*. Anna has a PhD in Sociology from La Trobe University.

Sam Carroll-Bell is a doctoral candidate at RMIT University, Australia. His PhD examines the worldviews and knowledge-based constructs of international development workers based in Timor-Leste. He is a founding member of Agile Development Group, a Cambodian development organization specializing in disability and inclusive design, social enterprise development and community-based agricultural programmes. Sam's research has appeared in journals including *Bijdragen tot de Taal-, Land- en Volkenkunde* and *Local Global*.

Alice Driver is a writer from the Ozark Mountains in Arkansas, USA. She is the author of *More or Less Dead: Feminicide, Haunting and the Ethics of Representation in Mexico* (2015) and the translator of *Abecedario de Juárez* (2022). She writes for *The New Yorker, The New York Review of Books* and *Oxford American*. Alice is currently working on the forthcoming books *The Life and Death of the American Worker* (Astra House) and *Artists All Around* (Princeton Architectural Press).

Madeleine Esch is an Associate Professor in the Department of English, Communications and Media at Salve Regina University in Newport, Rhode Island, USA. Her research addresses the intersection of nonfiction entertainment television, ideology and consumerism. Madeleine's most recent publication appears in the edited book *Beyond Princess Culture: Gender and Children's Marketing* (2019).

Caroline Fleay is an Associate Professor and Co-director of the Centre for Human Rights Education, Curtin University, Australia, where she teaches human rights and engages in research and advocacy with people from asylum-seeking backgrounds. She has written extensively about the impacts on people seeking asylum of indefinite detention and living on a temporary visa in the community. Caroline is also a board member of the Refugee Council of Australia and Co-convenor of the Western Australian Refugee and People Seeking Asylum Network.

Diane M. Foley is the founder and President of the James W. Foley Legacy Foundation, which advocates for the freedom of all American hostages and unlawful detainees and promotes journalist safety. The James W. Foley Legacy Foundation was started in 2014, one month after James Foley's public execution by ISIS in Syria. Jim was the oldest of Diane's five children. Before her non-profit work, Diane was a family nurse practitioner. She received both her undergraduate and graduate degrees in nursing from the University of New Hampshire, USA.

Helen Fordham is an Associate Professor in Media and Communication at the University of Western Australia, Australia. She is the author of *George Seldes' War for the Public Good: Weaponising a Free Press* (2019). Helen's research into public intellectualism, journalism history, media representation and Indigenous memoir focuses on exposing subordinated narratives that open up the possibility of change.

Alexandra Halkias is a Professor in the Department of Sociology at Panteion University in Athens, Greece, and Visiting Professor at the Media Discourse Centre of De Montfort University, Leicester, UK. She is the author of *Gendered Violences* (in Greek, 2011) and *The Empty Cradle of Democracy: Sex, Abortion, and Nationalism in Modern Greece* (2004), and editor or co-editor of several books including *Nation and Gender in Crisis* (2022) and *LGBTQ Politics in Greece* (2012). Alexandra's present research focuses on critical relationalities and the politics of vision, as well as gendered subjectivities in crisis and the role of nationalism and masculinities.

Shona Illingworth is an artist and Professor in Art, Film and Media at the University of Kent, UK. She has presented solo exhibitions nationally and internationally, including at The Power Plant (Toronto), FACT (Liverpool) and UNSW Galleries (Sydney); and participated in group exhibitions at the Wellcome Collection and Imperial War Museum (London), Museum of Modern Art (Bologna) and Akbank Sanat (Istanbul). A monograph on her work, *Shona Illingworth: Topologies of Air*, was published in 2022.

Christina Lee is a Senior Lecturer in English and Cultural Studies at Curtin University, Australia. She is the author of *Screening Generation X: The Politics and Popular Memory of Youth in Contemporary Cinema* (2010); editor of *Violating Time: History, Memory, and Nostalgia in Cinema* (2008) and *Spectral Spaces and Hauntings: The Affects of Absence* (2017); and co-editor of *Screen Tourism and Affective Landscapes: The Real, the Virtual, and the Cinematic* (2023). Christina's areas of research include cultural memory, spaces of spectrality and imagination, fandom and popular culture.

Julian C. H. Lee is an Associate Professor in Global Studies at RMIT University, Australia. His books include *Monsters of Modernity* (co-author, 2019) and the edited volume *Narratives of Globalization: Reflections on the Global Condition* (2016).

Susan Leong is Honorary Senior Research Fellow in the School of Arts and Humanities, Edith Cowan University, Australia. She is the author of *New Media and the Nation in Malaysia: Malaysianet* (2013), and co-author of *Global Internet Governance: Influences from Malaysia and Singapore* (2020) and *China's Digital Presence in the Asia-Pacific: Culture, Technology and Platforms* (2020). Susan's research centres on the intersections between technologies and societies, and includes work on diasporas, social imaginaries and digital Southeast Asia.

Julie Macken is a PhD candidate at Western Sydney University, Australia. Her research critically explores the treatment of refugees in Australia. She is a former senior writer with the *Australian Financial Review* and has worked as a political and media consultant, writing extensively on refugees, climate change, economics, human rights and political power.

Aya Ono is an independent academic based in Tokyo, Japan. Her research is interdisciplinary in nature and themes range from impact investing to care work migration. Her most recent publication is on Social Impact Investment in *Encyclopedia of the UN Sustainable Development Goals: Partnerships for the Goals* (2021). She is also a co-founder of Peace Palette, a community-based, peace-building NGO in South Sudan.

Kaye Quek is a Senior Lecturer in Global Studies at RMIT University, Australia. She is the author of *Marriage Trafficking: Women in Forced Wedlock* (2018). She has published in journals such as *Women's Studies International Forum* and *British Journal of Politics and International Relations*. Kaye is a member of the Coalition Against Trafficking in Women Australia, an organization that works to end sexual exploitation in all its forms.

Alicia Rana works in the social care sector and is a campaigner against modern-day slavery who is based in the South East of the UK. She has a particular interest in the recovery processes afforded to ethnic and minority communities within the governmental and social systems that should be supporting survivors of human trafficking. Alicia's personal experiences within that space support her work to bring awareness to the wider issue.

Sonia M. Tascón is a researcher and academic who works across the Schools of Media, Creative Arts and Social Inquiry and Allied Health at Curtin University, Australia. She has authored and edited several books, including

Visual Communication for Social Work Practice: Power, Culture, Analysis (2018), *Human Rights Film Festivals: Activism in Context* (2015) and, as co-editor, *Disrupting Whiteness in Social Work* (2020). Sonia's main areas of publication have been on the geopolitics of race, whiteness and post-colonialism, alongside human rights, refugee rights and the ethics of the other, as well as in film festival studies.

John Tulloch is Professor Emeritus in Media and Communication at Charles Sturt University and Adjunct Professor at the University of Newcastle, both in New South Wales, Australia. A history, sociology, media and cultural studies scholar, John has published over twenty books. Since he became a close-up victim of the 7 July 2005 terrorist attack on London, he has published a number of books focusing on images, icons and representations of risk across traditional and emergent media. Titles include *One Day in July: Experiencing 7/7* (2006) and, as co-author, *Icons of War and Terror: Media Images in an Age of International Risk* (2012) and *Risk and Hyperconnectivity: Media and Memories of Neoliberalism* (2016).

Acknowledgements

This book grew from an idea we had in 2016. Since then, worlds have been turned upside down, globally and at the level of the individual. For many of us, as we were thinking and writing about living with precariousness, we, too, were experiencing it. The confronting nature of precariousness and vulnerability can shake our very foundations; at the very least we are made deeply uncomfortable. But it can also shed light on how we endure those difficult moments, and can come out of them with different ways of thinking, seeing and feeling that allow us to live fully again. The editors wish to thank the authors who so generously shared their stories and insights in this book: Diane Foley, Julian Lee, Anna Branford, Sam Carroll-Bell, Aya Ono, Kaye Quek, Salem Askari, Caroline Fleay, Madeleine Esch, Ben Beitler, Julie Macken, Sonia Tascón, Alice Driver, Helen Fordham, Alicia Rana, Kevin Bales, Shona Illingworth, John Tulloch, Caterina Albano and Alexandra Halkias. It was an honour to work with you all.

Thanks go to Anne Allison for penning the Foreword to this book, whose own research on precariousness helped sow the seed for this project. And to Manu Brabo, *muchas gracias* for your generous spirit and for allowing us to use your photograph that captured precarious lives in a single frame.

We are incredibly grateful to the editorial staff at I.B. Tauris and Bloomsbury – Nayiri Kendir, Atifa Jiwa, Tomasz Hoskins and Katie Gallof – who took a leap of faith on the book concept, and helped us see it to completion. Thank you to Deborah Maloney and the Integra team, as well as Daphne Lawless, for getting us to the finish line. We thank the School of Media, Creative Arts and Social Inquiry at Curtin University, the School of Arts and Humanities at Edith Cowan University, and the School of Arts and Social Sciences at Monash University Malaysia for their support, as well as everyone who presented and participated in the *Precarious Times* symposium in 2016. The spirited debates reinforced that there was much more work to be done on the subject. Special mentions go to Rachel Robertson, Baden Offord and Suvendrini Perera, who were there from the beginning; and to Philippa Freegard for her ever-sharp copyediting skills.

Christina would like to thank her family – Eng Guan and Gerk Hong, Josephine, Jason, and little Olivia and Elijah – for their love, support and patience, even if they didn't always get what she was up to when she disappeared for long stretches to do 'book stuff'. Every academic needs sounding boards and soft landings, as well as distractions. Heartfelt thanks go to friends who were more than happy to oblige on one or all of these things: Suzy Galloway, Kirsten Hudson, Kerry James, Sook Kuan Chew, Pamela Kerpius, Ann McGuire, Serena McClellan, Russell Bishop, Anne Renucci, Damon Young, Adrianna Jankowiak, Yvonne Lewis and the JLC – Caroline Ng, Melissa Loh and Sarah Soon.

Susan would like to thank her family, Silverius, Claire, Sara and Elsie (1939–2018). To all the friends and colleagues: Emma Baulch, Terence Lee, Elaine Tay, Denise Woods, Thor Kerr, Kai-Ti Kao, Pat Chua, Anna Haebich and Helen Nesadurai; it is their interest and encouragement that sustained this project and made this book possible. Finally, two groups of people are owed special gratitude because without them the new direction in Susan's research would not have been possible: the symposium discussants whose conversations animated the stories told and the scholars, Anne Allison, Kathleen Stewart and Anna Tsing, whose works showed how the telling could be. Thank you.

Foreword

Anne Allison

As the editors of this wonderful volume point out, precariousness is nothing new in human existence. Our entanglement within multiple vulnerabilities goes back to time immemorial for all living entities including humans. And yet there is something quite particular about the contemporary moment when, as the editors write in the Introduction, 'for the majority of the middling masses today, precariousness has gained a newfound and everyday prominence'. Attentive to how 'a thin line separates us from crisis', it is not only the struggle to survive in times of climatic apocalypse, economic turmoil, housing and food insecuritization, and a yet-to-be-abated global pandemic that is challenging, but also the need and desire to cling to something along the way. The attachments we make, the hopes and aspirations that kindle the imagination, the everyday routines that anchor us – all of this can keep us going but also be a strain to keep up. How, then, do we maintain what Baruch Spinoza considered to be the basis of ethical life: continuing to feed whatever it is that increases the body's power to act?[1] To do so requires a modicum of surety about temporal horizons (the reason Spinoza didn't place much stock in hope, pinned as it is to a future whose outcome is in doubt) which is tremendously illusive today in times almost universally characterized as uncertain.[2]

Venturing into this terrain of considering how people actually live with threats to their livelihood, all the while forging patterns and paths that juggle the 'compounding of precarity' (Askari and Fleay) with what can be innovativeness (Esch) or even optimism of a 'reality-based' sort (Lee, Branford, Carroll-Bell, Ono and Quek), is what I see as the critically important contribution made by this volume. Coming at this from a diverse range of perspectives, backgrounds and cases – of both individual and collective trauma, and circumstances encompassing warfare, migration, sexuality, ethnicity, climate, academia, housing, mobility and citizenship – the authors are deft in an approach targeted more at strategies for living with precariousness than with political or psychic cures. In Susan Leong's keen observation in the opening chapter, precariousness has become ongoingly banal: a state that one doesn't climb out of any time soon, and perhaps never at all. To live, then, *with* precariousness may require tweaking one's imagination – readjusting ambitions, dreams, the lineaments of belonging. Something akin to, but rather different from, cultural theorist Lauren Berlant's notion of 'cruel optimism' where one remains attached to objects/persons/ pursuits that obstruct flourishing in life.[3] 'Nearly normal/nearly utopian' is what having a steady job means to the precariat protagonists Berlant examines in two films by the Dardennes brothers.[4] But, for them, this is a prospect forever littered with disappointment and despair. Might not 'living with precariousness' entail something rather different then? Letting go, perhaps, of one's attachment to the normal/normative, as in what Kathleen Millar discovers with *catadores* (garbage pickers) in Brazil in her book *Reclaiming the Discarded*, who find the flexibility, autonomy and ready-cash of this stigmatized work a good fit with lives that are always/already precarious.[5] So, too, with Leong who steps away from the grind of an academic career in order to prioritize the health and joy of life she can now more slowly enjoy. Perhaps it involves reassessing what we attach to, and how we can better live, despite the 'banal precariousness' of it all.

But, as Madeleine Esch warns us, precariousness is also a marketing opportunity, one in which clever new lifestyling designs aimed at reducing suffering and discomfort may be insinuated within the very socio-economic forms that contributed to this in the first place. This is exemplified by the Tiny House movement in the USA that, triggered by the shocking rise in rental and real estate costs and the accompanying spike in evictions and homelessness, markets downsized homes that are at once mobile, fashionable and cute. Even when more affordable than the going price of high-end urban property these days, such homes are still premised on the notion of a self-contained social (family) unit that acquires, and maintains, such a residence through private ownership. This very logic wounds, and precaritizes, so many lacking the jobs, financial resources, or intimate relationships to manage the upkeep of such a home, seen, even in the Tiny Home iteration, as a badge of social capital. To foster something more inclusive demands reconstructing what we imagine to be the measure, and means, of wellbeing in the first place. Maybe not a private home, but a commons more communally shared. This is what the feminist Care Collective has recently called for in their manifesto arguing that homes, built as dwellings for nuclear families, both extract and rely upon the unpaid labour of private members (disproportionately women) to care for the aged/children/diseased/vulnerable in society.[6] Far more equitable would be to cultivate what they call 'promiscuous care' to tend to any/everyone through such non-family-based infrastructures as basic income, universal health support, free childcare and affordable housing.

Living with precariousness would seem to beg for promiscuity in the sense not of random indiscrimination, but of opening up the horizons, strategies and connections for getting by in a world straddled by uncertainty and crisis. How precisely to do this, with what affects and effects for those involved, are issues that the authors of *Living with Precariousness* take up with smarts, sensitivity and soul.

Notes

1   Benedict de Spinoza, *Ethics*, ed. and trans. Edwin Curley (USA: Penguin Books, 1996).

2   Marc Abélès, *The Politics of Survival*, trans. Julie Kleinman (Durham, NC: Duke University Press, 2010); Anna Lowenhaupt Tsing, *The Mushroom at the End of the World: On the Possibility of Life in Capitalist Ruins* (Princeton, NJ: Princeton University Press, 2015); David Theo Goldberg, *Dread: Facing Futureless Futures* (Cambridge: Polity Press, 2021).

3   Lauren Berlant, *Cruel Optimism* (Durham, NC: Duke University Press, 2011).

4   Lauren Berlant, 'Nearly utopian, nearly normal: post-Fordist affect in *La Promesse* and *Rosetta*', *Public Culture* 19, no. 2 (2007): 273–301.

5   Kathleen Millar, *Reclaiming the Discarded: Life and Labor on Rio's Garbage Dump* (Durham, NC: Duke University Press, 2018).

6   The Care Collective (Andreas Chatzidakis, Jamie Hakim, Jo Littler, Catherine Rottenberg and Lynne Segal), *The Care Manifesto: The Politics of Interdependence* (London: Verso, 2020).

Introduction: Living with Precariousness

Christina Lee and Susan Leong

As fatality and caseload numbers from COVID-19 continued to dominate headlines in January 2022, a news story – one easily missed by international readers – appeared in several online news sites. It told of the death of Yao Pan Ma, a 61-year-old Chinese-American immigrant who passed away on New Year's Eve in 2021 in New York. He was the victim of an unprovoked violent assault in East Harlem on 23 April, targeted because of his ethnicity. Ma had been collecting cans to make money to support his family after the Chinese restaurant where he worked as a kitchen helper/cook closed in March 2020 when the city went into lockdown.[1] His attacker, a homeless man who had been in and out of the prison system, left him for dead on the sidewalk. Ma would die eight months later, having been put into a medically induced coma after sustaining severe injuries.

Ma's untimely passing brought into sharp relief the painfully real effects of living with precariousness during the pandemic. A husband and father loses his means of income because of state-mandated restrictions, which forces both him and his wife (who, too, has lost her job) into scavenging for recyclables to make ends meet. At the same time, amid growing frustration, anger, misinformation and politically-charged fearmongering surrounding the purported source of the virus, there is a rise in hate crimes against Asians in the West. Cause and effect seem straightforward here, and the event apparently an isolated case. However, the woeful circumstances that resulted in Ma's death are part of a much larger, complex story that precedes and will endure long after the pandemic. If anything, COVID-19 merely revealed and intensified the gaps in support and critical system failures that were already there, for instance, contingent employment, poverty, racism, and discrimination, to which many had previously averted their gaze.

Ma and his family were living in one of the world's wealthiest nations when he died. Yet there was little, if any, government assistance during their time of need. Having migrated from China to the United States of America with his wife in October 2018, when the pandemic hit Ma 'hadn't worked long enough to qualify for unemployment benefits'.[2] Despite being a trained dim sum pastry chef, he would face a similar plight to that of many new immigrants who encounter systems and structures that disadvantage them, in a society that often treats people from non-western countries as second-class citizens whose skills and contributions are devalued. Had the Ma family arrived even a year or so earlier, they might have been more established and better placed to gain access to financial support. Or if they had moved to a smaller city, their plight might not have been as easily anonymized. If Ma had been a trained nurse or bus driver rather than a chef, he may not have become unemployed as quickly. Finally, had Ma appeared to be of any but East Asian descent he might have escaped the ire of his assailant, himself a victim of misinformation and the lack of aid. Some would call it fate or bad fortune. What we see is an entanglement of multiple vulnerabilities here – an overlap of conditions that engender and reproduce precariousness, spaces that ensue from and encapsulate precariousness, and soft, human bodies needful of sustenance, coloured by prejudice and open to injury. How did such conditions come to prevail? What makes these spaces perilous? Are certain bodies more precarious than others, or are we all equally so?

We first broached the idea of 'living with precariousness' in 2016. It was a different era when we organized the *Precarious Times* symposium in Perth, Western Australia (where both editors live) to which we invited international and national speakers, including anthropologist Anne Allison whose work on precarity in Japan had been influential in the conception of the event's key theme. The panellists broached a diversity of topics, such as precarious memories, living and dying alone, haunted futurities, physical and social displacement, and the precariousness itself of re-presenting trauma, illness and disability in art and writing. Concurrently, another issue – the less-than-certain nature of our livelihoods in the university sector – became apparent during the sessions and coffee-break conversations. In some instances, it would surface as a Freudian slip, and in others it would occupy centre stage. Regardless of institution and country, there was a general consensus that the corridors of academia were groaning under the pincer pressures of shrinking budgets and bloated deficits, while teaching, research and outreach duties were being crammed into fewer hours and staffed by those on temporary and untenable terms. Insecurity of employment was the lament and we, the new precariat, were convinced that liberal capitalism was the culprit. Even so, beyond the symposium and our shared professional experiences, we had inklings that precariousness was affecting the world more widely than was recognized then.

The realization of precariousness as a common experience – as a shared condition and state of being – became the lynchpin of the book you hold in your hands. If precariousness is a banal part of life today – or to borrow from Allison, a 'general existential state' – we reason that accounts of its experience must also represent this breadth in scope, voice and language.[3] Hence, we invited mothers, journalists, human rights activists, scholars, teachers and survivors to share their stories with us. Rather than treat attempts to live with precariousness as isolated and individual exceptions, we reckoned that a book such as this would help us to see how others live with precariousness as akin to our own conditions of life.

Such a broadening of view called for a less narrow understanding of the term 'precariousness' than is accepted by academia. Already during the symposium there was insistence that the distinctions between 'precarious', 'precarity' and 'precariousness' imposed for theoretical explorations be rigidly retained because of their specific applications and associated meanings in different disciplines. There are some who are adamant that Judith Butler's post-9/11 discussion of precarious lives, as important reminders of our ethical stance on why some lives are regarded as less 'grievable' and 'livable', and her particular use of precarity be main frames of reference.[4] Others, like Franco 'Bifo' Berardi and Guy Standing, who have based their study of precariousness on labour issues and insecure employment, prefer the terms precariat and precarity.[5] In the field of anthropology, Kathleen Stewart seeks to understand and write of the precarious as affect, while Allison applies the term precarious to describe the erosion of familial and communal structures in Japanese society.[6]

It is not our intention to detract from the work of colleagues, but we propose that when an idea such as precariousness enters into everyday perception it inevitably loses some of its theoretical acuity. Strive as we might, life is never as neat as theorizations make it out to be. To delve fully into its affects we include older and other terms, like 'risk', 'un/certainty', 'insecurity' and 'disenchantment', that have been used to describe that feeling of deep-seated malaise we associate with 'living with precariousness'.[7] The nuances in these terms help convey the manifold ways precariousness can materialize and be articulated.[8] As the chapters in the book demonstrate, the entangled connections with other agents – human and non-human – that put us at risk are also the connections which make living with precariousness endurable. While the limits of book length make it impossible to address all forms of precariousness, we hope you see our point and the significance of our present endeavour.

Precariousness is not a new human experience. The unvarnished truth is that the poor, the marginalized, the displaced and the outsiders have lived on the edge throughout millennia. The millions who continue to flee their homes in search of refuge, and those forced to deny and disavow their identity and beliefs in exchange for survival testify to that. Lately, awareness of human vulnerability has been accentuated by the global spread of the SARS-CoV-2 virus. The prolonged pandemic, the emergence of variants and the corresponding countermeasures of lockdowns, restrictions, quarantine, vaccinations and masks since 2020 serve as ever-present reminders of how exposed humans are to upheavals over which we have weak to no control. Similarly, dire warnings of the Anthropocene and threats of the Earth's impending sixth mass extinction have schoolchildren out on the streets in protests while governments fiddle with carbon offsets and emission standards.[9] The life phase of this book – beginning as a particularly chaotic American administration rose to power, and ending as Russia invaded Ukraine – is a reminder that the freedoms and liberty of life must be continually fought for, impermanent as they are.[10] These are uncertain, troubling times where, to paraphrase Lauren Berlant, the optimism that drives individuals to expect progress toward the good life (financial stability, upward mobility, social and political equality, and so forth) are too cruel, because for too many the good life is not attainable.[11] How can human life continue to thrive, poised knowingly, as it were, on the brink of failure and disaster?

Urgent action is required. To stand by and watch while island nations sink below sea level and COVID-19 sufferers line hospital corridors would be indefensible. We do not trivialize these developments, but we aver that the turmoil experienced is not unprecedented. World-shattering changes have occurred in human societies before, for example, in previous centuries when the world proved not to be flat or when perceptions of traditional hierarchies in feudal societies were upset. Today, we see some of these as scientific and philosophical advancements. Nonetheless, the shift in worldviews demanded of those who lived through such changes must have been as turbulent, if not more so, an experience for those people as climate change and the pandemic is for us presently.

It is no overstatement to say that for the majority of the middling masses today, precariousness has gained a newfound and everyday prominence. There is an unsettling attentiveness to how thin a line separates us from crisis. A permanent job that has been made 'surplus to requirement', the unexpected diagnosis of a life-threatening illness, nature's unending cycles no longer a guarantee. As the natural historian Sir David Attenborough cautions in the documentary *Our Planet*: 'For the first time in human history, the stability of nature can no longer be taken for granted.'[12] To be clear, we do not claim the polysyllabic word 'precariousness' to be on the tip of everyone's tongue. Rather, what is different now is how accustomed we are to the visceral knot of precariousness, which has become an indelible part of our social imaginaries. Deprived of the stable foundations on which we have come to depend and expect, we might well ask, alongside philosopher Ludwig Wittgenstein, 'What can I rely on?'[13]

The struggle to find stable mooring amid a world in flux is an old battle. We want to redeem that labour by recasting precariousness as a shared reference of our time, as the authors in this volume have done. In widening the scope of precariousness and drawing on its antecedents as well as its emergent variants, we want to: (1) draw lessons from those who are coping with, resisting and have survived the harshness of precarious lives; (2) remind ourselves that however many times we hear it uttered in the media, these are not unprecedented times; and (3) recognize that we are not alone. Such an exercise attempts to reclaim the potential inherent in living with precariousness from the damage it can wreak.

The chapters

The subjects in this book run the gamut from manifestations of precariousness at a macro-level (global, national) to the micro-level. They span the impacts of global warming and the effects of neoliberalism on economies and social life, and include individual experiences of coping with illness, discrimination and the constant fear of threat to one's own life and those of loved ones. To bring some order to our endeavour, the book is divided into three parts: Precarious Conditions, Precarious Spaces, and Precarious Bodies. At the same time, and as Ma's death tragically illustrates, we recognize that none of these parts work in isolation and that they are entwined. Our reason for this organization is to draw attention to broader contexts that produce conditions and sites of precariousness, as well as personal, embodied experiences of vulnerability. The question of how we experience these different aspects of precariousness, live through them and learn from them animates and informs the chapters that follow. The goal of this book is to identify and think through precariousness as a defining experience in contemporary society that can be extended to, and yield insights on, issues beyond those surveyed in this volume.

In Chapter 1, Susan Leong takes her cue from scholars Brett Neilson and Ned Rossiter and attempts to pin down that third, unstable position of precarity as experience, within the continuum between theory and practice.[14] Leong sees this as a mode of experience she labels 'banal precariousness'. The adjective 'banal' is used here to denote the opposite of exotic. Leong argues that precariousness is banal because it is a chronic rather than acute condition of living. Nonetheless, being accustomed to precariousness does not lessen its impact nor detract from how it wears us down. The author's ficto-criticism approach explores the uncertainties and instability in current labour practices, the socio-economic challenges faced by migrants and how a change in one's employment, coupled with the effects of age and mental illness, can make 'partial persons' of us all. Through a combination of vignettes, interviews and reflections drawn from fieldwork, encounters, media discourses and policies in Malaysia, Singapore and Australia, the chapter unpacks and locates the idea of banal precariousness, and models it as an approach for comprehending precariousness as part of everyday life.

Kidnapped by ISIS in northern Syria while covering the Arab Spring in 2012, American conflict journalist James W. Foley was held hostage for almost two years before being publicly beheaded. This final act of barbarism was recorded and uploaded online by his captors in August 2014. Chapter 2, however, is less about Jim's untimely death than it is about his life's work to tell the truth and fight for freedom in the face of extreme risk. In this chapter, Diane Foley – Jim's mother – shares a personal account of her son's commitment to bear witness to atrocities in order to tell those stories to the rest of the world and give voice to the Syrian peoples' suffering. At the same time, she lays bare the precariousness of freelance journalism in conflict zones, from the mortal danger of reporting from the frontline to the prosaic worries associated with unstable employment. The Foley family, too, would encounter innumerable hardships and obstacles in their pursuits to find Jim and bring him back home safely, including a government unwilling to negotiate with terrorists. But even in the face of despair and grief, what emerges from this chapter is the need for moral courage during the darkest of hours.

In Chapter 3, Julian Lee, Anna Branford, Sam Carroll-Bell, Aya Ono and Kaye Quek argue that we are in 'pre-carious' times, where the present is full of signs that our future is inevitably carious and decayed. From the slow erosion of clear career pathways to the sweeping effects of environmental destruction, there seems to be a prevailing air of hopelessness as to our collective capacity to address the challenges of our time. This hopelessness largely stems from the lack of viable actions people can participate in. In outlining the intractability of the current situation, the authors seek ways of cultivating an empowering, reality-based optimism. It is an endeavour that is especially urgent in their profession of teaching young people at universities. The authors draw on philosophical works and their own pedagogical practices to propose different approaches for tackling social challenges. Importantly, the chapter incorporates the experiences and views of students who are, against the grain of widespread negativity, actively sowing the seeds of thoughtful optimism to effect positive change, and to remain buoyant in a pre-carious present.

In Chapter 4, Salem Askari and Caroline Fleay discuss the plight of asylum seekers who arrived in Australia via irregular means, and whose lives continue to be held in a state of limbo. Even after escaping violence and war in their home countries, life does not automatically settle into one devoid of precarity post-arrival to this island nation. Cruelly, this is by institutional design. In an effort to deter and punish unauthorized entries, successive governments in Australia have implemented punitive policies and regulations that have had corrosive effects on individuals and communities. Askari and Fleay explore the concept of compounding precarity in relation to the barriers faced by individuals when seeking employment, and their denied right to be reunited with immediate family members. This chapter draws attention to the profound suffering and psychological effects that arise from the uncertain immigration status of those seeking asylum. The authors draw directly from the first-hand experiences of those who have made the perilous voyage across oceans, only to be thrust into another uncertain existence at the final destination.

In Chapter 5, Christina Lee explores the 'ghost city' phenomenon in China that has become a symbol of the nation's aggressive mass urbanization and modernization in the western imagination. These newly built cities are distinctive for their haunting over-presence of empty spaces and under-presence of humans. Focusing on Ordos Kangbashi in the Inner Mongolia Autonomous Zone, Lee explores the various manifestations of precariousness that beset the city. At one end of the spectrum are the inherent risks of city-building master plans that depend on favourable conditions of a fickle global market and the unquestioning belief in the virtue of untrammelled progress. At the other, the city exemplifies the problematic erasure of the lived experiences of those who have built a life in this seemingly unhomely place, an erasure that creates a representational void which speaks only of loss, failure and haunted futures. Employing an autoethnographic and psychogeographic approach, the author contemplates how the intersection of local histories and the embodied experience of the city can cultivate a new capacity and openness to seeing other ways of *being* in a place and, thus, a re-thinking of what constitutes 'home'.

In Chapter 6, Madeleine Esch examines the Tiny House concept that has become a permanent fixture in the property-themed media landscape. Typically under 37 square metres (400 square feet) and often built upon wheeled trailers, these compact structures are admired for their small footprints, cost-effectiveness, portability and innovative designs. Esch analyses their media depictions in television series, documentaries and news reports to understand how these homes are rhetorically constructed as responses to financial precarity, and how this discourse is simultaneously resisted through an emphasis on freedom and choice. Fetishization of the Tiny House and its cute aesthetics work to assuage wider anxieties about challenges to affordable housing that are rarely given screen time. The author situates these celebratory representations of the Tiny House in relation to their use to combat the chronic urban homelessness throughout the United States. As a novel response to the instability of employment and a national housing crisis, Esch asks: how ought we to understand the nascent, contested Tiny House movement? And how might these tiny dwellings make us fundamentally re-evaluate what is 'the good life'?

In Chapter 7, Ben Beitler explores how telling a story about precarity draws our attention to vulnerable bodies at the same time as it exposes the politics of that representation. Beitler considers what it might mean to think about climate change in terms of interdependent bodies, through a comparison of two representations of environmental destruction: the nature documentary *Our Planet*, and Amitav Ghosh's novel *The Hungry Tide*. Side by side, these works are remarkable for the different sorts of environmental precarity they suppress or reveal. One captures the richness of life in diverse bioregions, and the threats to it due to climate change; this representation is dependent on making invisible the long history of colonial violence that has contributed to the present situation. The other experiments with representations of networks of bodies that would have us re-think how we come to know and experience the world, and what it means to live in this world with others on whom we rely for survival. This chapter ponders what an embodied representation of climate change might look like, and the politics that would motivate its creation.

In Chapter 8, Julie Macken and Sonia Tascón focus on two recent events in Australia that exposed the interconnectedness of its citizens and prompted collective responses for survival. The first was the devastating bushfire season dubbed the Black Summer that burned from mid-2019 to March 2020 on the east coast; the second, the spread of COVID-19 throughout the nation's population. As one petered out, the other gathered momentum. Both would test the limits of a neoliberal mindset that had fostered an 'every person for themselves' mentality, and would be forceful reminders of the essential function of public life and the common good. As Macken and Tascón show, at the centre of the fires and pandemic were community, connectedness and vulnerability – three things the neoliberal ideology cannot tolerate. The authors ask whether these events, and the pushback of a growing precariat class, offer a glimpse of the galvanizing potential of a new narrative of radical interdependency that rests on cooperation and care.

In Chapter 9, journalist Alice Driver documents the journey of Marfil Estrella Pérez Méndoza, a trans woman from El Salvador, as she seeks asylum in the United States. Marfil Estrella's life story is one of discrimination and violence that begins from an early age, initially at the hands of her own family, friends and community, and then the exploitative sex trade. A recurring theme is the abject breakdown of social structures and institutions that should have protected her. Tragically, such accounts are all too common for trans women in the Americas. This group is so dehumanized in society that intolerance leads to physical and social punishment, which often escalates to attempted annihilation. Marfil Estrella's and her friends' desperate attempts to transition (often via medically unsound ways) and cross national borders to find safety can be read as metaphors for the fraught journeys of trans women seeking to find acceptance and a home, within their own bodies and within the world. This chapter captures the dangers to one of the most marginalized groups in the Americas, for whom the human right to safety and freedom means, first and foremost, the right to exist.

In Chapter 10, Helen Fordham explores how precariousness affects both the quality of life of populations and the agency of individuals, through recounting the experience of placing her mother into residential aged care. As she witnesses her mother's increasing physical and mental vulnerability, what also becomes evident are the broader systems, processes, and cultural and political discourses that constitute her mother's life as marginal and manageable, and shape her options and choices as an aging citizen with cognitive decline. This chapter renders visible aspects of the findings of the 2021 Royal Commission into Aged Care Quality and Safety in Australia, which concluded that many elderly Australians have their human rights, dignity, agency and identity ignored by the systems of care designed to protect them. Drawing upon Butler's theory of precariousness, Fordham proposes that even as these systems limit the lives of the elderly, aged care settings can also serve as sites for a relational ontology of ethics and a re-imagining of equality based upon a recognition that humans are socially interdependent, and that all of life is precarious.

In Chapter 11, Alicia Rana and Kevin Bales illuminate the intersecting layers of precariousness arising from the lived experience of enslavement. Despite the severity of this crime, there is still confusion at global and local levels as to what the fundamental nature and causation of slavery is. This is evident in the dangerous lack of understanding of enslavement that has contributed to the problematic misidentification of the crime, its victims and perpetrators, not just by the public but also law enforcement agencies and other institutions. Focusing on modern slavery in the United Kingdom, Rana and Bales elucidate how being rescued from enslavement does not guarantee security, but can lead to another largely unrecognized, precarious reality – one without adequate access to health services, safe shelter, employment, education opportunities – and the increased likelihood of re-exploitation. Collaborating with a slavery survivor in the UK (the anonymous third author), this chapter is exemplary of the shift towards survivor-led research whereby listening to the voices of those with first-hand knowledge of slavery can inform meaningful change on the long road to freedom.

In Chapter 12, Shona Illingworth, John Tulloch and Caterina Albano reflect on the film *216 Westbound* and the experience of post-traumatic stress disorder. *216 Westbound* was created by artist Illingworth in collaboration with Tulloch, who is a survivor of the 7/7 London bombings in 2005. Tulloch was travelling on the Circle Line train and seated less than two metres away from Mohammed Sidique Khan when Khan detonated the explosive that killed seven (including the bomber) and injured many others. The authors explore embodied trauma – based on Tulloch's account of disorienting sensations of 'assembling and disassembling' – and how this trauma extended to the outside world. The shock waves of the blast would reverberate far beyond the crime scene. This would be seen in the images of the aftermath that were disseminated and exploited by the global media, and the British government's forceful response to re-establish order that entailed the submission of every individual to extreme state controls. Working across sound, image and film transcripts, the authors discuss the latent threat and fear that had, like the glass fragments deeply embedded in Tulloch's flesh, become lodged in the public and political imaginary, and continue to be felt today.

The final chapter looks at the strangeness of life brought on by COVID-19. Alexandra Halkias tracks several key moments in everyday scenes that register as 'small explosions' at an individual level. Articulations of embodied precarity in this 'new normal' can be seen in minor-but-significant actions and realizations: the now-expected practice of mask-wearing, modifications in the way we communicate with/to others online, altered priorities when grocery shopping, a wariness of human traffic in public spaces. Writing and reflecting on the situation in Athens, Greece – a country that was in its tenth year of a national debt crisis by the time the World Health Organization announced a global pandemic in early 2020 – the author examines how the taken-for-granted can be multifariously disrupted and how people struggle to adjust. Following a line of thinking by Anne Allison, this chapter ponders the re-making of life that emerges from the shared experience of precarity, and how we might use this moment in history to imagine new, meaningful relations with others that might mitigate the loneliness and strains of living with precariousness.

Notes

1   Gino Spocchia, 'Chinese immigrant attacked on streets of New York dies', *Yahoo News* (9 January 2022), https://sports.yahoo.com/chinese-immigrant-attacked-streets-york-113535042.html; Brittany Kriegstein and Clayton Guse, '"He is a kind person": anguished wife of Asian man in coma after beating on East Harlem street now fears for her own safety', *New York Daily News* (25 April 2021), https://www.nydailynews.com/new-york/ny-asian-man-attack-east-harlem-bottle-collector-20210425-ckg3y4b7lferbjv3cn4hczzxli-story.html.
2   Susan Haigh, 'Chinese immigrant attacked in NYC dies months later', *Associated Press* (9 January 2022), https://apnews.com/article/crime-new-york-new-york-city-homicide-hate-crimes-f159287b034a312e060a613aa5644ba7.
3   Anne Allison, *Precarious Japan* (Durham, NC: Duke University Press, 2013), 9.
4   Judith Butler, *Precarious Life: The Powers of Mourning and Violence* (London: Verso, 2004), xiv–xv.
5   Franco 'Bifo' Berardi, *The Soul at Work: From Alienation to Autonomy* (Los Angeles: Semiotext(e), 2009); Guy Standing, *The Precariat: The New Dangerous Class* (London: Bloomsbury Academic, 2011).
6   Kathleen Stewart, 'Precarity's forms', *Cultural Anthropology* 27, no. 3 (2012): 518–25; Allison, *Precarious Japan*.
7   See Ulrich Beck, 'Incalculable futures: world risk society and its social and political implications', in *Ulrich Beck: Pioneer in Cosmopolitan Sociology and Risk Society*, ed. Ulrich Beck (Heidelberg: Springer, 2014), 78–89; Mary Douglas, *Risk and Blame: Essays in Cultural Theory* (London: Routledge, 1992); Charles Taylor, *A Secular Age* (Cambridge, MA: Harvard University Press, 2007); Max Weber, *The Vocation Lectures: 'Science as a Vocation', 'Politics as a Vocation'*, eds. David Owen and Tracy Strong (Indianapolis, IN: Hackett Publishing, 2004).
8   While we argue that precariousness is a shared condition, this is not to suggest that there is a singular, universal experience of precariousness. There are varying degrees of vulnerability in different social groups.
9   The Anthropocene refers to the current geological epoch in which human activity has significantly altered the planet and which 'will remain a major geological

force for many millennia, maybe millions of years, to come'. Paul J. Crutzen, 'The "Anthropocene"', in *Earth System Science in the Anthropocene*, eds. Eckart Ehlers and Thomas Krafft (Berlin: Springer, 2006), 17.

10   The overturning of *Roe v. Wade* in the United States in 2022, nearly half a century after the Supreme Court's landmark decision that established a constitutional right to abortion, exemplifies the ongoing struggle for, and threats to, freedom and basic human rights.

11   Lauren Berlant, *Cruel Optimism* (Durham, NC: Duke University Press, 2011), 3.

12   *Our Planet*, 'One planet' (season 1, episode 1), prod. Adam Chapman, aired 5 April 2019 on Netflix.

13   Ludwig Wittgenstein, *On Certainty*, eds. G. E. M. Anscombe and G. H. von Wright (Oxford: Blackwell, 1969), 508.

14   Brett Neilson and Ned Rossiter, 'Precarity as a political concept, or, Fordism as exception', *Theory, Culture and Society* 25, nos. 7–8 (2008): 63.

Part One

Precarious Conditions

Banal Precariousness

Susan Leong

To be precarious is to be perched on the edge of an abyss from which the terror of the unknown looms. How, then, can an experience charged with high drama and extreme emotion be described as banal, that is, ordinary and common to all? How would such an experience be? Imagine, if you will, trying to make your way on foot across a vast landscape of sand dunes. It matters not whether you are going up, down or across because every step disintegrates as soon as you lay your weight on it. The trickling grains provide no foothold so standing still is not an option, and every centimetre gained leads only to the next stretch of shifting sand. This sense of *never quite* despite constant striving – whether the goal is to land a dream job, arrive at a desired destination, live the good life or achieve a level of fitness – is this chapter's concern. I call it *banal precariousness*. In earlier works, others have emphasized this notion using concepts such as risk and the lack of certainty and security to capture phenomena specific to spheres of life, such as medicine, migration, ethics, refugees, aging and labour.[1]

Borrowing from anthropologist Kathleen Stewart's approach of ficto-criticism, I use data gathered from ethnographic interviews and observations over many years, memoir and research, to build a creative narrative that helps me make a critical argument about banal precariousness. This story about banal precariousness has three sections built around experiences of mobility, work and the body in which, to quote Stewart, 'a form of sensing, thinking, or perceiving is emergent'.[2] The objective is to pin down what I believe is an elusive, widespread and damaging shared affect of our time. To be clear, while precariousness has always been a fact of life albeit often unacknowledged as such, it is my argument that it has never been as present, lurking and commonly felt beneath the rhythm of our days as it is now. Yet we have no helpful way of naming this uneasy undercurrent to life. Hence, my aim is that – as with children and the imagined monsters under their bed – by peering into the unknown, the terrors of banal precariousness may be named and tamed.

The three sections of this chapter and the concept of banal precariousness have unlikely beginnings. They are the result of research, conversations, inspiration, interviews, observations, exchanges with colleagues and personal lived experience. Like burrs from weeds picked up during a roadside ramble they have stuck fast for a decade, as I crisscrossed the Australian continent between Perth and Brisbane, hopped up to Kuala Lumpur in Asia, and finally returned to Perth in the midst of the COVID-19 pandemic. Their timelines overlap; there are no neat starts and endings. Nor has there been a eureka moment. Nonetheless, I believe banal precariousness is an apt description of an emergent phenomenon because it speaks of a pervasive helplessness, individually and collectively. Like Sianne Ngai in *Ugly Feelings*, my aim is to theorize 'social powerlessness'.[3] Working out this state of being, and working with words itself, is, to borrow a phrase, similar to 'feeling out the pitch of a note made by an imaginary tuning fork'.[4]

In its 'Stories about Words', the *Oxford English Dictionary* traces the root of 'precarious' to the Latin *precārius*, a word meaning 'given as a favour' or 'depending on the favour of another person' that may be withdrawn at any time.[5] Philip Armstrong adds to this the link between precarious and *precari*, that is, 'to ask, beg, pray'.[6] Favours obtained by entreaty remain at the pleasure of the giver so one begs for the gift, then prays that it not be taken away. From this root a 'semantic constellation' has spun – precarity, precariat, precariousness – each encapsulating a different aspect of human vulnerability in different contexts.[7] The history of the term spans centuries and its use remains varied and contested. In the 1970s when the notion of flexible workplace conditions began making inroads into established Fordist labour practices, the idea of 'precarity [as] rooted in the labour realm' became a reality for the working masses.[8] As flexibility and productivity became watchwords for businesses, social protections for workers receded further, prompting marginalized workers and the unemployed to mobilize across Europe in collective action and protest. One result was 'a new kind of social subject: the precarious worker'.[9] Eventually, contingent employment conditions also became the lot of the middle classes and white-collar workers in the 1990s, giving birth to Guy Standing's neologism of 'precarious' and 'proletariat' – the precariat.[10] Today, as the section on gig economy workers in Malaysia will show, the precariat is more prevalent than ever and a worrying plight even for young workers. In Australia, too, precariousness is no longer confined to Standing's precariat but has become a state of being that cuts across professions and geographical locations, from farmers and small business owners to engineers in cities and regional areas.

Precarity took on added weight and specific meaning after the catastrophic events of 11 September 2001. As an America in mourning responded with devastating force to attacks on home soil and the need for retribution threatened to overwhelm, Judith Butler's seminal book, *Precarious Life: The Powers of Mourning and Violence*, spoke to the inherent human vulnerability of as well as shared ethical obligation to those whose deaths qualify as 'grievable'. Butler calls out the unspoken 'hierarchy of grief' that governs how we deem some lives less worthy because they are seen as foes to our way of life, and other lives more valuable and their loss cause for deep mourning because they are our compatriots.[11] Since then, both precarity and precariousness have been applied as critical lenses for examining and understanding multiple situations.

As Donna McCormack and Suvi Salmenniemi put it, discussions of precariousness of life and precarity tend to fall into 'two main lines of inquiry'.[12] One strand is concerned with 'the use of precariousness and precarity to animate questions of what counts as human and of how vulnerability could form the basis for thinking ethical relationality'. This aspect is most closely associated with Butler's work. The second strand of precarity 'is mobilized to make sense of and theorize contemporary capitalism and its effects on life, labour and subjectivity'.[13] This is the more widely accessed and discussed aspect of precarity these days, especially in relation to deteriorating work conditions across industries.[14]

This chapter and its concept of banal precariousness belongs to the third, barely-mentioned strand as an exploration of the 'continued changing nature of precarization'.[15] 'Banal' is used to tease out and denote two qualities of contemporary precariousness. The first alludes to its unremarkable, innocuous nature. In that regard, the word functions similarly to Michael Billig's usage in *Banal Nationalism*, where he describes the unwaved national flag hanging in petrol station forecourts and prosaic phrases such as 'The Nation' that, whether noted or ignored, do not fail to give a tacit nod to the nation-state.[16] Although largely considered to be a part of the unnoticed, routinely familiar background of the everyday, these symbols are powerful because they reinforce and normalize specific understandings of how belonging, nationhood and inclusion operate. The contrast between the blandness of symbols and their power to animate emotions and action is, to my mind, a key feature of Billig's thesis.

In this chapter, 'banal' captures how far precariousness has sunk into our consciousness, 'unbound' and no longer 'limited to a specific context in which precarity is imposed by global events or macrostructures'.[17] Instead, it is to be found 'in the microspaces of everyday life and is an enduring feature of the human condition'.[18] Multiplied and amplified by networks of information, news and rumour, no threat to humanity is too distant, too minor or un-relatable. As offshore earthquakes and tsunamis destroy nuclear power stations, grounded vessels in the Suez Canal disrupt global supply chains, and a global pandemic creates chaos, the magnitude of these global events has made awareness of life's vulnerability inescapable. At the other end of the spectrum, precariousness can also be the outcome of human-scale, everyday occurrences. A fall, even a minor slip, can substantially lower the quality of life of an elderly person. The breadwinner's job loss can be the harbinger of homelessness for a family. A niggling ache can be symptomatic of a terminal illness. The structures around which our lives are built are fragile and our lives hang by a thread. Precariousness is banal because it is now common-to-all. The second quality of banal precariousness is attendant on its first quality of being innocuous. Although precariousness is, as I argue, more commonly felt than ever, that does not mean its corrosive character is any diluted or lessened. In fact, as the wearing effect that continuous drips of water have on stone attest, the damage may be slow but no less harmful. To recognize and limit its destructive erosion, it is imperative to see banal precariousness clearly for what it is and attend to its presence. Describing the visceral experience is the first step to such vigilance. In other words, what this chapter aims to do is to understand what Raymond Williams named a 'structure of feeling', wherein 'different ways of thinking' are 'vying to emerge in any one point in history'.[19] For me, personally, banal precariousness is an idea and experience that has gathered and grown over more than twenty years. It began with the sense of conditional belonging after the move to Australia in the 1990s. The niggling impression of an emergent phenomenon persisted, one for which I did not have the words to describe and share. I use a combination of personal, borrowed and fictional stories to do so in this chapter.[20] The point is to put a name to an intuition, to create an awareness of what it is we are all living.

Are you good enough?

We arrive in Perth from Singapore on 2 February 1998. It is eighteen months or so after the MP for Oxley, Pauline Hanson, declared in parliament that Australia was 'in danger of being swamped by Asians. … They have their own culture and religion, form ghettos and do not assimilate'.[21] The terms for our temporary residency visa are explicit. We have four years to operate a business, generate X amount of turnover over any two years, and hire Y number of Australian employees. This would earn us the chance to apply for permanent residence. Schooled in the productivity doctrine, we calmly accept the demand to prove ourselves deserving economic contributors. This is not far different from the expectations in Singapore, where working efficiently is a hallmark of society. As a young nation founded in 1965, a mere fifty-odd years ago, the need for social order and economic survival is deeply embedded in the Singaporean social imaginary. That working collectively and in accordance with the patriarchal government is vital to the harmony and prosperity of the entire country is an article of faith. All other considerations – political, cultural and social – come second to the economic. At the same time, the Singaporean psyche clings to the myth of meritocracy, that is to say, success comes to all those who work hard and everyone begins from a level playing field. Hence, one's beginnings, background and dis/advantages, from gender and race to socio-economic circumstances and education, supposedly have no significant impact on eventual success or failure in life.[22] Armed with this strange but potent mix of naivety and pragmatism, we blithely made our way to Australia, assured that we would be given 'a fair go'.

When individuals move from one city to another, one country to the next where there are no major differences in language, they expect to encounter sufficient familiarities to enable them to function from day to day. From such a base they can add fresh knowledge specific to their new surroundings and forge, hopefully, better lives. We envisaged being able to slip smoothly into life in Perth, largely because both countries use English as the language of business. What we found, to our chagrin, was that the navigation of even mundane tasks, such as signing up to a bank or phone account, involved ways that were surprisingly alien. On top of that, while the internet was already widely used, there were not very many resources developed with migrants in mind.

Frequently, in that first year in Perth, I felt helpless, powerless, ignorant of the ways of the world I had walked into, and reduced to an immensely frustrated, adult-sized ignoramus. For example, the wide choice of electricity suppliers versus a single publicly owned utility in Singapore required ploughing through multiple product disclosure statements written in legalese before we could select a service provider. Understanding that children were enrolled in public primary schools according to where they live so there is no substantial commute made for some head scratching for us, because in Singapore primary school placements were issued according to a child's order of birth in the family, familial alumni connections or religious affiliation. In Singapore, many choices as citizens and consumers were decided by default with there being only one option available. Without the tacit knowledge about how Australian society functions that locals possess, this filled me with a banal precariousness. It was possible to be fully part of an event one moment, then completely lost in the next because I had no map with which to navigate even the simplest of social niceties. One last example to illustrate: at the primary school my daughter attended parents were sometimes asked to 'bring a plate' to school events. Everyone assumes that you know that the plate you bring must be laden with food. There is nothing like being made to look a fool to give one a sense of being a not quite fully-paid-up member of Australian society. Yet, as I wrote in 2009, I was no longer a Singaporean either.[23]

To come back to the anxieties Hanson articulated in 1996, these were couched as those of 'ordinary Australians'. At the time, the country was drowning in record high double-digit interest rates (at its peak in 1990 at 17.5 per cent) and growing unemployment, so ordinary Australians railed against the perceived unfair handing out of benefits and opportunities to Indigenous Australians and Asian migrants.[24] Taxpayers' money must not be expended upon foreign aid, unfair benefits and non-assimilating migrants, they insisted. Rather, welfare benefits and Australian permanent residency should only be granted to those with proven merit. General hostility towards the not-yet-good-enough greeted us upon arrival in 1998. Two decades on, the nascent transactional logic that emerged previously continues to underscore the nation's current migration programme. Migrants to Australia are primarily understood through economic lenses. Not only must they bring money and employable skills into the country, they and their dependents must not draw on the public purse for health care, education and other forms of assistance – at least not until they have demonstrated themselves to be financial assets. This is despite findings that the flow of people, capital and talent of migrants is central to the nation's growth and future.

In 2015 I sit across from Raj, who was granted the same temporary business executive visa (subclass 457) to work and live in Australia for four years in 2004. He resides in Perth with his wife and two teenagers, one of whom is autistic. A technical sales manager with an outstanding career in Western Australia, he meets all the criteria for permanent residency but the application is repeatedly denied. Australian authorities baulk at taxpayers taking on the cost of caring for those with a disability. Raj and family were poised on the brink of being sent back to their home country for five years. Eventually, after multiple complex undertakings to personally bear the cost of care they are granted permanent residence. After the interview, Raj takes me to the family room and introduces Daniel, who sits watching television with his mother, Sami, who works part time as a teacher. They coax the teenager to shake my hand but he refuses to meet my eye. Sami seems disgruntled, perhaps unhappy with her husband's agreement to talk about the family's migration issues. Or perhaps the stigma associated with disability in the family survives the move to Australia.

The conditional belonging – belonging withheld until one proves being good enough – that Raj and his family lived with shadows my experience of migration, too. Never mind having jumped through the hoops of medical tests, validation of qualifications, valuation of assets, demonstrating decades of gainful, continued employment and proof of sound character: for six years, knowing that visas can be revoked for a multitude of reasons haunted my days and nights. Aside from the probability of not quite making the grade, by whatever yardstick the Australian government uses, there was always the nagging need to prove oneself part of a model minority of well-behaved, hardworking and modest ethnics.

In *Cruel Optimism*, Lauren Berlant frets over how those 'who have been working thinking other people are going to get stuff without working' turns into a question of *who* deserves the good life.[25] Compared to the rest of the world, Australia has had a relatively uneventful two decades, buoyed among other things by the continued demand from China for natural resources, and having sustained minimal impact during the 2008 Global Financial Crisis. Western Australia, in particular, benefited from a mining boom that saw record employment rates, ridiculous salary rises and soaring property values. Yet, we have not managed to escape the growing sense of pervading precariousness. Booms are inevitably followed by bust, so the economists say, and we brace ourselves for the eventual grinding halt. Most recently, it arrived in the form of a global pandemic. What the good life entails exactly has expanded, alongside the perception of threats facing it. At the same time, the question of who is deserving of it or at least the necessary resources to achieve it, remains hierarchical. Ordinary Australians maintain that 'our own citizens should come first' when it comes to early and easy access to the COVID-19 vaccine, expedited travel to and from the country, and various aid programmes. The rest of you must show yourself good enough for the good life.

Making work

Kuala Lumpur, 2018. It is late when I get into the silver hatchback. I am tired from a long day at the office and disinclined to chat as I usually do. Half dozing, I hear my Grab driver sighing several times during the start of what is always a long ride home because of heavy traffic. I take a peek and see a forbidding-looking man with a whiskery beard and a darkened, deeply unhappy countenance. 'How long have you been driving a Grab?' I chance. 'Two years already', he sighs again. 'Oh, what did you do before?' The unhappy tale unfolds. 'Actually, I have a master's in finance and administration', Ali reveals. 'I had a good job in the private sector but quit my job to take care of my father when he was very sick. Now he is better but I cannot get another job.' At 28, the last thing Ali expected upon his return to the workforce was continued rejection to more than three hundred applications. Deeply frustrated, Ali even wonders aloud, at one point, if his ethnicity (Malay) works against him. Unable to resist my didactic tendencies and eager to avoid the contentious topic of race relations in Malaysia, I counsel him on preparing custom cover letters and resumes instead of using generic ones. It is a pet topic and I wax lyrical. My advice seems to offer him a glimmer of hope. We arrive at the apartment and I alight, wishing him luck.

The conversation stays with me for days. What weighed most heavily on me was Ali's utter bewilderment at not having a job to return to, a promise that a master's degree and several years of relevant work experience should have delivered. Many of us do still expect to be rewarded for our work and effort. This is what we teach our children. 'No hat, no play', we say in Australian schools. No work, no reward – and by that logic, work always leads to reward. This, according to Erich Fromm, is 'the promise of domination of nature, of material abundance, of the greatest happiness for the greatest number, and of unimpeded personal freedom [that] has sustained the hopes and faith of the generations since the beginning of the industrial age'.[26] Denied work in the field he trained for, Ali's belief in his own future was shaken.

Youth unemployment remains high among graduates in Malaysia, and more so for those just starting out.[27] In 2018, when Ali and I had that chat, being an e-hailing driver was still regarded as a side hustle for earning extra cash. Most e-hailing drivers in the country work with Grab, one of Southeast Asia's largest online platforms. Most of those I spoke to between 2018 and 2020 considered such work a temporary solution. Like their overseas counterparts who might be working with Uber, Lyft, Didi or Ola, Malaysians working in the gig economy are classified as self-employed. This generally translates to a lack of employee benefits such as annual leave, medical benefits and some form of employer contribution to a provident or social security fund. Although some effort and protest at the lack of social protection has brought change, there is still little to no safety net for gig economy workers.

Another chat, another year, this time with Aziz, who drives a purple hatchback, decked out in matching upholstery and accessories. The 27-year-old says he was lucky to have obtained a car loan before he was let go at work. A local university graduate in finance, Aziz was unable to find another job and now relies on his car to earn a living as an e-hailing driver. The father of a six-month-old child, Aziz wants to be the sole breadwinner in his family so his wife can quit her job as an operations manager and look after their child. Reluctantly, he admits half of his current earnings go to monthly instalments for the vehicle and the rest go nowhere near fulfilling his self-imposed obligations as the 'head of the family'. Still, Aziz has pinned his hopes on starting his own business. He is cagey about product details but plans to sell a 'rare' kind of coffee and is optimistic it will lead to a better future.

On average there are more male than female e-hailing drivers in Kuala Lumpur, which makes Miriam stand out. In contrast to Aziz, she is more pragmatic and prepared for the travails of an unstable source of income. For Miriam, it is the flexibility of the gig economy that is most attractive. A single woman who needs only to support herself, she confides that she aims for a daily ride target of RM200 from which a percentage is set aside for her savings and another small sum is destined to be deposited into the voluntary Social Security Organization (SOCSO) scheme. Miriam's discipline and life goals are all mapped out. This was all before COVID-19. In 2018, the unemployment rate in Malaysia was 3.4 per cent and held steady at 3.3 per cent in June 2019. Under the grip of the pandemic, the unemployment rate rose to 4.9 per cent by June 2020.[28] The majority of the labour force, aged between 15 and 64 years, comprise just over 22 per cent of the nation's population of 32 million people, while those aged between 0 and 14 years form about 7.5 per cent.[29] Not surprisingly, the number of job seekers continues to grow every year. Within such a lackadaisical economy and competitive context, how would the likes of Ali, Aziz and Miriam fare now?

It is early 2020, and I am making the one-hour trip from my apartment to Kuala Lumpur International Airport. My Grab driver, Leo, is a former salesman in his late twenties, who resigned from his job a week before Malaysia instituted the strict Movement Control Order (MCO) to curb the spread of COVID-19. 'You been driving Grab long-term?' I ask. 'No miss.' Leo explains he has plans to supply a gap he sees in the delivery market and intends to develop the niche into a full-time business. 'Bad timing', I sympathize, referring to the pandemic. But Leo disagrees, maintaining he has always wanted to have a business of his own and the timing, good or bad, is irrelevant. It is unclear which of us he is trying to convince. In the interim, he does the sums very quickly, working out that if he continues to work 14 hours a day, 6 days a week, he can bring in RM10,000 (approximately US$2,400) a month. After the 20 per cent commission paid to the platform, the costs of fuel, maintenance and insurance, he takes home RM5,000 monthly – so long as he is willing to work twice as long as average at 84 hours a week.

The flexibility and autonomy of digital economy work is more illusion than reality for e-hailing drivers like Leo. The income level they need determines their hours. As soon as they stop driving, they stop earning. Furthermore, because they are self-employed workers of the informal economy, none among the four mentioned above, Ali, Leo, Aziz or Miriam, has access to the structures of company benefits. Instead, to get past what Ngai calls the 'general state of obstructed agency', they plan to set up their own businesses and manage their finances in order to reclaim some control over their precarious futures.[30] Their efforts go hand in hand with both state and federal government exhortations for Malaysians to embrace the promise of the imminent IR4.0 (Fourth Industrial Revolution). Smart technologies, artificial intelligence and autonomous machines sit alongside the pedestals on which the self-made billionaires of tech corporations – Elon Musk, Jeff Bezos and Jack Ma – are perched, held up as worthy exemplars of what can be achieved if one is bold enough. Beholden to digital platforms managed by opaque algorithms and left to the mercies of the on-demand economy, many Malaysians like Leo and Aziz buy into the myth of entrepreneurialism to fill the void of powerlessness. Sadly, as Silvio Lorusso explains, while what entrepreneurialism does on the surface is valorize 'individual initiative, action and risk, equating them to autonomy and freedom', what it ultimately creates is 'a paradoxical notion of autonomy ... because it generates more constraints'.[31] In other words, having taken charge of their own future, entrepreneurs have to proactively take risks, repeatedly betting on their futures and managing the mandatory 'speculative action'.

Partial persons

Academia, one would think, is a choice of career where age and experience would be advantageous. The more time one spends thinking about, writing and speaking of a research area or topic should only lead to greater delving and profound depths. For the tenured professors this is a comforting and welcome possibility. For the rest, semester/trimester-based contracts, short-term and part-time research gigs, and supply teaching are the more prevalent reality. Tenure is an endangered concept. Not that tenure is relevant in Australia where tertiary education is an industry, with the accumulation of profits overriding other rationales for existence. In this industry the main customers are students, especially foreign students who pay full fees. Their enrolments have replaced the government as the main source of university funding. Whatever government funds may be channelled to higher education are also dwindling with every year. The resultant fluctuations in annual funding have led to teaching and research activities being carried out by staff employed via contingent and exploitative contractual arrangements. Unable to budget beyond the thirteen-week cycle of semester, worn down by the compromises necessary to teach bigger classes with fewer hours, or frazzled and frayed by the constant need to seek further funding even while carrying out research, many skilled researchers and trained educators are leaving universities; some by choice, others through forced retrenchments or from disillusionment. The deplorable employment situation has been exacerbated since the COVID-19 pandemic due to travel restrictions and plunging international enrolments.

It is pointless pretending that higher education today is foremost about learning when more often than not it is entrepreneurialism that triumphs, for academics as well as students. As with all other enterprises, academia has become a sphere of activity where age eventually and inevitably becomes weakness rather than strength. Slow research, common in the humanities, arts and social sciences, that takes years to carry out and sometimes decades to prove its utility is now seen as *too* slow to satisfy ever-changing research bibliometrics, quality frameworks and university rankings. Slower researchers concerned not so much with the latest and greatest but rather with broader trends and longer-term implications are rapidly becoming surplus to requirements. Suddenly, like Stewart's mother remarked, '[my] work doesn't work anymore'.[32] It is too slow, has too low a media profile and attracts too few citations.

Of all the sections contained in this chapter, this is the hardest to write because it strikes closest to home. By the end of 2020, I had spent six weeks of six months in quarantine as I crossed the South China Sea and the Indian Ocean three times between Asia and Australia. The pandemic threw into sharp relief the effort it takes to keep alive a sense of meaningful work as an academic, to seek support and maintain good mental and physical health. From doctoral studies and research fellowship to full-time positions, my body has responded to the long and grinding stresses, first with hypertension and, later, hyperthyroidism. In late 2019, I was finally compelled to recognize that I needed more help with my mental health than my general practitioner could offer. Even the aid of a GP was resisted until an ex-colleague's open referral to her 'happy pills' made me face my own foolish cowardice. The admission that all that stood between me and a day spent mentally running around in circles was a tiny, white pill less than five millimetres across left big yellow bruises on my ego. Further admission that I needed specialist care required overcoming the surfeit of taboo and stigma that my Chinese heritage bequeathed on mental illness. My sister, Meng, pooh-poohed the idea when I spoke of consulting a psychiatrist: 'It's only temporary, right? Are you sure you really need to? It's not that serious, is it?' Her dubious comments were fraught with the unspoken fear and denial of a disgraceful familial taint. Mental illness runs in families – the ubiquitous 'they' say – and the afflicted are shunned. Will this trait be passed to my children? Have I done enough to bolster their self-esteem, foster resilience and awareness? Should I even be writing about this personal problem? Am I guilty of the criticism sometimes levelled at academics of navel gazing?

Surrendering to the limitations confronting me, I put in my resignation from my academic career, and withdrew gradually from editorial and major commitments, although I was fortunate enough to gain an honorary position at a Western Australian university. When colleagues ask me about it, it remains difficult to explain my decision and I resort to the convenient half-truth of burnout. Of the few who receive the truth, it is inevitably unwelcome, discomfiting news. A friend asked me if all my days are 'always like that'. That is to say, filled with the possibility of debilitating and complete depletion. 'Yes', I reply, without adding that I am poised on my tippy toes, between depletion and accomplishment each time I embark upon what were once routine activities – lecturing, teaching, research and writing. How do I explain the hovering greyness that can suddenly overwhelm without warning? The inertia and/or grief so numbing that nothing and no one can move me, apart from the urge of basic needs. Or that rush of energy that charges in and leaves in a heartbeat because ... because. On the outside, I look as per usual and can on occasion even push myself to function as of old. Imminent and chronic, depression means my state of mind is always precarious. The rewarding highs that flow from listening to the forces that drive me to achieve have to be carefully measured against the tensions that bedevil me. Equilibrium between these forces is fragile, still, not least because aging adds another insuperable force.

In Chinese, to denounce another with the phrase *ni bu shi ren* ('you are not a person') is to accuse that person of being less than human or, indeed, inhuman. Megan Steffen uses the phrase 'a real person' to query her experience of precariousness of having no money, no things, knowing 'everything could be gone in a moment', and 'when someone else has decided that you have nothing worth losing'.[33] If one is not a real person, then, one can be said to be not quite a person. Age and mental fragility make partial persons of us. Aging women become invisible. Older and slower academics become less useful. My own inclination is still to avoid mention of my mental state of health when queried. Friends and colleagues find my occasional angry bursts and sudden silences hard to comprehend but the bare truth embarrasses them.

To cope, I take myself home. My return coincides with the multiple lockdowns in various states across Australia. New South Wales and Victoria are the most badly affected. Due to the isolation and challenging social, economic and psychological conditions, the precariousness of mental equilibrium is now increasingly apparent across the board. The precariousness of my state of mind is one I live with all the time. It is ten months since I came home to Perth, and in two months' time I shall have stopped work for a year. Medicine, friendship, counselling, quietude, new passions, reawakened loves and rest help replenish the colours that leached from the contours of my being. Getting out of bed is less of an impossible mission. Music and exercise are rediscovered fun. The creativity of my early years and my penchant for cheeky mischief re-emerge. My urge to research is almost dormant but some ideas, such as banal precariousness, persist. Sometimes the greys still colour my days, and it is grey – that in-between, not black or white, or blue – that shades my life. The destruction of wars, famine, disease, waste, avarice, hubris, extremism and complacency is hard to ignore. I guard my equilibrium, cosseting myself with sights and words that nurture. A satisfying closure would be to speak of a return to being whole, triumphantly well and able to participate fully again. As if the last few years have been no more than a hiccup, a bump in the road that caused a detour. An alternate pleasing ending would be the manifestation of a brand-new pathway. No such developments have taken place and there is no return to normal. Banal precariousness is my constant state of being, but I am gradually reconciled to being a partial person. It leaves me space and time to become. I determine at l(e)ast to write as honestly and fearlessly as I can.

In closing

There are fewer and fewer among us who have not known what it is to leave home, town, state or country. Gainful, stable and fair employment is becoming more the exception than the rule. And while aging occurs to us all, mental illness is also rising in our societies. Most of the above could all be laid at the door of the COVID-19 pandemic, liberal capitalism and big tech corporations, but unpacking the conditions that give rise to banal precariousness do not speak to what it is to live with and experience it. Stories do. To make sense of the changes that take place on a daily basis, we need to share our individual and personal stories of what happens. Not so as to find deeper meaning or see the big picture, but merely to know we are not alone.

My inclination here is to provide a neat and positive conclusion but the best I can offer is another story. It is somewhat appropriate that this chapter, which started with a word-picture of a person trudging up and down sand dunes as a way of describing the experience of banal precariousness, ends with another image. The earth of Perth, Western Australia, where home is, is composed mostly of sand. Due to the sandy soils, the nickname given to West Australians by those who live in other Australian states is 'sandgroper'. The sandgroper is a long, thin insect that lives below the surface of sand, burrowing from place to place. Unlike the iconic kangaroo, koala, emu or quokka, sandgropers do not feature on Instagram. Nonetheless, the sandgroper is an insect that has evolved to thrive in its subterranean environment, developing powerful forelegs to part the soil ahead of it. Literally pushing at the shifting sands to make its own way, all the while protected from the burning sun by cool sand. So it is with how I live with banal precariousness, quietly and slowly making my way beneath the blazing stars parting grain after grain, day by day.

Notes

1   See Mary Douglas, *Risk and Blame: Essays in Cultural Theory* (London: Routledge, 1992); Dennis V. Lindley, *Understanding Uncertainty* (Hoboken, NJ: John Wiley & Sons, 2006); Victoria Baines, *The Rhetoric of Insecurity: The Language of Danger, Fear and Safety in National and International Contexts* (Abingdon: Taylor & Francis, 2021).

2   Kathleen Stewart, 'Precarity's forms', *Cultural Anthropology* 27, no. 3 (2012): 518.

3   Sianne Ngai, *Ugly Feelings* (Cambridge, MA: Harvard University Press, 2005), 2.

4   Kathleen Stewart, 'Writing, life', *PMLA* 133, no. 1 (2018): 187.

5   Peter Gilliver, 'Precarious', *Oxford English Dictionary* (16 August 2012), https://public.oed.com/blog/word-stories-precarious/.

6   Philip Armstrong, 'Precarity's prayers', *Minnesota Review* 85 (2015): 181.

7   Gabriel Giorgi, 'Improper selves: cultures of precarity', *Social Text* 31, no. 2 (2013): 71.

8   Alice Mattoni and Markos Vogiatzoglou, 'Italy and Greece, before and after the crisis: between mobilization and resistance against precarity', *Quaderni* 84 (2014): 57–58.

9   Mattoni and Vogiatzoglou, 'Italy and Greece', 57.

10 Guy Standing, *The Precariat: The New Dangerous Class* (London: Bloomsbury Academic, 2011).

11 Judith Butler, *Precarious Life: The Powers of Mourning and Violence* (London: Verso, 2004), 32.

12 Donna McCormack and Suvi Salmenniemi, 'The biopolitics of precarity and the self', *European Journal of Cultural Studies* 19, no. 1 (2016): 6.

13 McCormack and Salmenniemi, 'Biopolitics of precarity', 6.

14 See Brett Neilson and Ned Rossiter, 'Precarity as a political concept, or, Fordism as exception', *Theory, Culture and Society* 25, nos. 7–8 (2008): 51–72; Franco 'Bifo' Berardi, *The Soul at Work: From Alienation to Autonomy* (Los Angeles: Semiotext(e), 2009).

15 McCormack and Salmenniemi, 'Biopolitics of precarity', 6.

16 Michael Billig, *Banal Nationalism* (London: Sage, 1995), 38.

17 Nancy Ettlinger, 'Precarity unbound', *Alternatives: Global, Local, Political* 32, no. 3 (2007): 320.

18 Ettlinger, 'Precarity unbound', 320.

19 Raymond Williams, 'From *Preface to Film* (UK, 1954)', in *Film Manifestos and Global Cinema Cultures: A Critical Anthology*, ed. Scott MacKenzie (Berkeley, CA: University of California Press, 2014), 610–11; Oxford Reference, 'Structures of feeling' (2022), https://www.oxfordreference.com/view/10.1093/oi/authority.20110803100538488.

20 Pseudonyms have been used for the people I spoke with.

21 Special Broadcasting Services, 'Revisit Pauline Hanson's infamous maiden speech', *SBS* (last modified 1 August 2016), https://www.sbs.com.au/guide/article/2016/07/19/revisit-pauline-hansons-infamous-maiden-speech.

22 Loh Kah Seng, Thum Ping Tjin and Jack Meng-Tat Chia (eds), *Living with Myths in Singapore* (Singapore: Ethos Books, 2017).

23 Susan Leong, 'No longer Singaporean', *Continuum: Journal of Media and Cultural Studies* 25, no. 4 (2011): 559–72.

24 Special Broadcasting Services, 'The year of record interest rates – 1990', *SBS News* (last modified 1 January 2016), https://www.sbs.com.au/news/the-year-of-record-interest-rates-1990.

25 Paul Rand, 'Why chasing the good life is holding us back, with Lauren Berlant (ep. 35)', *University of Chicago News* (podcast) (4 November 2019), https://news.uchicago.edu/podcasts/big-brains/why-chasing-good-life-holding-us-back-lauren-berlant.

26 Erich Fromm, *To Have or To Be?* (London: Bloomsbury, 2013), 1.

27   Department of Statistics Malaysia, 'Graduate statistics 2019', press release (16 July 2020), https://www.dosm.gov.my/v1/index.php?r=column/pdfPrev&id=b3ROY1dj SVROS2ZhclZaUWhLUVp5QT09.

28   Department of Statistics Malaysia, 'Key statistics of labour force in Malaysia' (2020), https://www.dosm.gov.my/v1/index.php.

29   Pocket Stats Q3 2021, Malaysia, 'Demographic statistics by states' (2021), https://cloud.stats.gov.my/index.php/s/x4xSjTYRTuPCo8e.

30   Ngai, *Ugly Feelings*, 3.

31   Silvio Lorusso, *Entreprecariat: Everyone Is an Entrepreneur. Nobody Is Safe* (Eindhoven, Netherlands: Onomatopee, 2019), 65–66, 71.

32   Stewart, 'Precarity's forms', 521.

33   Megan Steffen, 'Real people: or, how I learned to stop worrying and love housework', *A Day is a Struggle* (14 October 2013), https://a-day-is-a-struggle. decasia.org/texts/real-people.html.

A Life for a Voice: The Work of Journalist James W. Foley Through the Eyes of his Family

Diane Foley

Greater love has no one than this: to lay down one's life for one's friends.

– John 15:13

Only Jim knows why he returned to the violent chaos of Syria as most journalists were leaving and the risks were growing. As his mother, I can only speculate from what I witnessed regarding his increasingly passionate commitment to give voice to the Syrian people's suffering.

Though he was dearly loved, I knew little about the man our oldest son Jim had grown into in his forty years. I knew he had taught underprivileged 10- to 14-year-old children in Arizona for Teach for America, obtained a master's degree in creative writing at the University of Massachusetts, and taught English at the Cook County Jail in Chicago while acquiring a master's degree from Northwestern University's Medill School of Journalism. But I did not know of his compassion, courage or talent until after he was killed.

I had no idea about the many lives Jim touched. I did not know he continued to mentor his Teach for America students until they reached out after his death to form the Phoenix Foley Alliance in his memory. Nor did I know he taught English in Holyoke, Massachusetts, as a Care Centre volunteer for unwed mothers. There he purchased the group's first recording device so they could tell their stories, an initiative that has grown into a public broadcasting radio programme with the University of Massachusetts.

When Jim chose to become a conflict journalist after years as a teacher and writer, we encouraged him because it seemed to meld his interest in people's stories with his writing talent. He initially went to Iraq in 2008, embedded with the Indiana National Guard and working with USAID in Baghdad. He further

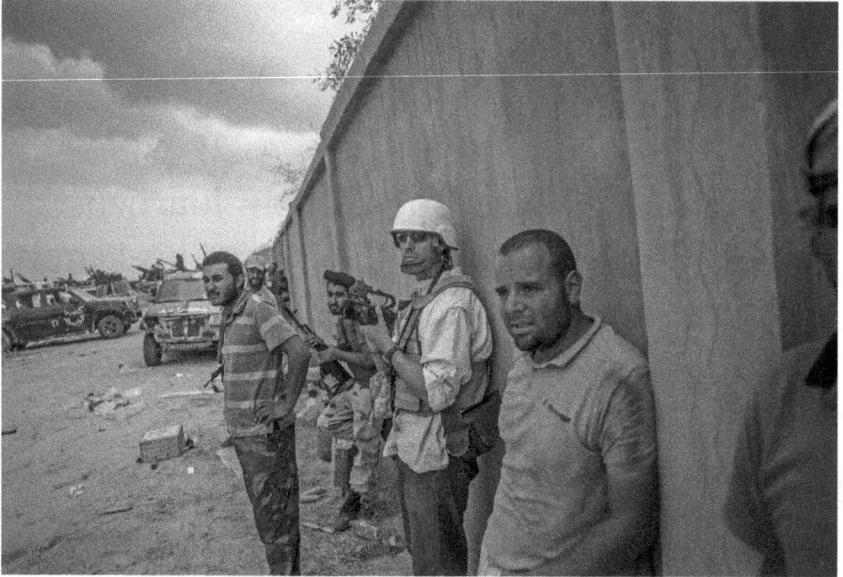

Figure 2.1 Jim Foley at the frontline in Sirte, Libya, October 2011. Image courtesy of Manu Brabo, 2011.

honed his reporting skills while embedded with the US Army's 101st Airborne Division in Afghanistan.

Thus, it was as a seasoned reporter that Jim began reporting on the 'Arab Spring'. I had worried about his two brothers in the US Army and Air Force and his sister, a Navy nurse. But I was ignorant of the higher risk facing freelance reporters in conflict zones. Jim had taken various safety training courses, learned from his time with the military and was doing everything he knew to keep safe.

Nevertheless, Jim was kidnapped in Benghazi, Libya, shortly after his arrival in mid-March 2011. On the morning of 5 April, he joined three colleagues – American freelance journalist Clare Morgana Gillis, Spanish photographer Manu Brabo and South African photojournalist Anton Hammerl – to travel to the frontlines of the conflict just outside Brega. After exiting their car, they were attacked with heavy gunfire. Anton was killed, while Jim and the two others were forcibly taken. Luckily, the event was witnessed by a *New York Times* reporter who identified the captors as soldiers loyal to Libyan leader Muammar Gaddafi. Kidnappings are most often unwitnessed, making the identification of captors and the location of hostages very difficult.

I was having lunch with my elderly mother when I received a telephone call from Peter Bouckaert, then emergencies director of Human Rights Watch, and then from my husband John, notifying us about Jim's abduction. We were in shock, clueless as to what to do. Within a few days, a person from the US Bureau of Consular Affairs called to confirm the terrible news. We were at a loss. We prayed, and prayed some more. During these forty-four days of terror, our son Michael took the lead, taking time off from work for multiple trips to Washington, DC, and for daily calls with concerned friends of Jim and two media companies that offered assistance.

Jim was a freelance journalist, not a staff reporter, so there was no security team to aid him. A contact from the US State Department faithfully called us weekly. One of the online news outlets that Jim was a correspondent for, the now defunct Boston-based *GlobalPost*, also offered help. However, it was ultimately a total stranger, David Bradley, owner of *The Atlantic*, already trying to locate Jim's colleague, Clare Gillis, who brought Jim home. Through research, David's team and Jim's friends identified Jacqueline Frazier, a Vermont native who had been the personal assistant to one of Gaddafi's sons. She immediately contacted David, flew to Libya and, using her government contacts, advocated for the hostages' release. Her efforts led to Clare, Jim and Manu being freed. Jim called me from his prison in Tripoli on the day before Easter saying he would be home for his sister Katie's college graduation ... and miraculously, he was.

Jim returned home filled with gratitude to his friends and family who had played a part in securing his freedom. He spent the next month visiting all who had helped and speaking at several schools of journalism about his experience. It was a euphoric time of thankfulness and hugs. Jim worked as an editor in Boston all summer, but he was restless. By the fall of 2011, he was back in Libya working with Human Rights Watch identifying Gaddafi weapons. He looked for steady employment with Human Rights Watch and the Committee to Protect Journalists, but there was no availability.

Jim was home for one final wonderful Christmas in 2011 and then returned to the Middle East by the New Year. Since the Arab hopes for freedom had spread to Syria, he decided to enter northern Syria across the Turkish border. He was reporting from there throughout 2012, flying back home in May for a fundraiser for his fallen colleague Anton Hammerl's children and again in October 2012.

That October was his last visit home. We celebrated his 39th birthday simply with his favourite Spanish paella. Several of Jim's friends argued with him not to return to the Middle East. John and I added our concerns for his safety, but he told me, 'Mom, I've found my passion. I must return'. I argued that he had so many safer options with his two master's degrees, writing and teaching experience. Jim seemed more sombre than usual but also more resolute about his need to return to Syria. He said, 'Mom, I have promises to keep'. Jim had spent months living with and among families and individuals in northern Syria. He was determined to bear witness to the horrific bombings and gassing of innocent civilians by the Assad regime.

The last day I spoke to Jim was on a brief phone call in mid-November 2012 while I was seeing patients in my family practice clinic. He offered his condolences upon the death of my elderly aunt. He reassured me that he would be home for Christmas. I never heard his voice again.

When John and I did not receive a call from Jim on Thanksgiving Day, we worried because it was odd not to hear from him on holidays. That feeling of foreboding was confirmed the very next morning when we received a call from Jim's colleagues, Clare Gillis and Nicole Tung, telling us our son had been kidnapped at gunpoint on 22 November, just a few miles from the Turkish border.

We were devastated. How could this be happening again? We did not know where to turn. Later that day, a representative from the US Bureau of Consular Affairs called to verify Jim's capture. The woman informed us that the Federal Bureau of Investigation would lead this investigation since the captors were unknown. She told us to expect a visit within the week.

An FBI agent did come to our home in Rochester, New Hampshire. He was nice, but seemed wholly unprepared for this assignment. We were stunned by his suggestion that we consider asking President Bashar al-Assad for assistance. The agent did not speak Arabic nor had he ever been to Turkey or Syria. He did not even ask for Jim's cell phone number. Three long weeks after Jim's capture, this FBI agent was on the Turkish border trying to make sense of the rumours and many conflicting leads about Jim's whereabouts. Jim had vanished ... there was no trace of him.

The FBI urged us not to convey to anyone that our son was missing, assuring us it would be better for Jim. It was a chaotic and confusing time. I tried to be calm and trust that Jim would be found and brought home soon, but inside I was overcome with terror and horrific anxiety.

We obediently went through Christmas telling no one but close family. By the New Year, we had decided to approach the media and go public with the news as we were hearing nothing from the FBI and were distraught.

As an independent conflict journalist, Jim had no security backup, minimal safety equipment and bare bones medical insurance. All he had was a passion to bear witness to the suffering people in Syria. He had not wanted to worry me about the dangers inherent in his chosen vocation so had not left any emergency information about his banking or social media passwords. He left no instructions, no last wishes.

Ultimately, I had to find attorneys who offered their legal expertise pro bono so we could obtain power of attorney allowing us to do basic things like stop the automatic payment for Jim's cell phone, end his newspaper subscriptions and so on. Jim had no dependents, apartment or vehicle, which would have complicated things further.

Both times Jim was taken hostage we did not know where to go to get help. We were an ordinary middle-class family, John a physician and I a family nurse practitioner. We had no knowledge of Washington, DC, or the issues of hostage-taking. Aside from dear friends, family and previous strangers like Phil Balboni, president and CEO of *GlobalPost*, and David Bradley of *The Atlantic*, we felt totally alone in our frantic pursuit to locate Jim and bring him home.

During the winter of 2013, I began frequent trips to Washington. The FBI agent assigned to us at the time seldom called. The few times he did, it was to gather information from us, never to offer any. *GlobalPost* had convinced its insurance company to offer a security team to find Jim. Thus initially, a security professional accompanied me on a few early visits to DC. However, this security team worked for the media outlet, not for us. They usually did not allow our family into their discussions and strongly insisted that Jim had been kidnapped by the Assad regime in Damascus. They would not consider the possibility, which we believed, that Jim was being held in northern Syria by another group and went to great lengths to persuade us, though they had no real evidence. So we increasingly felt at odds with the team and on our own.

We considered hiring our own security team but could not afford the prohibitive $4,000 daily fee. David Bradley offered the assistance of his staff at Atlantic Media once again. He was one of the true lights amid this darkness. He continues to support our family and other hostage families to this day.

To enable my monthly journeys to Washington, I had to quit my nurse practitioner practice. I would scour the internet for the cheapest ways to travel and cheapest places to stay. No one ever mentioned keeping receipts for the thousands of dollars we spent for possible reimbursement. No one ever mentioned, until after Jim died, that our government had funds to reimburse such travel and lodging. By then, burdened by disorganization and grief, I could not bring myself to find the receipts needed to submit for reimbursement. An FBI social worker would kindly call on occasion but offered nothing substantial. When I asked for help finding a counsellor for myself I was referred to an overwhelming website with thousands of counsellors!

I had to organize all my own meetings at the State Department and FBI. Some faces were familiar but others continually changed. Twice I was received at the White House by National Security Advisor Susan Rice, whom I had met when she was our United Nations ambassador. She was cordial and empathetic, repeating the refrain that 'Jim is our highest priority'. But she would refer me back to the FBI and State. I soon felt like I was going in circles, with no one taking responsibility to bring Jim home.

Finally, in the fall of 2013, we received word from two strangers that Jim was alive. The first, Dimitri Bontinck, a Belgian, reached out to inform us that his son Jejoen had seen Jim in a prison in Aleppo in northern Syria. Jejoen had been radicalized and gone to Syria to fight against Bashar al-Assad's regime, but he was subsequently imprisoned by ISIS, and then arrested upon his return home to Belgium. Then, Omar Alkhani, who had accompanied American Kayla Mueller, also a hostage, into Syria, reported hearing Jim's name and voice while in prison. Both of these good men contacted us and confirmed his detention with other Westerners. This news brought us renewed hope. These men had very detailed information to share with our FBI contact and the security team about where Jim was being held. However, since Jejoen was held in a Belgian jail and Omar was difficult to contact, it took more than a month for the FBI to debrief them. Then, at the end of November 2013, just over a year since Jim's abduction, our son Michael received the first email from Jim's captors, offering proof of life to questions we provided them.

Michael thought of three cryptic questions to which only Jim would know the answers. Every proof of life question was answered correctly. We knew by Christmas that these captors were holding our Jim. However, their demands for the release of all Muslim prisoners or €100,000,000 in exchange for our son's life were impossible for us.

In 2013, we had no idea that eighteen Western prisoners had been kidnapped by the violent jihadist group ISIS in Syria. There were four Americans, three British, four French, three Spanish, one German, one Russian, one Dane and one Italian national held together, beginning in the fall of 2013. They were all journalists and aid workers. Every nation negotiated separately for its citizens, except the United States and United Kingdom, which chose not to negotiate at all. Additionally, there were five international aid workers from Doctors Without Borders held separately by ISIS during that time frame; all were eventually released after negotiation.

We were threatened with criminal prosecution on three different occasions by our government if we tried to raise ransom for Jim's release and were clearly told that there would be no attempted rescue or negotiation through a third country. I was saddened and taken aback that our own government would threaten us.

A generous DC attorney had assured us there was no legal precedent to prosecute a family trying to secure the release of a family member, but we were very concerned about prosecution of any of our donors. Finally, in late 2013 and 2014, when it became obvious that the return of Jim and the other Americans was not a national priority, we embarked on raising pledges for a potential ransom for Jim's life. However, the emails from the captors stopped at the end of December 2013. They would not answer our emails or send any further communication until early August 2014, two weeks prior to Jim's murder.

In February 2014, the Spanish hostages held with Jim were released. In early March, I went to Spain to meet them, and then to Paris to speak with a French crisis group that was working hard to bring their French citizens home. On that visit, I met with a British hostage family member who was accompanied by a representative of the group Hostage UK, which supports the families of hostages. I was intrigued and honestly quite envious of such support, since I was most often alone amid my struggle to bring Jim home.

In the spring of 2014, we had most likely our last chance to rescue the four American and three British hostages. The released French hostages brought detailed information and communication avenues with the captors, but none was ever acted on to my knowledge. The freed Italian hostage, Federico Motka, travelled to the United States twice at his own expense to try to get help for Jim and the others from our government, but his essential information was heard only at low-level meetings with the FBI field agent assigned to our case.

Of the eighteen Western hostages taken by ISIS from 2012 to 2014, all returned safely home except for a Russian killed in captivity, and the American and British hostages whose countries adhere to a strict hostage policy of non-negotiation with terrorists. A similar non-negotiation policy exists for Canadian and Australian citizens kidnapped or unjustly detained while working or travelling abroad.

In 2014, the United States had no one responsible for securing the return of Americans abducted abroad, and no mechanism for interagency communication between the State Department, the FBI, our twelve intelligence agencies and the military. Our non-negotiation hostage policy prohibited the FBI from interacting with the captors of the four innocent Americans. Therefore, multiple opportunities to bring our Americans home were lost, leaving them to be abandoned and used as a propaganda tool by ISIS.

19 August 2020 started out a beautiful summer morning. I recall sitting on our screened porch with two FBI agents who oddly asked for DNA swabs, now twenty-one months after Jim's kidnapping. We dutifully complied with their requests for both Jim's DNA from an old toothbrush and our own mouth swabs. After the FBI agents left, I received a telephone call from a sobbing AP reporter asking me if I had looked on Twitter. I did so immediately and saw the horrific photo of Jim's severed head on his body. I refused to believe it and immediately reached out to the FBI for confirmation. No one returned my calls that day. Jim's murder was confirmed on the evening news by a short statement from President Barack Obama.

After the four Americans – journalist Steven Sotloff, aid workers Peter Kassig and Kayla Mueller, and Jim – were murdered and the outrage from our families and Congress, President Obama ordered the National Counterterrorism Center to conduct a total US Hostage Review, which identified the serious disorganization and lack of coordination that abandoned these American citizens to their captors. Those results prompted Obama to issue a Presidential Policy Directive in June 2015, leading to our present US government hostage enterprise to bring home Americans taken hostage abroad and to assist their families. In 2020, the Robert Levinson Hostage Recovery and Hostage-Taking Accountability Act was passed, adding criteria for the US State Department to identify wrongfully detained US nationals abroad and to use sanctions to deter both types of hostage-taking by state actors and criminals.

After Jim's murder, thousands of good people offered donations from around the world. We met Terry Waite, the British founder of Hostage UK, and the charity's director Rachel Briggs in London. We also heard from the released Danish hostage Daniel Rye Ottosen that Jim had spoken with Peter Kassig and Steven Sotloff in prison about starting an entity to help American hostages.

Within a month of Jim's murder, we established the James W. Foley Legacy Foundation. Its mission was to advocate for freedom for Americans taken hostage, to protect independent conflict journalists and to raise awareness about these threats to our freedom. Our first focus was to support American hostage families and returning American hostages. Our experience convinced us of the need for a confidential partner like Hostage UK in our own country that could accompany families throughout a hostage ordeal, helping and advising as needed. We felt strongly that American families needed nongovernmental advocates who could supplement what our government could or could not provide. We raised $200,000, which was matched by the Ford Foundation, to start Hostage US, similar to the organization that so impressed me in the UK.

Our beloved Jim spent the last two years of his life being starved, tortured and finally publicly beheaded for being an American and a journalist. But that is not the end of the story. As the European hostages were gradually released, we came to know the man our son had become. As the Spanish, French and Italian hostages came home, they each called to tell us stories about Jim. They told of his unwavering devotion to prayer multiple times daily and of the strength and hope it gave him. They told stories of the brotherhood that developed in spite of the horrific conditions they were enduring.

Our biggest solace was when Daniel Rye Ottosen was released at the end of June 2014. Since the American and British captives were not allowed to write to their families, Daniel had kindly memorized a letter from Jim to us and called to share it within forty-eight hours of his release. The letter contained a specific message for each family member and was filled with hope and love for all of us.

I prayed so hard that Jim would be strong enough to endure the hatred he was experiencing. That letter from Daniel, and stories from the other European hostages, assured me that God had enabled Jim to be compassionate and hopeful to the very end. That is what made an ordinary young man truly extraordinary.

Sadly, it was not until after Jim's very public execution that John and I began to understand how many lives Jim had touched. This is when we began to grasp the moral courage that he and other journalists have persistently shown the world. This is when we realized that Jim was handing over his commitment to fighting injustice and oppression through a free press and democracy for us to carry forward.

Jim's death opened doors at the White House, enabling us to make the return of American hostages a true priority. In June 2015, a new Presidential Directive established an interagency Hostage Recovery Fusion cell, Special Presidential Envoy for Hostage Affairs and a Hostage Recovery Group in the White House, whose sole mission is to bring Americans home. Since that date, hundreds of Americans have returned home. Unfortunately, US nationals continue to be taken hostage or be unlawfully detained since our adversaries have found hostage-taking a useful tactic to interfere with US foreign policy.[1]

After the horrific deaths of Jim and Steven Sotloff, the James W. Foley Legacy Foundation helped create the ACOS Alliance (A Culture of Safety Alliance), an unprecedented coalition of international media companies, press freedom nonprofits and freelance journalists working to improve the safety of independent conflict journalists.

We developed an undergraduate and graduate level James W. Foley Journalist Safety curriculum for university journalism programmes to challenge aspiring young journalists to prepare for the dangers inherent in their profession today. The curriculum uses the documentary *Jim: The James Foley Story*, directed by a childhood friend, Brian Oakes, to help explain the drive of conflict journalists to share the stories that the world would never hear without their courageous coverage.[2] It also explores the complexity of bringing citizens home from a kidnapping.

In 2012, Jim said, 'For some reason I have physical courage, but that's nothing compared to moral courage. I can go and get those shots, but if I don't have the moral courage to challenge authority, to write about things that are going to have reprisals on my career, we don't have journalism.'

Although Jim's story is a deeply personal one for our family, he represents the moral courage that is a guiding principle and aspiration for conflict journalists. Journalists, like Jim, risk their lives to give voice to others, to make a difference and to ascertain the truth for us. May we all aspire to be people of moral courage.

For further information, see:

www.jamesfoleyfoundation.org

www.foleyrun.org

Notes

1   The Foley Foundation continually updates the current public cases at www. jamesfoleyfoundation.org.

2   *Jim: The James Foley Story*, dir. Brian Oakes (New York: HBO, 2016). Documentary, 109 min.

Teaching for Buoyancy in the Pre-carious Present for an Evitable Future

Julian C. H. Lee, Anna Branford, Sam Carroll-Bell,
Aya Ono and Kaye Quek

The carious future

For those who spend their professional lives among young adults studying at university, there is a burgeoning anxiety about the future. Among many things, students are told that the 'job for life' is now history, and that they will have not only multiple jobs but multiple careers. This anxiousness has been compounded by the SARS-CoV-2 pandemic. In addition to the physical effects of the virus, health experts are also warning of the mental health consequences, including anxiety resulting from the fear of infection and the impacts of lockdowns and isolation. Indeed, COVID-19 has been described as 'the perfect vector for a mental health epidemic'.[1] But even before the pandemic, Greta Thunberg, who has come to be seen as articulating the climate concerns of young people, had asked, 'And why should I be studying for a future that soon will be no more, when no one is doing anything whatsoever to save the future?'[2]

In this chapter we dwell on the ways that, especially for young people, the present is 'pre-carious'. The evidence that the future *is* carious – decayed – seems everywhere, from environmental destruction to hard-won social advances being in jeopardy. Each summer seems to be the hottest on record; Greenland shed twelve billion tons of ice in 2019; extraordinary fire and heat ravaged the northern hemisphere in 2021; and bizarre and unnatural occurrences, such as a dead humpback whale being found in the Amazon rainforest, are omens of a 'nature in chaos'.[3] We are in the midst of the sixth mass extinction, whereby 'Earth is experiencing a huge episode of population declines and extirpations, which will have negative cascading consequences on ecosystem functioning and services vital to sustaining civilization'.[4]

Young people are increasingly seeking counselling for their concerns about the future, especially as it relates to the environment and climate crisis. This anxiety has received various labels, including climate anxiety, eco-anxiety and climate despair.[5] We are familiar with the concept of post-traumatic stress; however, the seemingly inevitable fate of our climate and environment is inducing pre-traumatic stress. Lise Van Susteren, who is attributed with coining 'pre-traumatic stress disorder', explains that when we have it, 'we have in our minds images of the future that reflect what scientists are telling us; images of people and animals suffering because of dumb choices we are making today'.[6] The trauma to come is made more palpable when the future that is feared is already being lived by growing numbers of people whose worlds are already decaying or decayed. Concerning the environment, Lucienne Cross observes that the conviction of many young people 'is simply not mirrored by those in power [leading] young people to feel hopeless and powerless in the face of such a large and impending catastrophe'.[7]

The advent of COVID-19 – itself a global event that has engendered a sense of despair and futility – has only added to the deep pessimism in terms of our collective capacity to address some of our most stubborn social challenges. The World Bank, for example, stated that up to 115 million people who had recently escaped extreme poverty were expected to be pushed back into it 'by the convergence of COVID-19, conflict, and climate change', bringing the total number of those living on less than $1.90 a day up to 729 million.[8] Even before the pandemic, and despite unprecedented levels of global cooperation, coordination and funding, the rates at which poverty was being reduced had already begun to slow.[9] COVID-19 has also exacerbated the many insecurities, inequalities and outright violence that has been part of the lived experience for women the world over. UN Women reports that since the initial outbreak, 'all types of violence against women and girls, particularly domestic violence, has intensified', leading them to designate it as a 'shadow pandemic'.[10] To put this into pre-COVID-19 context, in Australia, where we write from, 'One in five women will experience sexual violence and one in two will experience sexual harassment in their lifetime'.[11] International reports and evidence meanwhile suggest that around 35 per cent of women have been 'subjected to physical and/or sexual intimate partner violence, non-partner sexual violence, or both at least once in their life … This figure does not include sexual harassment'.[12]

This chapter describes our reflections and responses as people who have taught at Australian universities in relation to an air of pessimism to which academics have contributed. Our intention is to explore a central feature of the present gloom, which is the apparent lack of viable remedies which people can choose to become involved with in order to work against their carious future and for a brighter one, allowing them to stay buoyant in the present. We do this via an engagement with the opinions of author and political commentator Will Self, who takes to task the influential philosopher Slavoj Žižek and his book *The Courage of Hopelessness*. We then draw on the works of anthropologist Michael Jackson and philosopher Alfred Schutz, whose notion of 'the purpose at hand' is useful in pointing us towards the options for addressing the circumstances in which we find ourselves. The chapter concludes with reflections on the ways we have attempted to enable and empower students, and dare we say, give them some cause for grounded optimism.

Before proceeding, a note on the authorship of this chapter is required. The decision to have multiple authors signals our wider view that any undertaking to deal with major issues must be collaborative. Many an article seeking to counsel readers about their fear of the future asserts that working with others is known to help with feelings of despondency.[13] Claudia Lang, an alumnus from the International Studies undergraduate degree at RMIT University into which the authors have all taught to various extents, observed with respect to her work as a facilitator for the organization Climate for Change:

> I have felt much more positive and hopeful about the world when working as part of a team. I've since found that this is what makes me hopeful about the climate crisis, and life generally. Everything's far more achievable when I feel connected to the people and places around me.[14]

It is in this spirit that our collaboration in the chapter occurs. At the same time, there are occasions where our individual recollections and experiences are identified. In these instances, we refer to ourselves in the third person by first name.

Paralysis

In stark contrast to Barack Obama's platform of audacious hope, today hopelessness seems much more tangible. In front of an auditorium of audience members in 2017, in an event of verbal jousting at which Will Self interrogated Slavoj Žižek about his (then new) book *The Courage of Hopelessness*, Žižek asked Self, 'Do you know what is happening today?' Self replied:

> I think the light at the end of the tunnel is the approaching train. I agree with
> you. And I assume you agree with the International Panel on Climate Change,
> that if there is a 4 per cent or 5 per cent rise in global temperatures by the end of
> this century, we're all toast, and I don't mean that metaphorically.[15]

In this conversation, there was no disagreement as to the urgency for something to be done with respect to diverse dangers – including environmental ones – imperilling us. Rather, the contest focused on what actually to do and Self's inability to get Žižek to articulate any concrete actions. Self's interest in a programme of action was pre-empted a month earlier, where he lamented that 'the problems we face frankly are so difficult and intractable that it paralyses us'.[16]

When discussing the scale and consequences of global phenomena with the appropriate gravitas, we can readily induce in our selves and our students the paralysis of which Self speaks. One year, Julian had included in a globalization class a magazine article by Emeritus Professor of Politics Robert Manne titled 'Diabolical: why have we failed to address climate change?'[17] The piece draws on an array of texts that explore the causes of our inaction and summarizes the key reasons for the failure that include deeply ingrained human psychological dispositions, climate change denial and the ascent of neoliberalism. Manne avers:

> At the very moment when the neoliberals came to dominate the political
> economy of advanced capitalism, a rational response to climate change required
> powerful government regulation and intervention, state action to rein in the
> activities of the fossil-fuel corporations, state industry policies investing
> heavily in renewable energy, high tax on carbon pollution, recognition of the
> catastrophic potential of market failure. These were precisely the policies and
> attitudes that neoliberals had cast into the rubbish bin of history and that they
> most abhorred.[18]

Julian's objective had been to provide students with an accessible and informed analysis of the complexity of social and political impediments to tackling climate change, and to examine a case study from multiple angles to form a comprehensive picture of the problem at hand which could be later applied to other situations. Instead, teaching staff in that globalization class found that students were overwhelmed by the reading. The breadth of issues and depth of entrenched systems that conserve a trajectory towards climatic and political insecurity made the problems of the world look insurmountable.

But as Self argues, hope is in itself not a means by which large complex problems can be solved. After Self made critical comments about political speech writers during a talk at University College Dublin, an audience member suggested that Self take a less negative view of those politicians who were 'standing up [and] encouraging the best in you'. Self replied that:

> We're in a political culture, and certainly have been since the sixties … in which civil society and civil institutions [are] fraying. People don't feel the natural connection between their engagement, you know, from family, to community, to wider society. That's where the problem lies. It doesn't matter how high flown the rhetoric is, if people are not in a kind of environment in which their positive inclinations are given institutional form all around them, then they're not going to do anything. That's what we saw with Obama: 'Hope! Hope! Hope!' But what then?[19]

Sam and Julian recall a heartfelt conversation in one of the globalization classes at which the topic of 'what to do' about large-scale problems arose. The tension lay between the poles of whether small individual actions, such as buying fair-trade chocolate instead of cheaper alternatives, were actually useful, or whether real change was dependent on the actions of large institutions, particularly governments, working alone or in concert with other governments. We had sought to steer a path between a dispiriting critique of individual efforts, which we affirmed still had their place, while asserting the need for the larger scale and collaborative interventions. This sentiment was cogently captured several years later by Lang, a student who had taken the class in a different year. In a piece for student magazine *Here Be Dragons*, she wrote with respect to making ethical personal choices that:

> The issue is that they place the burden and responsibility to act on the individual, and distract from the root causes of corporate greed, unfettered economic growth and the rise of the individual, which have brought us here in the first place. … Talk to other people, join a local action group, participate in our democracy, call out the worst offenders of climate pollution.[20]

Apparent in the students that the authors of this chapter encounter is a genuine desire to make a positive impact, but also an uncertainty as to how. This desire to know what to *do* was also evident in the exchange between Self and Žižek. While Žižek had no substantive answers to Self's repeated solicitations as to how we should respond to pressing problems, Self likewise did not proffer specific actions, which is indicative of an impasse endemic in the academy:

Žižek: Why do you read prescription into everything that I say?

Self: Because if I read your stuff as *descriptive* it doesn't really take me anywhere. It's the ghost of prescriptivism lingering around your prose that draws people to it. I think people *do* want to hear what your prescriptions are. They don't just want to hear your *des*criptions, or we'd just read you as a cultural critic, and you would have no, no tension or significance as a philosopher at all.[21]

Students readily pick up on the hesitancy of those who teach them to outline salutary ways to respond. Another alumnus from the same degree referred to earlier, Megan O'Malley, who co-founded the ethical fashion blog Walk Sew Good, conveyed her experience of the degree to Julian in a conversation:

A lot of the subjects talked about what you shouldn't do, and how you shouldn't behave. But they didn't give you a way to contribute to the world. It was just like, 'Don't do this. Don't do this. Don't do this'. I was like, 'Why am I doing this degree? I can't do anything!'[22]

O'Malley's comments gesture to a more widespread confinement of people's aspirations to *do something* about their carious future through the systematic closing down of options. We now explore this predicament through the existential and phenomenological philosophies of Jackson and Schutz.

The purpose at hand

… what is possible for a person is always preconditioned by the world into which he or she is born and raised, but a person's life does more than conserve and perpetuate these pre-existing circumstances; it interprets them, negotiates and nuances them, re-imagines them, protests against them, and endures them in such complex and subtle ways that, in the end, human freedom appears as 'the small movement which makes of a totally conditioned social being someone who does not render back completely what his conditioning has given him'.

– Michael Jackson, quoting Jean-Paul Sartre[23]

Helping us to work through paralysis and pessimism is the work of anthropologist Michael Jackson, who has considered the ways people 'struggle for being'.[24] He writes that 'the *question* of being is universal, and constitutes a starting-point in our attempt to explore human lifeworlds as the sites of a perennial struggle for existence', and that human existence is 'continually at *risk*'.[25] The threat and damage that may be caused to one's being – one's self and sense of self – may present itself in a multitude of ways. One's self, one's being, may be endangered by physical harms but also more symbolic harms, such as being regarded as unworthy of recognition. Furthermore, one's sense of self is imperilled by changes to the world and the concrete aspects with which one had worked out a *modus vivendi*.[26]

Enabling us to understand the concrete circumstances in which people struggle and act is the notion of the lifeworld, which is the world of people's daily life. According to Alfred Schutz, 'The world of everyday life is the scene and also the object of our actions and interactions. We have to dominate it and we have to change it in order to realize the purposes which we pursue within it among our fellow-men.'[27] That is, our everyday life is the stage on which we seek to realize our deep and human goals and we act in it and upon it in conjunction with others who are likewise pursuing their goals. Schutz goes on to describe people as located, at any given moment, within a biographically determined situation. This situation 'includes certain possibilities of future practical or theoretical activities which shall be briefly called the "purpose at hand". It is this purpose at hand which defines those elements among all the others contained in such a situation which are relevant for this purpose.'[28] And here, the purpose at hand guides our attention to both the goal we might have at hand in a given moment and those elements of our environment which we can make use of in pursuit of that goal.

We might conceptualize the response of a person to their 'purpose at hand' with an image of a person in a room with multiple doors through which they can choose to pass in light of their circumstances and objectives. Whenever confronted with a situation with which we must wrestle, we can enumerate various options – each option is like a door – and the end of the exercise results in us going through one of them. The choices considered are understood in what phenomenology terms the 'natural attitude'. The natural attitude refers to common sense and taken-for-granted ways in which members of a given society understand their world and account for events in it. This would include commonplace ideas, idioms, techniques and rituals, which will vary from society to society (as well as within segments of a society). One example might be explanations of misfortune; whereas some societies will explain negative events in terms of random 'bad luck', other societies will do so in terms of malevolent intentions by others, or capricious deities.[29] The different explanations lead, in turn, to different courses of action and remedies when undesirable events transpire. A phenomenological approach is more concerned with people's worlds as they appear to them, and less so with 'reality'.

Recalling Self's comment that we live in a political culture where 'civil society and civil institutions are fraying', and the sense of paralysis referred to earlier, it is natural that, when faced with the scale of the problems, we readily feel daunted and without options. In spite of this, what we equally see in students is Jackson's existential drive to make an impact, and in their case, a deep-seated desire to have a positive influence on the world that must not be underestimated or neglected. Coupled with that is the necessity to think carefully about how we present to students what the problems at hand are, and their relationship to the options they have for addressing them.

The land of endless critique

Addressing issues that are complex and overwhelming can be done in a way that both confronts the realities of the problems at hand without leaving an audience of students and others in unhelpful despair. Whether despair is unhelpful is, however, contested. In *The Courage of Hopelessness*, Žižek states, 'It is only when we despair and don't know any more what to do that change can be enacted – we have to go through this zero point of hopelessness.'[30] For Žižek, crises are the instigators of change, provoking this zero point of hopelessness that stirs us towards what really needs doing. In conversation with Self, Žižek remarked, 'My pessimism is at the same time a cause of optimism. Don't worry! There will be new crises. And I mean this very seriously.'[31] Self interjected shortly after, saying, 'Slavoj, you gotta do better than this, man. You gotta do better than these pathetic one-liners.' In attacking these 'one-liners', Self highlighted Žižek's lack of a substantial and constructive response to that which he criticized, for what course of action was the audience supposed to take?

Self's disparagement of Žižek's book in that dialogue and in a review for *The Guardian* still leaves us with the question as to what we should do.[32] Furthermore, as Amitav Ghosh reminds us, *knowing* what we should be doing in this era of climate change is very different from doing it, even if we are convinced of that action's rightness. He states:

> Contrary to what I might like to think, my life is not guided by reason; it is ruled, rather, by the inertia of habitual motion. This is indeed the condition of the vast majority of human beings, which is why very few of us will be able to adapt to global warming if it is left to us, as individuals, to make the necessary changes.[33]

Ghosh's 2016 book *The Great Derangement: Climate Change and the Unthinkable* interrogates the lack of attention to climate change in 'serious' literary fiction, rendering literature complicit in the concealment of this issue. He lambasts this failure of recognition as 'an aspect of the broader imaginative and cultural failure that lies at the heart of the climate crisis. … the climate crisis is also a crisis of culture, and thus of the imagination'.[34] If 'things are what they are experienced to be', it would be wise to heed Ghosh's critique of literature and art, and to apply it more generally, when he says that it participates in 'modes of concealment that [prevent] people from recognizing the realities of their plight'.[35]

Such debates are neither unique to climate change nor the preserve of authors like Žižek, Self and Ghosh. For instance, the academic discipline known as Development Studies has for most of the last seven decades been the site of intense debate and critical scholarship with many of its key protagonists arguing both for and against the efficacy and 'ethicacy' of its practice. In one of its most dramatic and challenging turns, several critical thinkers – drawing inspiration from the advent of new social movements in South America during the 1990s and a wider post-modern questioning of Western forms of knowledge – would go on to produce a radical stream of scholarly literature known as 'post-development'. These authors claimed that the discourse of development encouraged people to perceive themselves as 'undeveloped' and requiring specific kinds of 'knowledge' and 'planning'.[36] Within this dynamic the language of development itself discreetly positioned Western society as a universalized ideal while simultaneously sweeping away local values, knowledges, lifestyles and histories. As a result, development theory and practice, it was argued, often took on an uncritical and un-reflexive mode of self-replication, allowing little in the way of negotiation and contestation of ideas. Moreover, this literature spoke to what it saw as a series of unequal power relationships that in effect limit a society's capacity to 'dream again their own dreams' and to 'trust their own noses'.[37] This was not to single out and apportion blame to those individuals who had dedicated their lives 'to working with the poor'; rather it was a forceful rejection of the wider structures at play. As Thomas Yarrow and Soumhya Venkatesan neatly summarize:

> The [post-development] critiques reveal how an overtly benign impulse to eradicate poverty and promote positive social change often ends up reinscribing the very forms of inequality 'development' purports to overcome. Thus it has been suggested that in their discursive construction of ideas of 'poverty', development institutions objectify an un-differentiated and passive 'third world', whose problems are erroneously attributed to the actions of the people living there. In this way development institutions justify their own activities by locating the 'solutions' in the supposedly superior forms of 'expertise' that Western development professionals bring.[38]

Development and its promise of social progress was said to be little more than a sleight of hand, whereby the application of Western knowledge gradually subjugated the people of the global south under the pretence of freedom and prosperity. Authors like Arturo Escobar would depict development as a 'Frankenstein-type dream' and 'an apparatus that links forms of knowledge about the Third World with the deployment of forms of power and intervention, resulting in the mapping and production of Third World societies'.[39]

The blistering critique of development frequently left workers and scholars cold if not confused about how, or even if, they should engage with the subject of poverty. This was due in no small part to post-development offering little in terms of tools or a way of navigating the multifaceted ethical questions it had opened up.[40] Post-development itself was soon to become the subject of its own scrutiny, charged with being guilty of the same sort of discursive essentialism it had exposed in the language of development.[41] Development scholar George Curry contended that in its outright rejection of all development-related activity, post-development denied the possibility for any improvement to people's 'health, education, and material well-being'.[42] So, if not development, then what? How else would poverty and hunger be alleviated? And for those wanting to contribute to the material wellbeing of people around the world, where and how should they proceed? Development Studies and its practice had reached a critical moment but in so doing it also seemed paralysed. Once again Yarrow and Venkatesan succinctly capture this moment:

> Although this post-development critique has pertinently highlighted how apparently 'neutral' and 'objective' developmental discourses often end up justifying political inequality, it has led to an increasingly acute impasse. In their wholesale rejection of 'development', these critiques have tended to foreclose consideration of how or whether it is possible to retain hope in the vision of a better or more just future.[43]

Here, we pause and reflect on our work as academics and teachers. One regularly hears academics criticize a policy, law or whatever else, and follow it by saying it is not their place to offer an alternative. However, we must be aware of the profound effect of dwelling in the Land of Endless Critique. Far from suggesting that we do not critique nor teach our students the invaluable skill of critical thinking, the outcome of witnessing this time and again will be that many will believe that whatever they might imagine or do will be assailed and undermined, rendering them embarrassed or even ashamed. Recycling waste plastic and paper, or using re-usable coffee cups, might be a way to reduce pressure on resources, but perhaps the psychological comfort that recycling gives us impedes us from adopting better and more radically sustainable behaviours.

An example to illustrate this point brings together the existential and phenomenological perspective outlined in this chapter, and perhaps demonstrates its utility. In 2016 Julian was circulating around a classroom, visiting numerous student conversations. One group was excoriating 'voluntourism', where (usually privileged) people pay an organization or company to enable them to volunteer and help a community in an underdeveloped country. Over the past few years, Julian had regularly heard such lambastings of voluntourism for diverse reasons, including the potential for it to undermine employment opportunities in the place of destination and to perpetuate profitable forms of misery.

While not doubting the usefulness of critiquing voluntourism, Julian suggested to this table of students that they consider why voluntourism exists and the pathways that people travel towards participating in it. One of the things that the phenomenon of voluntourism suggests is that there is this desire and will – the existential drive – by many people to make a positive impact in the world and for others that they do not even know. And then imagine someone who decides they are not being fulfilled in their job and they want to lead a more meaningful life, but they are not enrolled in a degree like the students and so do not have access to the insights in it. What are they to do? How are they to react to their situation? Carrying out web searches on the internet may quickly lead them to volunteer tourism programmes. In terms of their options – their phenomenological experience of their choices – there are few. While the criticisms of voluntourism are warranted, it may be more productive instead to locate it in a broader debate in order to channel the positive desires and energies of people in genuinely constructive ways. At this point in Julian's suggestion, one student at the table admitted that she had participated in (what she now knew to be) voluntourism in the recent past and had found the experience enlightening, despite having qualms about it now in retrospect.

We suggest that it can be possible to participate in a critique of something, but to do so in a way that does not disempower. It is possible to channel attention towards reflection and direction for gainful action, without shaming or embarrassing those who have acted with good intentions. This is not to advocate mollycoddling, sugar-coating or evading hard truths. The ways we structure our conversations can be profound. As O'Malley expressed in 2018, 'The fear of failure and of doing the wrong thing paralyses people from doing anything. They are like, "Oh well. It's too hard. I won't do anything".

One possibility for exploring a different mode of engagement may lie within the tones and attitudes conveyed in the teaching space on the evolution of a discipline's key ideas. Anna notes that this idea is highly relevant to her own background in Sociology, a field in which it can be tempting to explore the historical sequence of modifications, reformulations and changes-of-direction as a string of fairly obvious responses to ignorance and oversight (sometimes wilful) on the part of past theorists and thinkers. Sometimes imposing this kind of narrative structure onto the evolution of ideas can be difficult to avoid, for example, when identifying the colonizing potential of development theory or the heteronormativity of ideas and definitions like marriage being the 'union of a man and a woman'. There are costs when this approach becomes a kind of *modus operandi* within university discourse, one of which is unwittingly laying the groundwork for a culture whereby new ideas are rendered implicitly dangerous for students, becoming an open invitation for disdain and disgrace. This can cultivate a mentality whereby students choose the safe role of critic above the risky role of the imaginer in the very setting where new ideas could grow, and in the pre-carious era in which they are vital.

Critique is, of course, a crucial component of a culture of growth, and accountability is indisputably necessary where ideas have caused, and are causing, harm. However, critique and accountability can be offered while recognizing the context and the history of the issue at hand. Key possibilities may lie, again, in the way the histories of our ideas are taught and discussed. 'What problems did this idea cause, and for whom?' can be asked alongside 'How could those problems have been foreseen?' and 'What new ideas did the problematic ideas make possible?' Flowing into a present-tense application, this contextualized approach to critique may embolden thinkers in articulating new ideas. If a blunder can be characterized as the moment at which an idea's wrongness comes into sharpest focus, its value as a moment of clarity for others striving in the field is surely worth highlighting. Without undermining the need for accountability where harm is done, it can be acknowledged that a field becomes stronger when, say, its thinkers come to realize that a key term is inappropriate, or that a demographic has been missing from the data, or that a crucial viewpoint has been excluded. In this context, disdain for Žižek's 'pathetic one-liners' has served as just such a crystalline moment. We must all do better than this.

So, then, what to do? A test to our imaginative abilities will be how we conceive of the causes of our predicaments. We often readily assign blame for one or another tragedy. However, it can be harder to see behaviours as being conditioned by the larger context, or system, within which they occur. As Fred Kofman and Peter Senge state:

> There is no enemy out there to blame. … Nor will blaming ourselves individually help. The causes lie in collective behaviors and unintended side effects of actions that make individual sense. There is no blame, there is no guilt, just a need to think differently.[44]

Whatever one might make about the principle in systems thinking of 'there is no blame', it does helpfully ask us to think about occurrences beyond the immediate actors and their immediate circumstances, which for many people is to think differently about things.[45] In the image of the person with several option-doors to choose from for their purpose at hand, endless critique has the effect of closing doors. In the concluding section of this chapter, we share some of the ways, including using systems thinking and 'creative ideation' tools, that we have used with students.

Installing doors

Globalization classes and their accompanying textbooks are usually structured around a series of 'ands' – 'Globalization and culture', 'Globalization and crime', 'Globalization and the economy' – which may help students know more *about* an aspect of their world, but will often be unclear as to how to actively engage *with* the world about which they are learning. There are alternatives, however. Systems thinking offers one such alternative, given its focus on holistic and inclusive analyses and its adoption by various non-government organizations including Oxfam.[46] In thinking on the current state of affairs, for instance, if climate change, global poverty and social inequalities are understood as a series of interconnected human constructs that are largely of our making or neglect, rather than a natural phenomenon or an inevitable state of being, then such ideas can be deconstructed and reworked to create more sustainable futures. By focusing on the inter-relationships and the way they are perceived and bordered by various groups, systems thinking encourages people to see how the social, cultural, political, environmental, spiritual and economic arenas intersect and influence one another in complex and uneven ways. Comprehending these dynamics and the various perspectives that people have on them is what gives us the foundation to talk, plan and act in a way that is attuned to each other's needs and to forge new, more sustainable systems.

Systems thinking is advocated by Leyla Acaroglu, an alumnus from the authors' university, who has founded change-enabling organizations such as the UnSchool and Disrupt Design which draw on systems thinking perspectives. For her and others, holistic systems thinking attempts to counter the flaws in deeply ingrained reductionist thinking. Acaroglu writes:

> Systems thinking is a way of seeing the world as a series of interconnected and interdependent systems rather than lots of independent parts. As a thinking tool, it seeks to oppose the reductionist view – the idea that a system can be understood by the sum of its isolated parts – and replace it with expansionism, the view that everything is part of a larger whole and that the connections between all elements are critical.[47]

Whereas others have detailed what systems thinking is and its benefit to scholars and activists, as well as the dangers of reductionist (aka linear) thinking, of relevance in the present discussion is its positive impact as a pedagogic tool. A colleague of Sam and Julian's, who has taught for several years in the globalization class mentioned in this chapter, commented that they felt 'our systems thinking activities empowered students and brought home that global issues aren't insurmountable'. Similarly, a number of Sam's students informed him of how the systems thinking activities had given them the perspective and confidence to take their studies in new and unanticipated directions. In the words of one student, 'the problems are still massive, you know, it's not like they've gone anywhere, but with systems thinking, I have a place to start and a way of understanding them properly or maybe a way that I can work with others to understand them better'.

In addition to learning about and creating systems maps for given issues, the classroom activities in question were developed by Acaroglu (in collaboration with others), and were from a range of tools aimed at 'educators, creatives and facilitators [to] activate positive social and environmental change in creative and fun ways'.[48] Sam and Julian's globalization class has used the 'Game Changer Game' and the 'Designercise Ideation Toolkit', while Kaye has employed the former in her global feminisms class. These toolkits contain structured tasks designed to assist participants to first identify a pressing matter (small or large), and then to inspire creative ideas and actionable plans by shifting peoples' perspective with role-plays, exemplars of past interventions or engaging teamwork. For example, in the Game Changer Game, groups of five to ten people have two minutes to develop an intervention for an identified issue by drawing inspiration from a card that they are given. These cards briefly detail ways in which a real-life problem was addressed, such as encouraging physical exercise through making stairs in a subway more fun by turning steps into piano keys that played music.

In prompting students to engage with an issue, the games led to their outlining genuine social and international problems, and responding with creative and often viable ideas as to how they might be tackled. As significant as the actual ideas was the atmosphere that was generated. Despite the gravity and immensity of some of the topics broached, students often reacted in the same way – with excitement and enthusiasm, and sometimes laughter, after initial tentativeness because of the newness and ostensibly unserious nature of the task. The value of such activities lies in the intellectual and emotional impact. Intellectually, they break a problem down into manageable fragments, which can become the focus of one's efforts, rather than a nebulous abstract issue. Rather than simply presenting various options, these exercises created new ones. In the image of a person with option-doors to choose from, these activities break through walls and create doors that were not there before. Emotionally, the levity-despite-gravity fosters buoyancy and agency in place of hopelessness and helplessness.

Systems thinking implies a collaborative approach as the processes that contribute to a given phenomenon and the stakeholders who ought to be included are diverse. It also advocates against 'solutions' and linear utilitarian thinking that is a problematic trait in a range of fields, including Development. Reflecting on the desire by many people from privileged backgrounds to 'fix' major issues, Clare Talwalker suggests that the 'utilitarian approach today gives a privileged role to those thought to know best about what will produce the greatest good for the greatest number – these are usually experts from the comfortable classes of society'.[49] Through her own teaching in a class on poverty, Talwalker explains how she guides her students away from instrumental and unilateral approaches towards ones that have at the outset equitable engagements and collaborations with the communities of interest. This has 'meant backing away from a programmatic approach and a concrete goal and instead opening up to the unpredictability of what other people think and do'.[50]

It is in this spirit of interest in and engagement with others that Aya, a graduate of the Bachelor of International Studies, started her journey with Peace Palette. Co-founded in 2012 with friend and former child soldier in Sudan, David Nyuol Vincent, this not-for-profit organization works for peacebuilding in what is now South Sudan, which gained independence in 2011 after Africa's longest-running civil war. The first projects did not have the impact or longevity that was initially hoped for due to insufficient cash flow. However, the organization placed an emphasis on collaboration to make the operation sustainable by gaining insights, feedback and engagement with communities in South Sudan, leading to the true ownership of the objectives of Peace Palette on the ground. The organization itself draws heavily on the insights and networks of Vincent.

Based on its collaborative model, Peace Palette developed its main continuing project, Sport for Peace, which has achieved a degree of success. This initiative provides a platform for young people to participate in the Peace and Reconciliation Basketball League (PRBL), which involves people from areas that experience frequent inter-tribal cattle raids. As part of the basketball tournament, which is wholly staffed and run by local South Sudanese, players receive training that plants the seed of personal transformation to be Peace Ambassadors so as to bring the peacebuilding message and tools back home. This approach draws on participatory rural appraisal (PRA) where the co-founders of Peace Palette 'hand over the stick' to local staff and young people who then are invested in the process of peacebuilding in the precarious post-conflict setting.[51] The PRBL is broadcast nationally on television and is now part of a community calendar. The frequent cattle raids and tribal conflict have dramatically reduced, and the way locals deal with serious conflicts has shifted from revenge killing to dialogue for compensation.[52] Aya's experience with Peace Palette, and especially the inclusive and participatory nature of its work that moves away from utilitarian thinking of 'fixing' a problem towards collaboration, is evidence that gains can be made in contexts where the difficulties seem intractable and a gloomy future inevitable.

Cultivating students' belief in an evitable future presents challenges not only in the teaching of doomsday scenario topics but also in relation to local social issues. For instance, gender-based violence offers a compelling example of the presently fraught and equally pre-carious times in which we live. For our students in Melbourne, there is ample reminder of the enormity of the test we are facing in the phenomenon of male violence against women. In recent years, the subject has gained traction in the public consciousness with initiatives like the development of national 'action plans' on gendered abuse, community awareness and education campaigns run by state and non-state actors alike, and sustained reporting in news media.

The high-profile rapes and murders in Melbourne of two young women – both similar in age to the majority of our students, and one of whom was a university student at the time of her death – have undoubtedly impacted on students' own sense of security, of their present as well as their future, signalled in their referencing of the cases in class.[53] The occurrence of the crimes combined with extensive media coverage contributes to a pervasive despair – in the university and beyond – that casts violence against women as perpetual. Against this background, teaching on the topics of rape culture, male sexual entitlement and constraints on female sexual agency is precarious, especially when one is conscious of not wanting to diminish the hopefulness of students for a society where such things do not exist.

Yet in teaching feminist theory on sexual violence and rape culture, Kaye noticed students frequently find space for hope where we might expect to find only despair. The cautious optimism derives in large part from her students' engagement with a chapter from sociologist Lynn Phillips' work, *Flirting with Danger*.[54] In the assigned chapter, Phillips draws on interviews with US female college students to identify a range of techniques used by her participants to negotiate experiences of sexual inequality, discomfort and injury in their everyday lives. Female students frequently report feelings of 'relief' and 'excitement' at seeing their own experiences of an unequal (hetero)sexual culture, which privileges male pleasure and desire over those of women, mirrored and so clearly expressed in academic work. Phillips gives a language to a problem (in this case, constraints on female sexual agency) that many students encounter but, prior to the reading, had not yet been able to fully articulate. The power to name is thus frequently experienced as *empowering*, giving rise to an emerging sensibility based on recognition of the fact that those concerned with it are better equipped than before to counter destructive norms that perpetuate coercive (hetero) sexual relations.

Lastly, but not inconsequentially, students tend to view the class discussion, anchored initially by Phillips' work, as an opportunity to unpick the ubiquity of sexual coercion in everyday heterosexual relations. In other words, having gained the language and conceptual tools with which to think through the challenges of rape culture in their own lives, many students observe their potential to affect change in small but meaningful ways. Over the years, more than one male student has noted to Kaye that the Phillips' chapter and subsequent tutorial debates have given rise to a newfound desire to ruminate on, question and ultimately undo instances of male sexual privilege among their peers and in their community; privilege which they had previously not been conscious of. Students, both male and female, have commented that their experience of the class, and the exchanges therein, have been energizing, forming a basis for starting conversations for change with their friends and partners. When Kaye asks students for their thoughts about the Phillips' reading a common refrain is an immediate 'I've given it to all my friends!' The overall sentiment from that part of the course was that the way it is does not have to be the way it always will be, with newly discovered language and concepts forming a path forward for constructing a brighter future via conversation and collaboration.

Conclusion

Experiences of gains made in difficult circumstances are good for their own sakes, but also for enabling people to understand that advances per se can and do occur. In the present climate of anxiety over our carious-seeming future, it is imperative to prepare students to navigate the world critically, constructively and collaboratively with others. Supporting Lang's sentiments in the introduction of this chapter, Professor of Psychology Art Markham enjoins his audience to 'get together with people and actually try to build a plan to solve [issues]', and that 'feel[ing] like you are part of a community that is trying to achieve a goal [is] something that can actually make the present a deeply wonderful place to be'.[55] As people working in universities, we appear at a critical moment in our students' lives and history, where we have the opportunity and obligation to equip them with knowledge, skills and, as importantly, the disposition, to make a positive difference in their chosen realm of endeavour.

Notes

1   Idura N. Hisham, Giles Townsend, Steve Gillard, Brishti Debnath and Jacqueline Sin, 'COVID-19: the perfect vector for a mental health epidemic', *BJPsych Bulletin* 45, no. 6 (2021): 332–38.

2   Greta Thunberg, *No One Is Too Small to Make a Difference* (London: Penguin, 2019), 11.

3   Jonathan Jones, 'Why we can't help but see the whale in the forest as an omen', *The Guardian* (27 February 2019), https://www.theguardian.com/environment/ shortcuts/2019/feb/26/why-we-cant-help-but-see-the-whale-in-the-forest-as-an-omen.

4   Gerardo Ceballos, Paul Ehrlich and Rodolfo Dirzo, 'Biological annihilation via the ongoing sixth mass extinction signaled by vertebrate population losses and declines', *Proceedings of the National Academy of Sciences of the United States of America* 114, no. 30 (2017): E6089. https://doi.org/10.1073/pnas.1704949114.

5   See Molly S. Castelloe, 'Coming to terms with ecoanxiety', *Psychology Today* (9 January 2018), https://www.psychologytoday.com/gb/blog/the-me-in-we/201801/coming-terms-ecoanxiety; Zing Tsjeng, 'The climate change paper so depressing it's sending people to therapy', *Vice* (27 February 2019), https://www.vice.com/en_au/article/vbwpdb/the-climate-change-paper-so-depressing-its-sending-people-to-therapy.

6   Quoted in Ben Brooker, 'I'm afraid something might be coming', *Overland* 230 (2018): 41.

7   Lucienne Cross, 'Climate anxiety: is hopelessness preventing us from confronting our biggest challenge?', *Inhabitat* (24 July 2019), https://inhabitat.com/climate-anxiety-is-hopelessness-preventing-us-from-confronting-our-biggest-challenge.

8   World Bank, 'Poverty: overview / context' (7 October 2020), formerly available at: https://www.worldbank.org/en/topic/poverty/overview#1.

9   World Bank, 'Poverty'.

10 UN Women, 'The shadow pandemic: violence against women during COVID-19' (2020), https://www.unwomen.org/en/news/in-focus/in-focus-gender-equality-in-covid-19-response/violence-against-women-during-covid-19.

11 Bianca Fileborn, 'Acting on gender-based violence must be a priority for the next federal government', *The Conversation* (7 March 2019), https://theconversation.com/acting-on-gender-based-violence-must-be-a-priority-for-the-next-federal-government–110765.

12 UN Women, 'Shadow pandemic'.

13 See Penny Sarchet, 'Stressed about climate change? Eight tips for managing eco-anxiety', *New Scientist* (21 October 2019), https://www.newscientist.com/article/2220561-stressed-about-climate-change-eight-tips-for-managing-eco-anxiety/; Miki Perkins, '"We can't let this happen": how ordinary people handle climate distress', *The Age* (11 August 2021), https://www.theage.com.au/national/we-can-t-let-this-happen-how-ordinary-people-handle-climate-distress-20210811-p58hpw.html.

14 Personal correspondence with Julian Lee (2019). Permission acquired to quote and name.

15 How To Academy, 'Slavoj Žižek vs Will Self in Dangerous Ideas', filmed 18 May 2017 in London, video, 1:17:33, https://www.youtube.com/watch?v=CId1iOWQUuo.

16 UCD, 'Will Self | Q&A with UCD Clinton Institute for American Studies', filmed 31 March 2017 at the Royal Irish Academy, Dublin, video, 22:18, https://www.youtube.com/watch?v=qOP4XV7iQgw.

17 Robert Manne, 'Diabolical: why have we failed to address climate change?', *The Monthly* (December 2015–January 2016): 24–34.

18 Manne, 'Diabolical', 32.

19 UCD, 'Will Self'.

20 Claudia Lang, 'A convenient lie', *Here Be Dragons* 6 (2019): 10.

21 How To Academy, 'Slavoj Žižek'.

22 Personal correspondence with Julian Lee (2018). Permission acquired to quote and name.

23 Michael Jackson, 'Introduction: phenomenology, radical empiricism, and anthropological critique', in *Things as They Are: New Directions in Phenomenological*

Anthropology, ed. Michael Jackson (Bloomington, IN: Indiana University Press, 1996), 30.

24 Michael Jackson, *Existential Anthropology: Events, Exigencies and Effects* (New York: Berghahn Books, 2005), xx.

25 Jackson, *Existential Anthropology*, xii, xiv, original emphasis.

26 Michael Jackson, *The Politics of Storytelling: Violence, Transgression and Intersubjectivity* (Copenhagen: Museum Tusculanum Press, 2002), 71–72.

27 Alfred Schutz, *Alfred Schutz on Phenomenology and Social Relations: Selected Writings*, ed. Helmut R. Wagner (Chicago: University of Chicago Press, 1970), 73.

28 Schutz, *Alfred Schutz*, 73.

29 William O'Barr, 'Culture and causality: non-western systems of explanation', *Law and Contemporary Problems* 64, no. 4 (2001): 317–23.

30 Slavoj Žižek, *The Courage of Hopelessness: Chronicles of a Year of Acting Dangerously* (London: Penguin Books, 2018 [2017]), x.

31 How To Academy, 'Slavoj Žižek'.

32 Will Self, 'The Courage of Hopelessness by Slavoj Žižek review – how the big hairy Marxist would change the world', *The Guardian* (28 April 2017), https://www.theguardian.com/books/2017/apr/28/courage-of-hopelessness-slavoj-zizek-review.

33 Amitav Ghosh, *The Great Derangement: Climate Change and the Unthinkable* (Chicago: University of Chicago Press, 2016), 54.

34 Ghosh, *Great Derangement*, 8–9.

35 Ghosh, *Great Derangement*, 11.

36 See Arturo Escobar, *Encountering Development: The Making and Unmaking of the Third World* (Princeton, NJ: Princeton University Press, 1995); Wolfgang Sachs, *The Development Dictionary: A Guide to Knowledge as Power* (London: Zed Books, 1992).

37 Gustavo Esteva, Salvatore Babones and Philipp Babcicky, *The Future of Development: A Radical Manifesto* (Chicago: Policy Press, 2013), 55.

38 Thomas Yarrow and Soumhya Venkatesan, 'Anthropology and development: critical framings', in *Differentiating Development: Beyond an Anthropology of Critique*, eds. Soumhya Venkatesan and Thomas Yarrow (New York: Berghahn Books, 2012), 2.

39 Arturo Escobar, 'Reflections on "development": grassroots approaches and alternative politics in the Third World', *Futures* 24, no. 5 (1992): 419; Arturo Escobar, 'Imagining a post-development era', in *The Power of Development*, ed. Jonathan Crush (London: Routledge, 1995), 207.

40 Jan Nederveen Pieterse, *Development Theory* (London: Sage, 2000), 119–22.

41 George Curry, 'Moving beyond postdevelopment: facilitating indigenous alternatives for "development"', *Economic Geography* 79, no. 4 (2003): 405–23.

42 Curry, 'Moving beyond postdevelopment', 406.

43 Yarrow and Venkatesan, 'Anthropology and development', 2.

44 Fred Kofman and Peter Senge, 'Communities of commitment: the heart of learning organizations', *Organizational Dynamics* 22, no. 2 (1993): 11.

45 Pamela Buckle Henning and Wan-Ching Chen, 'Systems thinking: common ground or untapped territory?', *Systems Research and Behavioral Science* 29, no. 5 (2012): 479.

46 Kimberly Bowman, John Chettleborough, Helen Jeans, Jo Rowlands and James Whitehead, 'Systems thinking: an introduction for Oxfam programme staff', *Oxfam: Policy and Practice* (2015), https://policy-practice.oxfam.org. uk/publications/systems-thinking-an-introduction-for-oxfam-programme-staff-579896.

47 Leyla Acaroglu, 'Problem solving desperately needs systems thinking', *Medium* (3 August 2016), https://medium.com/disruptive-design/problem-solving-desperately-needs-systems-thinking-607d34e4fc80.

48 Leyla Acaroglu, 'Toolkits', *Leyla Acaroglu* (2021), https://www.leylaacaroglu.com/toolkits. The authors of this chapter have no vested interests related to the products discussed here and no personal connection with Acaroglu.

49 Clare Talwalker, 'Fixing poverty', in *Encountering Poverty: Thinking and Acting in an Unequal World*, eds. Ananya Roy, Genevieve Negrón-Gonzales, Kweku Opoku-Agyemang and Clare Talwalker (Oakland, CA: University of California Press, 2016), 133.

50 Talwalker, 'Fixing poverty', 144.

51 Robert Chambers, 'Participatory rural appraisal (PRA): analysis of experience', *World Development* 22, no. 9 (1994): 1253.

52 Radio Tamazuj, 'Cattle keepers, farmers commit to peaceful co-existence in W. Bahr el-Ghazal' (23 May 2021), https://radiotamazuj.org/en/news/article/cattle-keepers-farmers-commit-to-peaceful-co-existence-in-w-bahr-el-ghazal.

53 The cases referred to here are the rape-murders of Palestinian woman Aiia Maasarwe in January 2019 and Australian woman Eurydice Dixon in June 2018.

54 Lynn Phillips, *Flirting with Danger: Young Women's Reflections on Sexuality and Domination* (New York: New York University Press, 2000).

55 Antony Funnell, 'Why we see the past through rose-coloured glasses, but not the future', *ABC News* (29 August 2019), https://www.abc.net.au/news/2019-08-29/humans-pessimistic-by-nature-but-future-not-all-bad/11452114.

'Will there be a day that I say I am an equal human being?' Living With the Compounding Precarity of Seeking Asylum in Australia

Salem Askari and Caroline Fleay

Introduction

Salem: As a young man coming from a deprived and impoverished part of Afghanistan, where people are judged based on their physical appearance, religious beliefs and race, it has always been my dream to live a life where I am treated as an equal to my fellow citizens.

I ran away from injustice, discrimination, hatred and persecution, in the hope of a better life where I can exercise my freedom of expression and beliefs without the possibility of being threatened by the government or other groups.

I always admired Australia for its passionate advocacy about human rights injustices around the world. It seemed to me that whenever there was a human rights violation in any part of the world, the Australian government voiced its concern. I found this encouraging. However, I now know that this is not always the case and there are significant human rights issues within the country that are barely acknowledged.

For instance, there are over 30,000 refugees and people seeking asylum currently living in Australia who have been here for almost a decade now. I am one of them. Many of us have been working hard, learning a trade or profession to support ourselves and our families, and also contributing to the economy. Despite the difficulties we have endured, we persist in our efforts to establish a new life and not be a burden on the community.

Yet after nearly a decade, we still cannot apply for a permanent visa or be reunited with our families, and continue to face barriers in employment and other social conditions due to our temporary visa status. This greatly compounds our fear and uncertainty.

***

Precarity is about 'conditions of vulnerability'.[1] Although it is something that all humans potentially face, precarity is often unequally distributed, dependent on the dominant values of a society which determines whose lives are to be protected and nurtured, and whose are not.[2] This can be witnessed in government policies imposed on particular groups of people that lead to differential treatment and varying levels of aid. For some, this creates extreme conditions of precarity and an 'associated sense of insecurity' that manifests in multiple spheres, often at the same time, including employment, housing and welfare supports.[3] Australian policies and laws for people seeking asylum can be understood in this way.

The number of people forcibly displaced worldwide due to crises, such as persecution, conflict and violence, has doubled over the past decade to reach 82.4 million in 2020.[4] This includes 26.4 million refugees and 4.1 million people seeking asylum.[5] However, as outlined below, Australia accepts relatively few refugees from offshore locations, and given its geographical isolation relatively few people seeking asylum arrive through irregular means, that is, by boat. Despite this, successive governments have imposed punitive rules and regulations that have debilitated the lives of many seeking protection. A person may be removed from a place that poses imminent danger to life, but their arrival to this island nation does not automatically guarantee their safety and stability.

This chapter explores the intersection of multiple conditions of precarity that many people from asylum-seeking backgrounds who arrived in Australia over the past decade continue to endure. We first outline the country's policy framework for people seeking asylum, then follow it with a discussion of the concept of compound precarity in relation to employment and the denial of the right to live with one's family, before concluding by reflecting on the mobilizing potential of precarity. We draw on Salem's experiences as someone who sought asylum in Australia after arriving by boat in 2013 and who continues to live on a temporary protection visa, to illustrate the daily realities of existing in a state of limbo. We acknowledge that even though each individual's journey to freedom and safety is unique, there are common experiences. As a human rights scholar and advocate, Caroline first met Salem in 2015 and for the past five years they have engaged in advocacy and research together in response to this compound precarity. Therefore, we also draw here on our knowledge of the policy landscape and involvement in the Western Australian Refugee and People Seeking Asylum Network that is underpinned by the right to seek asylum.[6] The indented sections denote where Salem's own experience is discussed, while all other areas incorporate Salem's and Caroline's reflections.

Policy context

Prior to the COVID-19 pandemic, the Australian government granted 13,171 resettlement visas for the 2019–2020 annual intake of its Refugee and Humanitarian Program.[7] The programme includes people who arrive in the country to resettle and those who apply for refugee status after arrival. In 2020, Australia ranked third in the world (after Canada and the United States) 'for the number of its resettlements from other asylum countries', but any assessment of these numbers has to take into account that less than 1 per cent of the world's refugees are resettled each year, with the vast majority residing in countries neighbouring the one they fled.[8] As of mid-2021, 85 per cent of the world's 26.6 million refugees were hosted in developing countries.[9]

Australia's meagre contribution to international humanitarian efforts is even more pronounced when considering its handling of vulnerable groups. While people resettled under the offshore component of the Refugee and Humanitarian Program receive a permanent visa and government-funded supports and services, people seeking asylum post-arrival must often wait for lengthy periods of time for their refugee claim to be finalized, with minimal access to social welfare and other government-funded services. According to the Australian Human Rights Commission, 'current temporary protection arrangements discriminate unjustifiably against certain asylum seekers based on their mode of arrival, and may effectively operate as penalties for irregular entry'.[10] Those who arrive by boat, which is often the only way people without a valid visa can attempt to enter Australia, have been subjected to especially severe measures. One of these is mandatory detention, first enshrined in law in 1992, which involves imprisonment of a person (including children) in an immigration centre until their refugee claim has been accepted, regardless of the length of time this processing may take, or until the Minister for Immigration exercises their discretion to allow the person to live in the community as they wait for their claim to be finalized. From 1999 to 2008, and again from 2013, Australia has granted only temporary protection visas to refugees who arrived by boat. Between 2001 and 2008, and since 2012, Australia has employed the practice of transporting people to detention facilities on Nauru in Micronesia and Papua New Guinea's Manus Island for offshore processing, without any prospect that they would be resettled in Australia.[11]

To understand this treatment of people seeking asylum, it is necessary to acknowledge the nation's colonialist history. As Chris Sidoti observed, Australia has had two obsessions since the British landed in 1788 – 'locking people up' and the perceived threat of being invaded by large hordes of people from Asia.[12] Founded as a penal colony, the beginnings of Australia as a nation-state – understood here as a 'white Australia' – involved incarceration of convicts from Britain and Ireland, and also the locking up and massacre of many First Nations peoples who were seen as inferior to the colonizers. The colonial mentality is deeply embedded in Australian society and most clearly borne out by the nation's policies towards, and treatment of, those deemed less than or unworthy of being part of the country. For example, its contemporary manifestations can be clearly seen in the imprisonment of First Nations people in Australia far in excess of any other racial group, despite the recommendations of various inquiries that call for systemic change, and the inhumane detainment on an indefinite basis of people seeking asylum.[13]

In addition to its deeply entrenched practice of incarceration, Australia has a long history of inhibiting non-white people from entering its borders. Up until its official demise in 1973, the White Australia immigration policy was designed to limit non-British migration as much as possible, reflecting fears of the 'other'; any 'group or race that is perceived as the most important threat to the existence of a nation or national identity'.[14] For instance, the Immigration Restriction Act which came into law in 1901 'gave immigration officers the power to make any non-European migrant sit a 50-word dictation test' in any European language, and after 1905 it could be given in any prescribed language.[15] This made the test impossible for many to pass, and especially targeted people of Asian descent. But it is not only the blatant racism and lingering effects of these early immigration policies that is relevant here. As Robert Manne argues, their absolutism is now embedded in Australia's 'immigration culture of control' – whereby the Australian government must retain the capacity to control and order who is allowed to enter the country.[16] This helps, at least in part, to explain the extent to which successive governments have sought to deter and punish the arrival of people by boat who are seeking asylum.

These policies became particularly harsh during the first half of the eleven years of the conservative Coalition Government (1996–2007) when there was a spike in the number of people seeking asylum, many fleeing violence and persecution in countries such as Afghanistan, Iran and Iraq. In the immediate wake of 9/11 and rising anti-Muslim sentiment, the government conflated the arrival of people seeking asylum from Muslim-majority countries with terrorism and used this to justify how it responded to unauthorized entries into the country. This played a critical role in its electoral success in November

2001.[17] With significantly declining boat arrivals in the subsequent years, as well as growing opposition to the Coalition Government's strict policies, by the time the Labor Government was elected in 2007 there was space for supporting more humane policies.[18]

However, after several years, increasing numbers of people seeking asylum began to arrive by boat and the political rhetoric and accompanying policies surrounding this issue began to harden once again. From July 2012 until June 2013, some 25,000 arrivals were reported, which was the highest annual number ever received. Although this figure is comparatively very small on a global scale, the Labor Government nevertheless retained the use of mandatory detention and re-introduced offshore sites of detention as part of its increasingly hard-line approach to border security. After the re-election of the Coalition Government in September 2013, policies became even more punitive. While the right to work began to be granted to people seeking asylum who were living in the community, 'fast track assessment' of their protection claims was adopted. Despite its name, this process has been characterized by long delays in processing and restricted access to independent review of decisions that refused protection.[19] Furthermore, those found to be refugees have only been granted temporary protection and issued either a three-year Temporary Protection Visa (TPV) or a five-year Safe Haven Enterprise Visa (SHEV). These visa holders are not privy to the full range of government-funded supports and services that permanent residents and citizens enjoy, nor are they permitted to apply for immediate family members to join them in Australia.

Unlike TPV holders, SHEV holders may become eligible for permanent residence provided they first meet the SHEV pathway requirements, and then the criteria of one of the few permanent visas on offer. The pathway requirements are satisfied if, for at least three and a half years while on a SHEV, an individual has been either employed in a designated regional area and/or enrolled in and physically attended full-time study in a regional area, and not received social security benefits.[20] Given that most SHEV holders lived and worked in non-regional areas for some years before being granted the visa, they are understandably reluctant to leave their employment, healthcare services and the community supports they have developed. Even for those who have fulfilled the work or study criteria in a designated regional area, options for permanent residency are limited. Of the small number of visas available to them, most are skilled visas that require high levels of skill and English language proficiency that are beyond the reach of most SHEV holders.

Therefore, while there are some prospects for SHEV holders to apply for a permanent visa at the end of the five-year period, the criteria that must be met are onerous and unlikely attainments for the majority. Along with TPV holders, most people on a SHEV, such as Salem, can only re-apply for another temporary visa.[21] The impacts of this policy landscape are profound as people must undergo a seemingly unending cycle of uncertainty. In the following sections, we discuss how precariousness compounds for asylum seekers in relation to work and involuntarily living apart from their family for years, without any end in sight.

Precariousness in employment and precarious work

Precarity that is inherent in a temporary status leads to precarity in a range of economic and social conditions, the most obvious being financial insecurity and the inability to fully participate as a citizen in society. John van Kooy and Dina Bowman explore the intersections between an uncertain immigration status and multiple levels of employment precarity, highlighting how they 'combine and compound the insecurity and alienation felt by asylum seekers' in Australia.[22] They argue that the restrictive policies force people to live in such a way that effectively narrows their coping strategies and reduces self-agency. As van Kooy and Bowman observe, 'people seeking asylum expend their energies on individual coping and survival strategies, such as "keeping quiet" to preserve employment relationships and attempting to avoid recognition as asylum seekers'.[23]

Writing on labour insecurity more generally, Iain Campbell and Robin Price argue that there are several overlapping levels that allow us to conceptualize employment precarity, two of which are directly relevant to our immediate discussion – precariousness in employment and precarious work. Precariousness in employment refers to 'objective job characteristics that involve insecurity, such as a low level of regulatory protection, low wages, high employment insecurity and a low level of employee control over wages, hours and working conditions', and precarious work is 'waged work exhibiting several dimensions of precariousness [that] are often, though not always, non-standard jobs'.[24] Research on the employment of people from refugee backgrounds in Australia who are on temporary visas has shown that the majority experience downward occupational mobility, and often only find low-skilled work that is poorly paid.[25]

Employment precarity is intensified by numerous impediments to finding secure full-time work that are unique to this group. In the first instance, they may be overlooked by prospective employers during recruitment. People from asylum-seeking backgrounds have stated that it is common for employers to ask for a prospective employee's visa status, preferring someone with permanent status.[26] More insidiously, they can encounter structural discrimination that is 'reinforced by mainstream prejudices and negative stereotyping of racially and culturally different immigrants and refugees by employers'.[27] The existence of such prejudices and stereotyping is reflected in the findings of a national survey of Australian Muslims conducted by the Australian Human Rights Commission in 2019. Almost half of the respondents (48 per cent) reported unfavourable treatment while looking for employment or in the workplace, and the majority believed that this was based on their religion, race or ethnicity.[28]

Attaining an education, often as the first step towards a career pathway and job security, can pose an insurmountable hurdle for many. Those on a temporary visa who can enrol in higher education would be classified as 'international students', and would need to meet expensive up-front tuition fees unless they have been awarded a university scholarship or been granted access to vocational TAFE courses at domestic student rates by the state or territory government where they reside. In addition, they would not be eligible for government-funded student financial supports.[29] Such factors make it difficult to gain the qualifications for skilled employment positions. With limited options and opportunities to earn an income, temporary visas can expose people from asylum-seeking backgrounds to mistreatment in the workplace.

> This has been my experience. When I got the chance to go to school in Afghanistan, I put so much effort into becoming educated with the hope of going to university. However, this all changed when I arrived in Australia in 2013.
>
> As a Hazara child descended from generations of deprivation and poverty, I was the first in the whole history of my family to go to a publicly funded school which taught mathematics, geometry, literature and English language. Everyone, including my parents and other villagers, were supportive of myself and my siblings going to school and learning the 'Modern Knowledge'. The stories of becoming a doctor, engineer, politician or lawmaker were the sweets of every gathering, meeting and local *jirgas* (assembly of elders on important public matters). I remember listening to elders praising someone who could speak fluently in another language, doctors who could treat patients and engineers who could build roads and irrigation canals. All of these individuals had a very special place among community members. By the time my father decided to move to the city in order for us to have access to better schools, I had realized that going to school was a necessary and vital tool for a future career.

My father provided me with every support that I needed to continue my education. He made multiple journeys to Iran for work and stayed there, away from us all, for up to four years at a time, doing difficult labouring tasks to provide enough money for us to go to school and pay for the private tutor to teach us English. It got to a point that my father suffered from a hernia due to the heavy lifting that he did for work over a period of thirty years, but he did not quit. He would wrap his abdominal area with a long piece of cloth and continued the same job for a very long time, despite his critical health condition. My father would say, 'I cannot afford to treat myself now, because all my children are at school, I don't want their studies to be disrupted by my inability to support them'.

When he was in Iran, he experienced a lot of difficulties navigating his way in and out of the city because he could not read and write and had to rely on instinct or people's honesty. He had many incidents where he wished he was at least able to read and write. He used to say, 'You have everything. You must rescue yourself from the harsh labour and dark fate that I had, to provide food for us. Do not waste your time. Grab the opportunity and make a better future for yourself.'

My father's words instilled optimism, hope and a dream in me so profound that it made me believe that I can get to anywhere I want, if I have good qualifications. Therefore, I told myself that I will get the highest level of education possible and one day I will run for presidency in the new Afghanistan. It may seem farfetched now. But in those days, I carried that great ambition with me, day and night. When I graduated high school, I chose to study social sciences, politics and philosophy, to gain a good grasp of how society works.

Unfortunately, from 2010 the security situation in Afghanistan began to deteriorate, and by mid-2012 I made the very difficult decision to flee the country. Despite the pain and misery of leaving my family and my country behind, I still had this ambition to pursue my studies in Australia. I had heard numerous stories about how countries like Australia value education.

I remember reminding myself that I would lose the close proximity of all my friends, classmates and even my family, but that I would at least gain a good quality education in a prestigious university in Australia. This would often console me to cope with being so far away from everyone I had ever known and loved.

But after three months of immigration detention and then being allowed to live in the community in Australia, by late 2013 I realized this dream was lost. After so many failed attempts to enrol myself in some sort of educational environment that I could afford, and get back on track with my studies, I finally quit. I realized that it was a government policy to deny me affordable access to education. For the first three years of my life in Australia, I did not have permission to work either which finally killed my enthusiasm, eagerness and passion to study.

When I finally got permission to work in 2016, I needed to find employment and work as hard as I could to support my family back in Afghanistan. Given that there were no government support services available to help people like me, I had to find employment on my own.

I had no previous experience in any industry, so it was difficult to convince someone to give me a job. Finally, through community connections, I managed to get a job as a stonemason in a stone benchtop factory in mid-2016, which paid me a low wage for two years until I learned the trade and gradually could make a decent income out of it. However, I recently found out that the job I had been doing for the last five years meant I had been working in an environment with toxic silica dust that can cause silicosis.

We were never trained or warned about the damage of this toxic dust. We were never provided with personal protective equipment. The only point of focus was how many jobs we could finish by the end of the day. Despite all of this, I continued the job because my SHEV status meant there was the slim prospect of getting permanency through a skilled migration visa, if I could meet the pathway requirements of the SHEV and those of a skilled visa.

The difficulty was that if it did become possible for me to apply for a skilled visa, stonemasonry was the only skill I had, and on top of that the visa required an employer to sponsor me. Therefore, no matter how dangerous or toxic the work environment was, I stayed and put up with it, in order to gamble my luck for permanency. I was stuck with a job that horrified me every moment that I cut and polished those slabs, eight hours a day. There was no other option for me to get myself out of this endless precarious situation.

But this job came to an end in early 2021 when I found out my friend and workmate had contracted silicosis. I left the job but feel like I now live with even more precarity. I don't know what is going to happen to my visa status. As silicosis is a progressive disease, what if I develop it in the future, even though my test results are negative now? I am on a six-monthly check-up routine to monitor if there are any new developments in my lungs. Thinking about this can keep me awake at night, with many disturbing and stressful 'what if' and 'how come' questions.

An Australian study found that higher education is considered by many people from asylum-seeking backgrounds to be 'an important tool for developing the capacities and knowledge to sustain their livelihoods and to contribute to their communities and to society'.[30] Yet, as Salem's account shows, an inability to undertake higher education was a significant first barrier, which then effectively excluded him from being able to apply for skilled positions. In the absence of government assistance to find work, Salem was left with no choice but to rely on community or informal networks. Such a predicament is more likely to lead to poorly regulated, insecure work. For Salem and his co-workers, these compounding factors constrained them to paid work in dangerous conditions, in the hope that this might one day help them to satisfy the conditions of the SHEV and be granted a permanent visa.

Precarious life without family

Arguably, an overemphasis on the physical safety of people from asylum-seeking backgrounds upon arriving in Australia has been to the detriment of fully understanding the acute psychological impacts of remaining on a temporary protection visa. This includes the serious mental health ramifications of being denied access to family reunion and being forced to live without one's family (which shall be discussed further shortly). Research has shown that living with uncertainty for a prolonged period contributes to mental deterioration, despair and suicidal ideation.[31] In Australia, an increased incidence of post-traumatic stress disorder and depression for people on temporary visas compared with those on permanent visas is evident.[32] There are multiple aspects of the process of seeking asylum itself that can be re-traumatizing.[33] After escaping persecution and having to leave home and family, individuals undergo the stress of building a new life without sufficient supports and rights, as well as a complex and drawn-out administrative process to be recognized as a refugee. Being granted a temporary protection visa means inevitably having to face the claims process again. As one participant on a TPV expressed in a 2018 study:

> [as] a person who came here on a boat and had some trauma in the past, the journey was traumatic, detention centre is trauma, living in Australia and in limbo for years is traumatic, sometimes it's even worse than what you experience in life because when you're in [your home country] … when you come here you don't work and study, you have all this time to think about all that happened and all that is happening to you and it is a lot more difficult and you're in a country with no contact, with no community, no family support.[34]

Being denied the opportunity to apply for family reunion is especially damaging to an individual's mental health and wellbeing. The close presence of one's family offers more than emotional comfort, important as it is to us all.

Familial relationships provide both support networks and motivational strength for individuals facing challenges. The ordeal of living without one's family is magnified by not knowing if or when one may ever be able to bring them to Australia.

> Being forced to remain on a temporary protection visa means living without your family. The emotional and psychological side of this story is not often shed light upon. At a time of crisis people need care and compassion, people need human touch. For me, that is the unconditional love and support of my family which has bonded us together since my childhood. I need their trust and emotional support, and many others in my situation need this too. It is very important to take notice of the significance of the family in a refugee's life, and the loss of this when talking about precarity.
>
> It is devastating to leave your loved ones behind when you are forced to seek asylum. Because of the risk involved in taking this perilous journey, it is often safer for one person to flee on their own than having the whole family with them. Therefore, when a refugee leaves their family behind, it does not mean that they are not important. It is rather the opposite. That is why many refugees hope to be able to secure a safe pathway for their families to be reunited with them. That is why they may make the hardest choice of running away alone.
>
> I know from my friends who are in the same situation that I am not alone in experiencing this. The past decade-long separation from our families has pushed us into a corner with unimaginable mental trauma, pain and guilt. We feel responsible for our families who are stuck in war-torn countries. Yet, we cannot do anything to help them or get them to safety. We cannot even apply to get our partner and children to join us in Australia. Some people end up harming themselves out of sheer desperation, with the belief that this is the only way to put an end to this mental torture.
>
> Such self-harm has to be understood from their reality as people who have been persecuted, tortured and lost family members in wars, have fled their country to seek refuge in another which is a signatory to the UN Refugee Convention. But they then find themselves locked up for months, if not years, then released from detention on a never-ending series of temporary visas, and restricted from applying to get their family to join them in Australia. This comes as a shock at first, and then becomes intolerable after ten years.

The distress that is caused by family separation is now more widely appreciated given that many across the globe who may not have experienced this before are now doing so due to pandemic-related border restrictions. Given the multiple traumas people from asylum-seeking backgrounds are likely to experience before seeking asylum, and upon their arrival to Australia, it is particularly important that they be in close contact with family and others who are significant to them. As Louise Newman and Sarah Mares write, 'Prolonged and indefinite separation from family members increases the risk of complicated grief, persisting PTSD and depression. It can be associated with continuing anxiety about the lost family member, adds to a sense of powerlessness and can be associated with a continuing sense of injustice.'[35] Enduring this for years, along with the knowledge that your family's own situation is deeply volatile and dangerous, creates a level of extreme precarity that heightens the insecurity and vulnerability already felt by a person – all are barriers to feeling safe.

> Sometimes when the issue of safety of people on temporary protection visas comes into a conversation, authorities put forward the most disingenuous statements that one can imagine, such as 'refugees on temporary visas are safe here, we have given them protection'. But how can a person feel safe when their families, including their children, are living in countries where they fear for their lives every day?
>
> These comments suggest we are not appreciative of the fact that we are living in a country that has provided us with safety and security. The problem with this sort of narrative is that it does not differentiate between *being* safe and *feeling* safe. To me, 'being safe' represents the safety of my physical being, while 'feeling safe' represents the psychological and mental health side of my story. To live a safe life, I need to have both factors.
>
> I can be safe in physical surroundings where I can get my basic needs met if my sole purpose is to stay alive. But this is like keeping an endangered bird inside a cage and claiming that it is safe. This is an understanding of protection as a cage only.
>
> I cannot feel safe in such a restricted framing of protection. I need to have a place to call 'home', and the peace of mind of being able to live with those who I love. Having a sense of belonging to them and they to me, being able to do the most basic things like having a cup of coffee with my family in a café.
>
> That is when I will feel safe and protected. I will then feel respected as a human being with rights.

Contrary to assumptions that granting temporary protection to someone in Australia allows them to be 'safe', this does not assure any long-standing feeling of safety. First of all, being safe is compromised given there is the real prospect that Australia's protection can be revoked when the person's refugee claim is next considered. Secondly, the ability to feel safe goes beyond the barriers imposed by the temporary nature of the protection visas that many refugees in Australia are forced to live with. For many people, feeling safe is inherently connected to their family's situation and whether they can live with them or not. This is yet another layer of distress and insecurity that is forced on people in Australia on temporary protection visas, compounding their experience of precarity even further. As Salem expresses it, the forced separation from family communicates that this group of people is not equal to others in Australia, thus preventing them from living fully as human beings.

Conclusion

While precarity relates to conditions of vulnerability, some also see its mobilizing potential – for those experiencing it and those who are witnessing its effects on people they feel connected to.[36] Referencing Judith Butler, Michele Lobo writes that 'precarity that is differentially allocated can contribute to collective responsibility through the ethical demand from the other to whom we are exposed and to whom we are bound', and, therefore, can help to 'mobilise struggles for freedom from oppression'.[37] This is the experience of both the authors of this chapter. We see precarity as a trigger for collective responsibility and collective action. We speak in particular from the standpoint of our own mobilization – Salem as a person who endures this precarity, and Caroline as an Australian citizen who has come to know him and many others in a similar situation and who witnesses their experiences of compound precarity on a daily basis.

As part of our collective action and responsibility, we have taken a leading role in the WA Refugee and People Seeking Asylum Network to advocate for the rights of people from asylum-seeking backgrounds. As well as assisting people with their access to the immigration authorities and refugee support agencies, it has been essential to listen to the stories of those who exist in a constant state of vulnerability and to enable these accounts to be visible to others. This has required facilitating meetings between Australian government officials and people seeking asylum to make sure the decision makers hear from those directly affected by their policies. We see this collective action as a type of coping mechanism, even a matter of survival.

We agree that precarity can prompt collective responsibility and action, but it is the *intensity* of its impacts that we see as being a vital trigger to mobilization. Through our witnessing of those who continue to endure extreme levels of suffering, and Salem's own acute experiences, we have joined with others in taking collective action. But at the time of writing (January 2022), this mobilization is yet to shift the Australian government's punitive policies. The positive outcomes of being involved in this action are still far outweighed by the extent of the suffering and trauma generated. Therefore, we caution that any possibility of mobilization in a situation of precarity must also consider the severity and longevity of the effects of that condition. Mobilization in the form of collective action is important, but the gains must not detract from attention given to the profoundly negative impacts of this precarity.

I sometimes wonder, will there be a day that I say, today I am who I was born to be:

A free man, independent.

An equal human being.

Today I live for myself.

Today I am going to knock off work, and go to visit mum and dad.

Today I will take my partner to a restaurant.

Or just simply go to a house where I feel I am home.

Notes

1   Michele Lobo, 'Living on the edge: precarity and freedom in Darwin, Australia', *Journal of Ethnic and Migration Studies* 47, no. 20 (2021): 4620.

2   Judith Butler, 'Precarious life, vulnerability, and the ethics of cohabitation', *Journal of Speculative Philosophy* 26, no. 2 (2012): 148.

3   Iain Campbell and Robin Price, 'Precarious work and precarious workers: towards an improved conceptualisation', *The Economic and Labour Relations Review* 27, no. 3 (2016): 315–16.

4   United Nations High Commissioner for Refugees, *Global Trends: Forced Displacement in 2020* (Copenhagen: UNHRC, 2021), https://www.unhcr.org/flagship-reports/globaltrends/.

5   According to the 1951 United Nations Convention Relating to the Status of Refugees (as amended by the Protocol Relating to the Status of Refugees 1967), a refugee is someone who has a well-founded fear of persecution on the grounds of their race, religion, nationality, membership of a political social group and/or political opinion, should they return to their home country. A person seeking asylum has sought refugee status in another country but has not yet had their refugee claim finalized.

6   The Western Australian Refugee and People Seeking Asylum Network was formed in 2017 to advocate as a collective to the state and federal governments for greater access to supports and services for people from asylum-seeking backgrounds. The

network comprises people from asylum-seeking backgrounds, academics, lawyers, individual activists and representatives from refugee support agencies and church groups.

7   Department of Home Affairs, Australia Government, 'Australia's Offshore Humanitarian Program: 2019–20' (2020), https://www.homeaffairs.gov.au/ research-and-stats/files/australia-offshore-humanitarian-program-2019-20.pdf.

8   RMIT ABC Fact Check, 'Alex Hawke says Australia's resettlement of refugees ranks third-highest globally. Is that correct?', *ABC News* (14 September 2021), https:// www.abc.net.au/news/2021-09-14/fact-check-does-australia-s-resettlement-of-refugees-rank-third/100436334.

9   United Nations High Commissioner for Refugees, 'Refugee data finder' (2021), https://www.unhcr.org/refugee-statistics/.

10   Australian Human Rights Commission (AHRC), 'Lives on hold: refugees and asylum seekers in the "Legacy caseload" (2019)' (Sydney, NSW: AHRC, 2019), 12, https://www.humanrights.gov.au/our-work/asylum-seekers-and-refugees/ publications/lives-hold-refugees-and-asylum-seekers-legacy.

11   For a detailed discussion of Australia's mandatory detention and offshore processing, see Jane McAdam and Fiona Chong, *Refugee Rights and Policy Wrongs* (Sydney, NSW: University of New South Wales Press, 2019).

12   Chris Sidoti, 'Foreword', in Don McMaster, *Asylum Seekers: Australia's Responses to Refugees* (Melbourne, VIC: Melbourne University Press, 2001), v.

13   In particular, see 'Indigenous deaths in custody 1989–1996: a report prepared by the Office of the Aboriginal and Torres Strait Islander Social Justice Commissioner for the Aboriginal and Torres Strait Islander Commission' (Australia: AHRC, 1996), https://humanrights.gov.au/our-work/indigenous-deaths-custody.

14   McMaster, *Asylum Seekers*, 3.

15   National Museum of Australia, 'White Australia policy' (last modified 31 August 2021), https://www.nma.gov.au/defining-moments/resources/white-australia-policy.

16   Robert Manne, 'How we came to be so cruel to asylum seekers', *The Conversation* (26 October 2016), https://theconversation.com/robert-manne-how-we-came-to-be-so-cruel-to-asylum-seekers-67542.

17   Ian McAllister, 'Border protection, the 2001 Australian election and the coalition victory', *Australian Journal of Political Science* 38, no. 3 (2003): 445–63.

18   Caroline Fleay, *Australia and Human Rights: Situating the Howard Government* (Newcastle upon Tyne: Cambridge Scholars Publishing, 2010), 117–33.

19   Caroline Fleay, Mary Anne Kenny, Atefeh Andaveh, Salem Askari, Rohullah Hassani, Kate Leaney and Teresa Lee, '"Doing something for the future": building relationships and hope through refugee and asylum seeker advocacy in Australia', in *Handbook of Migration and Global Justice*, eds. Leanne Weber and Claudia Tazreiter (Cheltenham: Edward Elgar Publishing, 2021), 281–82.

20 The regional stipulation was added to the SHEV pathway requirements as part of a political compromise between the Australian government and a minor party in order to gain the latter's support for the legislation in December 2014. It was to encourage SHEV holders to fill labour shortages in regional areas.

21 AHRC, 'Lives on hold', 12.

22 John van Kooy and Dina Bowman, '"Surrounded with so much uncertainty": asylum seekers and manufactured precarity in Australia', *Journal of Ethnic and Migration Studies* 45, no. 5 (2019): 705.

23 van Kooy and Bowman, 'Asylum seekers', 705.

24 Campbell and Price, 'Precarious work', 315.

25 Val Colic-Peisker and Farida Tilbury, 'Employment niches for recent refugees: segmented labour market in twenty-first century Australia', *Journal of Refugee Studies* 19, no. 2 (2006): 203–29.

26 Caroline Fleay, Lisa Hartley and Mary Anne Kenny, 'Refugees and asylum seekers living in the Australian community: the importance of work rights and employment support', *Australian Journal of Social Issues* 48, no. 4 (2013): 485.

27 Val Colic-Peisker, 'The "visibly different" refugees in the Australian labour market: settlement policies and employment realities', in *Refugees, Recent Migrants and Employment: Challenging Barriers and Exploring Pathways*, ed. Sonia McKay (New York: Routledge, 2009), 67.

28 Australian Human Rights Commission, 'Sharing the stories of Australian Muslims report (2021)' (Sydney, NSW: AHRC, 2021), 45, https://humanrights.gov.au/our-work/race-discrimination/publications/sharing-stories-australian-muslims-2021.

29 Lisa Hartley, Caroline Fleay, Sally Baker, Rachel Burke and Rebecca Field, *People Seeking Asylum in Australia: Access and Support in Higher Education* (Perth, WA: Curtin University, 2018), 6, https://www.ncsehe.edu.au/wp-content/uploads/2018/11/Hartley_PeopleSeekingAsylum.pdf.

30 Hartley et al., *People Seeking Asylum*, 2.

31 Mary Anne Kenny, Carol Grech and Nicholas Procter, 'A trauma informed response to COVID-19 and the deteriorating mental health of refugees and asylum seekers with insecure status in Australia', *International Journal of Mental Health Nursing* 31, no. 1 (2022): 62–69.

32 Elizabeth Newnham, April Pearman, Stephanie Olinga-Shannon and Angela Nickerson, 'The mental health effects of visa insecurity for refugees and people seeking asylum: a latent class analysis', *International Journal of Public Health* 64, no. 5 (2019): 763–72.

33 Nicholas Procter, Mary Anne Kenny, Heather Eaton and Carol Grech, 'Lethal hopelessness: understanding and responding to asylum seeker distress and mental deterioration', *International Journal of Mental Health Nursing* 27, no. 1 (2018): 448–54.

34 Hartley et al., *People Seeking Asylum*, 33.

35 Louise Newman and Sarah Mares, 'Mental health and wellbeing implications of family separation for children and adults seeking asylum', in *Together in Safety: A Report on the Australian Government's Separation of Families Seeking Safety* (Melbourne, VIC: Human Law Rights Centre, 2021), 20, https://www.hrlc.org.au/reports/2021/9/1/together-in-safety-report.

36 Louise Waite, 'A place and space for a critical geography of precarity?', *Geography Compass* 3, no. 1 (2009): 413.

37 Lobo, 'Living on the edge', 4620, 4621.

Part Two

Precarious Spaces

Haunted Futures: (Making) Home in the Ghost City of Ordos Kangbashi

Christina Lee

This chapter begins with a story of a place and its haunted futures.

One late September evening in 2016, I left the sprawl and chaotic energy of Shanghai and flew into Ordos – a city comprised of the three districts of Dongsheng, Azhen and Kangbashi – which is located in the middle of the Gobi Desert in the Inner Mongolia Autonomous Zone in China. The city's grand design was apparent even from the sky, with the lights of Ejin Horo Airport highlighting its undulating curvature that made it look like a grounded spacecraft of tomorrow. In the main hall, around the rim of the rotunda that had been inspired by the sun with spokes radiating from the centre, a sprawling tableau featured the proud histories and myths of Mongolia. The airport inspired awe, but there was also a nagging bleakness that stemmed from its unrealized potential. This was intimated by echoes of footsteps and luggage wheels reverberating in the partially illuminated terminal. Janitorial staff swept floors and wiped down rails that were already spotless, and the taxis lined up outside looked like they had just been rolled off an assembly line and were ready for delivery, rather than waiting for service. When I located a group of taxi drivers, they seemed genuinely surprised at the prospect of a client. While many of my fellow travellers had boarded a shuttle bus into the city, the others had simply vanished.

During the first half of the forty-minute journey from the airport to Dongsheng, I noticed about two other cars on the freeway. The under-utilization of this major thoroughfare was accentuated by the frequent stop-start motion of the taxi that would come to a halt at automated pedestrian crossings even where there were no pedestrians. With me unable to speak Mandarin or Mongolian, and the driver unable to speak English, the awkward silences were interrupted only by the hum of the vehicle and the crosswalk lights beeping. I wondered whether

Figure 5.1 Ordos Museum, Kangbashi. Christina Lee, 2016.[1]

my front-seat companion thought this whole situation as absurd as I did. On occasions, a lone figure or a small group of people appeared in my peripheral vision walking along the side of the freeway. In the darkness, even-darker outlines of buildings became discernible and broke flat stretches of nothingness. Some were isolated single or double-storey constructions, and others were residential apartment complexes from which no light emanated.

In Dongsheng, the bright lights of commercial buildings above gave the impression of busyness, but at ground level the streets were notably still. At the Crowne Plaza Hotel where I was to stay for the next week, a bulb behind one of the letters of the hotel's sign had blown. The hotel interior was dimly lit and there were but a handful of staff and guests around as I checked in. The unlit chandelier in the foyer was at once a grand and pointless gesture. Welcome to Ordos, the 'city of the future' … and the pre-eminent ghost city of China.[2]

***

According to Wade Shepard, over the next two decades, 'China will build hundreds of new cities, thousands of new towns and districts, erect over 50,000 new skyscrapers, wipe untold thousands of villages off the map, and relocate hundreds of millions of people.'[3] This accelerated construction work is part of the country's master plan for modernization and urbanization. Ordos has come to represent both this ambition and one of the by-products of this process: the modern 'ghost city' that is distinctive for its severe under-population.[4] In this chapter, I focus on Ordos, and more specifically Kangbashi New District, to examine the multiple layers of precariousness that beset these new developments. At the macro level, these cities can be extremely susceptible to external shocks, such as those from an unpredictable global market, that renders them high-risk ventures and precarious places to reside. At the local level, there *are* people who have managed to build a life in these seemingly unhomely cities, yet they remain haunted by a persistent denial/non-recognition of their existence in dominant representations that continue to 'evacuate' the city of human life. Using the methods of autoethnography and psychogeography – chosen because both connect personal, embodied experience to the broader socio-cultural context – I explore the presences not visible on the master plans and maps of the (ghost) city, which force a re-thinking of ways of *being* in a place and, thus, the concept of 'home' itself.

Planning (ghost) cities of the future

China's ghost cities first gained attention worldwide in 2009 when Al Jazeera correspondent Melissa Chan reported on Ordos Kangbashi as 'brand new and built in just five years and meant for one million residents. But no-one's moved in. The city stands empty.'[5] Not long after, photo essays in *Time* featured Ordos as a desolate frontier town bereft of human occupation and activity.[6] Although Ordos may appear to be an exceptional cautionary tale of disastrous urban planning, ghost cities are an increasingly common, albeit unintentional, outcome of mass urbanization and modernization that is occurring at breakneck speed throughout the country. This process involves internal migration of rural dwellers to built-up areas, and the creation of infrastructure to accommodate the swell in city populations projected over the next several decades. Shepard describes the scale of this movement of people:

> Within the past thirty years 400 million Chinese, more than the entire population of the United States, have transitioned from rural to urban areas; throughout the first decade of the twenty-first century the country's urban head count was growing by the population of Australia annually. But China's not done yet. By

governmental decree, 300 million more people are expected to become urban by 2030, the much-portended year when the country is expected to have 1 billion city dwellers. This means that 1.4 million Chinese, roughly the population of Estonia, will need to urbanize each month for the next sixteen years.[7]

Urban expansion in China is a political and practical strategy. It is an administrative exercise that includes re-zoning rural into urban areas, and renaming and expanding the borders of existing places; but it also encompasses the physical transformation of landscapes, such as levelling mountains and demolishing established settlements, to make way for new cities. City-building has become an integral strategy for nation-building, functioning as a main source of revenue and a measure of the achievements and political might of local authorities in advancing the national agenda.

Ordos illustrates the drivers that have enabled rapid urban development in China, as well as the conditions that give rise to the ghost city. The region underwent a re-classification in 2001, with its conversion from the prefecture-level Yeke-juu League to Ordos Municipality granting local authorities greater economic and administrative powers, and conferring Ordos with the prestigious status of a city. Prior to this, the discovery of extensive reserves of natural resources in the region in the late 1990s created a lucrative extractive industry that saw one of the most impoverished and largely rural parts of the Inner Mongolia Autonomous Zone quickly ascend to become one of China's wealthiest areas. Over the next decade, Ordos would produce approximately one-sixth of the national coal reserve, one-third of the national gas reserve and 65 billion tons of rare earth minerals.[8] This period coincided fortuitously with a threefold increase in demand for coal since 2000 and reforms in coal pricing that led to historically unprecedented profits.[9] The taxes and fees levied on coal-mining firms alone generated more than half of Ordos Municipality's revenue.[10] As a point of comparison, the city's per capita GDP exceeded that of Shanghai and Beijing in 2007, and that of Hong Kong in 2010.[11] High revenues from the mining industry and Ordos's newly minted city status were the green lights to initiate large-scale construction projects.

From 2001, urban space was increased and basic infrastructure and housing stock was improved throughout Ordos. Kangbashi New District, however, would be the region's showcase and symbol of prosperity and culture. Situated approximately 25 kilometres from the already-established Dongsheng, construction of Kangbashi commenced in 2003. Originally, it was to spread over 355 square kilometres to accommodate one million people.[12] Unlike its older neighbour, with its relatively poor infrastructure and chaotic layout, this new district would actualize the nation's vision of urbanity: modern, orderly, clean, a paragon of architectural feats. Between 2003 and 2010, there was swift development of commercial and residential properties, government and cultural infrastructure, and transportation networks. Kangbashi boasted state-of-the-art amenities, including a sports stadium, museum, library, cultural arts centre and theatre, which were distinctive for their innovative and ostentatious designs. The market entry of multinational franchises, such as McDonald's and Subway, signalled that Ordos had gone global. With public confidence running high, investors poured their money into a speculative property market in anticipation of handsome gains to be reaped in the future. Due to limited investment opportunities, existing property laws and low rental yields in China, many properties were purchased for their resale value and would, as is common practice, remain unoccupied for years in the meantime.[13]

The short- and long-term plans for Kangbashi were dependent on favourable conditions in the global economy, and were propped up by the shared belief in unstoppable growth. As the city's fortune was tethered so tightly to the resource sector, this meant that any ripples in the international market were amplified at a local level. When demand and the price of coal declined sharply in 2011, the resource that had been vital to Ordos's success became its Achilles' heel. This blow was accompanied by the spectacular fallout of Ordos's real estate market that had been characterized by high interest rates, informal lending services and an over-reliance on private investors and capital from the coal industry. Emblematic of Ordos's volatile financial position, the local real estate industry exposed a vulnerable, unsustainable system with few fail-safes in the event of an economic downturn. Bankruptcy and defaults on property repayments increased, and the promise of future buyers for investment properties-in-waiting dissipated. Less than a decade after the beginning of the boom era, the dream was over. Plans for Kangbashi were subsequently scaled down partway through construction for a population of half a million, and then to 300,000.[14] In 2017, the population of permanent residents was 153,000.[15]

Mapping the city, erasing the people

Kangbashi is a place that seems to make little sense, a perception accentuated by the mismatch between its cavernous architecture and sparse inhabitants. Like so many other new towns and cities in China that function as 'trophies commemorating the rise of the municipalities that built them', the district's grand designs have resulted in a place that does not seem built to scale for humans.[16] People feel like an afterthought in the master plans, dwarfed as they are by row-upon-row of residential towers, vast boulevards, sprawling public squares and imposing monuments that one would expect to see in a metropolis of millions. The epic dimensions of the built environment exacerbate the surfeit of space. The bronze statues in Genghis Khan Square, for example, are statement pieces that make 'people strolling by look like listless, tiny ants'.[17] In Kangbashi and Dongsheng, it is difficult to ignore the over-presence of vacant and under-utilized spaces, and the jarring contrast between abandoned and neglected modern ruins that sit among active construction sites. Ordos captures the arresting strangeness of living with contradiction, that is, living with emptiness and excess, with the old and new, with slow decay and rapid progress. In 2015, journalist Jody Rosen commented that 'Ordos is not empty, but it is odd'.[18] But the city's design is not the only reason for the leitmotifs of barrenness and oddity that afflict it.

Focus, too, has been pulled *away* from the human element in Ordos. As Max Woodworth avers, China's ghost cities have been 'aestheticized from the outset' in photography as spectacles of ruin and economic collapse, and

Figure 5.2 Abandoned construction site, Dongsheng.

'studiously voided of humans'.[19] I became uncomfortably aware of this in my own documentation of the city, which had initially involved playing a calculated waiting game, specifically waiting for passers-by to exit the frame before taking the shot of an *emptied* landscape. This photographic act risked replicating a type of 'representation void, a petrified place that speaks only of loss, of a helplessness' of Ordos's citizens.[20]

Notwithstanding the seductive and suggestive qualities of China's spectral cityscapes that make them sites of fascination, in other respects the vision of a de-populated city is perhaps inevitable. After all, how can we even begin to imagine the estimated 300 million Chinese to be urbanized by 2030, as predicted earlier by Shepard, let alone the 1.4 million people on the move, month after month, without being overwhelmed by the scale of change and its social impacts. As the 'massive numbers blur into meaninglessness', we are no longer able to see the people.[21] The clinical precision of these statistics, the unifying narrative of national advancement, and the equally unifying counter-narrative of urban failure are tempering factors that make comprehensible that which is otherwise incomprehensible.

Here, maps provide a useful way to understand how China's ghost cities have been conceptualized, while simultaneously raising critical questions about the representational politics surrounding them. As with master plans, maps visualize and order the world into logical and 'relevant' spatial information. This organizing principle is reassuring because it allows us to know the world around us. Governments, institutions and capitalist structures rely on these features of maps and plans to draw investment and inspire confidence. In order for maps to be legible and make sense, they require abstractions and selections to be made; however, there are implications in making things absent or not locatable on the map. Proponents of critical cartography have shown that mapping is a political act that produces 'specific spatial knowledges and meanings by identifying, naming, categorizing, excluding, and ordering'.[22] As Jeremy Crampton aptly articulates, relations of power are embedded in mapping as it is 'involved in *what* we choose to represent, *how* we choose to represent objects such as people and things, and *what* decisions are made with those representations'.[23] We might ask: what is at stake in mapping the ghost city without people?

Sociologist Iain Chambers writes that:

Maps are full of references and indications, but they are not peopled. ... It permits us to grasp an outline, a shape, some sort of location, but not the contexts, cultures, histories, languages, experiences, desires and hopes that course through the urban body. The latter pierce the logic of topography and spill over the edges of the map.[24]

Maps convey a stable terrain, but their 'references and indications' fail to capture the fullness of human activity within it. Even though people and their movements are implied and imagined on maps, it is always in expected and conventional ways, for instance, people using spaces in predetermined ways and travelling along clearly marked out passageways. Returning to Crampton's point on the exclusionary and inclusionary process of map-making, this is evident in the 'unseeing' of those who are considered marginal or counter to the overarching purpose of the map, such as the homeless and other undocumented populations.[25] They do not 'fit' on the map because they do not conform to the metanarrative of a place. In the case of Ordos, the lived experiences of residents and workers are often rendered invisible or downplayed in representations, whether through omission in accounts or in the characterization of its citizens as lacking agency.

In order to engage with the fugitive presences that might not be captured in dominant, official representations of the (ghost) city, in my field research in Ordos I utilized an autoethnographic and psychogeographic approach. Both methods call for self-reflection as a way of understanding the world, at the same time as they query those understandings. Autoethnography connects personal experience to the broader culture and cultural practices, and allows the researcher to 'become more attuned to the subjectively felt experiences of others'.[26] This was especially appropriate in this present study where 'others' have been erased from the environment and its imaginings. As Carolyn Ellis writes, autoethnography 'requires that we observe ourselves observing, that we interrogate what we think and believe, and that we challenge our own assumptions'.[27] Psychogeography is the exploration of (often) urban environments through the activity of walking. It is an unplanned journey, or *dérive* ('drift'), to borrow from Guy Debord and the 1950s French Lettrist Group who pioneered it as an experimental strategy for traversing through the city's landscape. Through its focus on the emotional and behavioural effects of an environment, its ambience and its local histories, psychogeographic practice facilitates an embodied experience of place.[28]

To create space for alternative readings of the city, over a one-week period I undertook unplanned drifts through Kangbashi and Dongsheng. Local histories and the unmapped/unmappable intersected with my own experience of being in those places. Travelling with a local translator, we conducted unstructured interviews (predominantly in the form of casual conversations) with people in various sites of work and leisure. Other instances of the fieldwork were more akin to urban exploration, that is, seeking out environments that would normally be classified as 'off limits'. We observed Ordos from above, below, at street level, and from inside. The drifts took us from abandoned residential precincts on the outskirts of town to the unfinished floors of towers in the Central Business District; from the retail and cultural centres associated with the communal life of a place to the motorways and subterranean parking lots.

Against the flow of Ordos's vehicular culture, we navigated the urban environment mostly by foot.[29] The physical act of walking allowed for a '*migrational*, or metaphorical' space to emerge from the 'clear text of the planned and readable city', to use Michel de Certeau's words.[30] It was an invitation to veer off prescribed pathways, to slow down and pause on quotidian, often unnoticed details that might provide an alternative to the all-too-common ghost city story that equates absence with a void. As Merlin Coverley says, walking 'allows one to challenge the official representation of the city by cutting across established routes and exploring those marginal and forgotten areas often overlooked by the city's inhabitants'.[31] In this research, that exploration encompassed the overlooked inhabitants themselves. Although walking through and actively engaging with the city was always going to unearth unexpected things, I had not anticipated where it would eventually lead me … back home.

Home-making in the unhomely city

While the appearance of emptiness can indicate loss, it can also signal other ways of *being*. Throughout Ordos, there were signs of diverse actors occupying what I had first thought to be untenanted spaces, and using them in informal ways that they were not planned for. In one of the CBD towers, a shopkeeper had set up a bed next to the counter to provide comfort and respite during the frequent periods of inactivity. In a nearby residential zone, the rows of incomplete complexes, piles of debris and dust whirls proffered a forlorn sight of dereliction and barrenness that came undone when I peered into one of the ground-floor apartments and spotted dried human faeces in the corner of a room. At the foot of that building was a hutch that had been cobbled together from chicken wire and wooden boards, and was home to several rabbits that were skirting around fresh cabbage leaves scattered on the ground.

Each encounter and trace overtly challenged the dominant discourse of an uninhabited (and uninhabitable) ghost city, and revealed the gap between the locals' ways of knowing and being, and my own positioning. After a brief sojourn in Kangbashi's public library, my assessment of its inadequacy was contradicted later that day by an elderly man we met on a bus who was making his way to that venue. He told us that he felt fortunate to live in this town with its many conveniences, facilities and activities for retirees; and commented favourably on the lack of crowds and pleasant weather. Two high school students in a fast food restaurant shared that they liked living here, and that increasingly more people were coming. A security guard from Shanxi Province, who was working in Building 5 in the CBD, told us Kangbashi was 'just like his home, just not a lot of people ... it's a really comfortable place to live'. Another security guard at the Great Theatre of Ordos, a 27-year-old man, said that he enjoyed the clean air, the green lands and wide roads, as well as the social aspect of the town; playing basketball and pool were two of his favourite pastimes.[32] His responses did not align with what Glenn Albrecht calls solastalgia, which occurs 'when there is recognition that the beloved place in which one resides is under assault (physical desolation)', which undermines 'a personal and community sense of identity, belonging and control'.[33] To make way for Kangbashi, two old ethnic Mongolian villages were cleared away.[34] The security guard was one of those former denizens whose pastoral homestead no longer existed. Prior to 2003, this

Figure 5.3 Convenience store at the base of a CBD tower, Kangbashi.

place had been his home. In 2016, it was now a different sort of home. As part of an ethnic minority that has been displaced several times over, he had found a way of living with and adapting to change. Or perhaps he saw the change as superficial because home is home, whatever building is imposed on it.

I turn here to what geographers Alison Blunt and Robyn Dowling describe as a critical geography of home. The authors identify home as the relation between a place/site and a spatial imaginary that is imbued with feelings and cultural meanings.[35] 'Home does not simply exist, but is made', they argue, whereby everyday practices become critical in tying together the materiality of place with emotions and social relationships, and in constituting identities.[36] This multifaceted idea of home problematizes its idealization as a fixed entity – its homeliness supposedly deriving from an inherent stability and authenticity rooted in origins and heritage – which tends to neglect the active process of home-making.

The varied ways of identifying with a place are particularly salient in the experiences of migrants, who must negotiate a new space to re-build a home away from (original) home, and find a sense of self and belonging. This was demonstrated in a study of internal migrants in China that was conducted by Dror Kochan.[37] Kochan found that the ancestral home (*laojia*) was a nostalgic point for some that evoked yearning for a previous home, thereby making the adjustment to a new locale more difficult, while for others it was regarded as a burden. Many cited mobility and flexibility as major factors in building their new urban identity, which contradicted the common assumption that we find comfort in and seek out, by default, that which is constant and stable. For some, their lack of property ownership and limited possessions meant the freedom to move to another place that was more desirable (for instance, a location closer to work or to the city centre) and to form new relations.

As a new district, the majority of residents and workers in Kangbashi have migrated from elsewhere, whether it was a neighbouring town – as was the case for many civil servants whose offices were relocated from Dongsheng to Kangbashi to boost the population – or settlements in other parts of the country. For Kangbashi's occupants, home-making practices and the symbolic meanings associated with the site have been vital to making homely a city that has been touted as estranging and unliveable.[38] Looping back to the guard at the Great Theatre of Ordos, after he gave us a tour around the venue, he agreed to pose for a photograph. In his crisp uniform, I half-expected the stern expression of a man on duty. Instead, the camera captured a warm, wide smile. Upon returning to Australia, I learned from a colleague that the ornate gold panelling on the

Figure 5.4 Security guard at the Great Theatre of Ordos, Kangbashi.

building's interior that the guard stood in front of was an intricate Mongolian pattern. Traces of the man's former home and hidden meanings in the place surfaced where I had previously detected none.

On 'doing' a critical geography of home, Katherine Brickell contends that drawing public attention to domestic issues 'can and should be complemented by academics' efforts to transform or at least make sense of their own negative or challenging experiences of home(s)'.[39] As I travelled through Dongsheng and Kangbashi, after several days I felt a simultaneous homecoming and homesickness in Ordos. It was not unlike the sensation of re-visiting my childhood home of Goldsworthy in the Pilbara region of Western Australia in 2008, fifteen years after it was bulldozed.[40] As with Ordos, the prosperity of this remote mining town was due to its abundance of natural resources; in this case, iron ore. As a child, I vividly recall my family and the rest of the townspeople converging on the sports field to watch the fireworks display that had been put on by BHP to celebrate another successful year. The mining industry was thriving, and life was good. But after a few years the supplies of ore were depleted, and the town was eventually closed in 1992. Then commenced the process of removing all structures, digging up the foundations and undertaking landscaping and reseeding to return the 350-hectare site 'back to nature'. Shortly after, Goldsworthy disappeared from the maps.

For those passing by the site of the old township today, it is an unremarkable patch of bushland and red dirt. And yet, the town-that-no-longer-exists remains for me, and for many of the ex-residents, still our home; full of signs gesturing to the lives once lived there. In the way that others cannot conceive of the site as homely, I started to rethink my own assumptions about the unhomely nature of Ordos. Its vacant spaces began to transform (for) me.

In Ordos, I took photographs of the built environment that identified the unmistakably ghostly qualities of the city. Half-finished buildings resembling partially skeletal concrete carcasses; intersections where the lights signalled for no traffic; cultural precincts frequented by few, if any, patrons; rows of plastic chairs overlooking a school sports field that were fading and cracking; an entertainment centre (named 'Future World') that was mostly untenanted inside and in a state of disrepair outside. At the same time, the impulse to fixate on such images slowly shifted. The camera's memory cards began to fill with pictures of human activity that are so often omitted from the expected tableaux of Ordos. They included both extreme long shots of anonymous individuals dwarfed by the towering structures around them, and the more intimate portraits of people we encountered in the city. A street cleaner during his break; a curious child poking her head out from behind the curtain draped over the entrance to her home; a group of boys riding their bicycles and shooting hoops outside the library; a mother and her young children during their stroll at dusk around the main plaza; e-bikes lined up outside a fast food joint; families and friends gathered for the musical fountain show at the artificial lake; old beer bottles discarded in an unfinished apartment.

There were familiar, homely presences throughout Ordos, even if just the traces remained. On occasions where I had become lost in Kangbashi and Dongsheng, or was taken on an outing by my translator, surprise would come to be replaced with the *anticipation* of turning a corner to find a street filled with vendor carts, restaurants, karaoke lounges, shops and city parks, which was, above all, 'peopled'. I stopped seeing still lives, and started to see a city in transition – uncertain as it was. At that point, Chambers's idea of things that are not easily rationalized, that 'pierce the logic of topography and spill over the edges', made sense.

Figure 5.5 Future World entertainment complex, Dongsheng.

Figure 5.6 Street cleaner, Dongsheng.

Coda

In many respects, this research was about experiencing the subject as a way of coming to terms with it. Intensely destabilizing but also liberating, the fieldwork and project were akin to research freefall. The abandonment of maps was not only for methodological reasons, but, admittedly, also borne out of necessity. Upon arrival at the Crowne Plaza Hotel, and before I had secured the services of a translator, I was provided with a map of Dongsheng to navigate the town. The document was written in Chinese (which I could not read), and ultimately proved useless because it was woefully out of date. Pictorial representations of landmarks and roads that I had to rely on no longer corresponded to what was actually on the ground. Quite literally, I could not follow the map. This research project began as an investigation of the exceptional state of ghost cities but, like my psychogeographic wanderings, drifted unexpectedly into a study of the meaning of (their/my) home amid precarious conditions. Traversing beyond the inked borders of the map and including the people allowed a *becoming* of the city.

Even my translator had drifted from her initial outlook on the terminal ghost city. A native of Dongsheng, with Mongolian and Han Chinese parentage, Laura Wang had witnessed Kangbashi rise from the desert. When I first met her in 2016 – then a 24-year-old teaching English at a language school – she was vocal in her disapproval of Kangbashi, the wasted resources to build it, and the disappearance of historical sites in the pursuit of national progress throughout Ordos. At Ordos Museum, we came across a photograph that showed a traditional marketplace where her father once had a stall. Now gone, replaced by a more modern structure, her nostalgia for it was palpable. Although she had an uncle who worked and lived in Kangbashi whom she had visited several times, the place still felt like a foreign land to her.

Six months later, Laura had secured a job at a public school in Kangbashi. In October 2017, she wrote to me about the lights of the town: 'I will send you some pictures about Kangbashi if I hang out during the night time. It's very beautiful. They did a lot of work for the UNCCD meeting 2 months ago.'[41] In April 2021, she informed me that the housing prices had skyrocketed, with the prices of this fourth-tier city close to that of a first-tier city. New developments were drawing more residents. Laura wrote:

> Because people are getting more used to live [sic] here instead of just driving back and forth between Dongsheng and Kangbashi for work, they enjoy living

here. Remember the empty building neighbourhood? They are all finished and a lot of people moved here. I think it's definitely worth coming over again to see how everything has changed. I can show you around in my school as well.[42]

These accounts, over time, are a reminder that China's 'new towns are ongoing dynamics of change and becoming', rather than cenotaphs to inertia.[43]

To experience Ordos's excesses and contradictions is to be confronted with a challenge – that is, to acknowledge and accept other ways of seeing and experiencing places – and to disinvest from the totalizing narrative of ghost cities as dead spaces, where the future is already haunted by failure. It is to also write back into the landscape those human presences that have been marginalized, and subjected to representational erasure and a state of non-existence. I think back to the people we met in Ordos and the contentment many had found there; they saw open spaces as freedom where others could not see beyond a wasteland. This city in the Gobi Desert brought me back to my hometown near the edge of the Great Sandy Desert, almost 7,000 kilometres away; a place that is to the untrained eye inhospitable hinterland and little else. Against the compulsion to know and control our environments, any meaningful, critical engagement with China's ghost cities comes with the caveat that the answers to our questions may be, according to the logics we apply, irrational, unpredictable, emotional and not fixed. This unknown territory is risky business that requires venturing off the planned and readable map.

Notes

1   All images in this chapter are copyrighted by Christina Lee, 2016.

2   Melia Robinson, 'Surreal photos of China's failed "city of the future"', *Tech Insider* (30 January 2016), https://www.businessinsider.com/chinese-ghost-town-2016-1.

3   Wade Shepard, *Ghost Cities of China* (London: Zed Books, 2015), 5.

4   Although many of these ghost cities are classified as towns, I use the more commonly recognized phrase 'ghost city' that appears in scholarly literature and the media.

5   Melissa Chan, 'China's empty city', *Al Jazeera* (10 November 2009), http://www.aljazeera.com/news/asia-pacific/2009/11/2009111061722672521.html.

6   See Michael Christopher Brown, 'Ordos, China: a modern ghost town', *Time* (n.d.), http://content.time.com/time/photogallery/0,29307,1975397_2094492,00.html.

7   Shepard, *Ghost Cities*, 7.

8   Christian Sorace and William Hurst, 'China's phantom urbanisation and the pathology of ghost cities', *Journal of Contemporary Asia* 46, no. 2 (2016): 311.

9   Max Woodworth, 'Frontier boomtown urbanism in Ordos, Inner Mongolia Autonomous Region', *Cross-Currents: East Asian History and Culture Review* 1, no. 1 (2012): 83.

10 Zhanlin Zhang cited in Woodworth, 'Frontier boomtown', 84.

11 Sorace and Hurst, 'China's phantom urbanisation', 311.

12 Shepard, *Ghost Cities*, 68.

13 Max Woodworth and Jeremy Wallace, 'Seeing ghosts: parsing China's "ghost city" controversy', *Urban Geography* 38, no. 8 (2017): 1275.

14 Wade Shepard, 'An update on China's largest ghost city – what Ordos Kangbashi is like today', *Forbes* (19 April 2016), http://www.forbes.com/sites/wadeshepard/2016/04/19/an-update-on-chinas-largest-ghost-city-what-ordos-kangbashi-is-like-today/.

15 Xinhuanet, 'Across China: from ghost town to boomtown – the new look of boomtown' (29 June 2017), http://www.xinhuanet.com/english/2017-06/29/c_136402110.htm.

16 Shepard, *Ghost Cities*, 70.

17 Christina Lee, 'Building the new urban ruin: the ghost city of Ordos Kangbashi, Inner Mongolia', in *The New Urban Ruins: Vacancy, Urban Politics and International Experiments in the Post-Crisis City*, eds. Cian O'Callaghan and Cesare Di Feliciantonio (Bristol: Policy Press, 2021), 79.

18 Jody Rosen, 'The colossal strangeness of China's most excellent tourist city', *The New York Times* (6 March 2015), https://www.nytimes.com/2015/03/06/t-magazine/ordos-china-tourist-city.html.

19 Max Woodworth, 'Picturing urban China in ruin: "ghost city" photography and speculative urbanization', *GeoHumanities* 6, no. 2 (2020): 239, 240.

20 This research shared many of Paul Dobraszczyk's concerns in his work on the Chernobyl zone and Pripyat, namely the compulsion to acknowledge only tragedy and loss. He writes, 'Chernobyl represented an opportunity to discover a secret world in ruins, one that might challenge existing certainties and provide liberating alternatives'. Paul Dobraszczyk, 'Petrified ruin: Chernobyl, Pripyat and the death of the city', *City* 14, no. 4 (2010): 373, 372.

21 Shepard, *Ghost Cities*, 7.

22 Jeremy Crampton, *Mapping: A Critical Introduction to Cartography and GIS* (Chichester: Wiley-Blackwell, 2010), 9, 45.

23 Crampton, *Mapping*, 41, original emphasis.

24 Iain Chambers, 'Cities without maps', in *Mapping the Futures: Local Cultures, Global Change*, eds. Jon Bird, Barry Curtis, Tim Putnam, George Robertson and Lisa Tickner (London: Routledge, 1993), 188.

25 Scholars and practitioners in critical cartography and counter-cartographies have experimented with different and participatory ways of mapping that generate alternative spatial knowledges, such as the movements of migrant street vendors. See Annette Kim, 'Critical cartography 2.0: from "participatory mapping" to authored visualizations of power and people', *Landscape and Urban Planning* 142 (2015): 215–25.

26 Arthur Bochner, 'Putting meanings into motion: autoethnography's existential calling', in *Handbook of Autoethnography*, eds. Stacy Holman Jones, Tony Adams and Carolyn Ellis (Walnut Creek, CA: Left Coast Press, 2013), 53.

27 Carolyn Ellis, 'Preface: Carrying the torch for autoethnography', in *Handbook of Autoethnography*, eds. Stacy Holman Jones, Tony Adams and Carolyn Ellis (Walnut Creek, CA: Left Coast Press, 2013), 10.

28 Phil Baker, 'Secret city: psychogeography and the end of London', in *London: From Punk to Blair,* 2nd edition, eds. Joe Kerr and Andrew Gibson (London: Reaktion Books, 2012), 277.

29 Taxis, buses and e-bikes were used when covering long distances, such as when commuting from Dongsheng to Kangbashi. Taxis and buses provided further opportunities for striking up conversations with the locals.

30 Michel de Certeau, *The Practice of Everyday Life*, trans. Steven Rendall (Berkeley, CA: University of California Press, 1984), 93, original emphasis.

31 Merlin Coverley, *Psychogeography* (Harpenden: Pocket Essentials, 2006), 12.

32 It is possible that interviewees spoke favourably about Ordos because they did not want to be seen as criticizing the efficacy of local party leadership. In order to encourage genuine responses, the local translator led the engagements with interviewees and adopted a relaxed, conversational approach. In other studies of Kangbashi, interviewees similarly commented on its positive aspects, such as it 'being quiet, spacious, distant, slow-paced, reminiscent of simpler "rural" life, and amenable to ad hoc social interaction'. Duo Yin, Junxi Qian and Hong Zhu, 'Living in the "ghost city": media discourses and the negotiation of home in Ordos, Inner Mongolia, China', *Sustainability* 9, no. 11 (2017): 12.

33 Glenn Albrecht, 'Solastalgia', *Alternatives Journal* 32, no. 4/5 (2006): 35.

34 Shepard, *Ghost Cities*, 71.

35 Alison Blunt and Robyn Dowling, *Home* (London: Routledge, 2006), 2.

36 Blunt and Dowling, *Home*, 23, 24.

37 Dror Kochan, 'Home is where I lay down my hat? The complexities and functions of home for internal migrants in contemporary China', *Geoforum* 71 (2016): 21–32.

38 Yin, Qian and Zhu, 'Ghost city', 1, 2.

39 Katherine Brickell, '"Mapping" and "doing" critical geographies of home', *Progress in Human Geography* 36, no. 2 (2012): 237.

40 Christina Lee, 'Home is where the hearth *was*: remembering and place-making a vanished town', in *Spectral Spaces and Hauntings: The Affects of Absence*, ed. Christina Lee (New York: Routledge, 2017), 51–69.

41 Personal correspondence with Laura Wang (24 October 2017). UNCCD refers to the thirteenth meeting of the Parties to the United Nations Convention to Combat Desertification that took place in Ordos on 6–16 September 2017.

42 Personal correspondence with Laura Wang (16 April 2021).

43 Yin, Qian and Zhu, 'Ghost city', 2.

Upgrading Downsizing: Tiny Houses as a Response to Precarity

Madeleine Esch

'It feels so spacious!' declares Nicole, touring for the first time the Hawaiian-inspired tiny home on wheels in Texas she will share with her husband. They marvel at the designer touches – green glass splashback in the kitchen, corrugated steel shower surround in the bathroom, custom storage for golf clubs and even a compact enclosed patio for their dog. Featured in an episode of reality TV series *Tiny House Nation*, the trendy, fit, white, twenty-something couple plan to use their house on wheels to travel the country while working from home as self-employed online marketers.[1]

'It's just a gorgeous little thing', 60-year-old Gladys, an African-American woman who suffers from severe arthritis and uses a walker, says of the tiny house she rents-to-own for $350 a month in Detroit, Michigan. It is one in a cluster of such homes that are part of nonprofit Cass County Community Social Services' response to chronic homelessness in the post-industrial city. As a *New York Times* article on the development describes it, a tiny house village 'can offer reassuring domestic coziness for residents, and its nonthreatening appearance also appeals to wealthier neighbors, who might have raised "not in my backyard" objections to nonprofits' proposals for more institutional designs'.[2]

As the aforementioned examples suggest, the tiny house is a multivalent site that, as journalist Jim Wilson writes, is a form of 'affordable living for hipsters and homeless alike'.[3] For the relatively privileged who opt to downsize, such dwellings are extolled as offering freedom and flexibility; for the underprivileged, they are pathways to security and stability. In the past decade, domestic architecture with a smaller footprint has coalesced under the sign of the 'Tiny House'. The Tiny House signifies a diminutive, detached housing unit that has taken on an outsized cultural significance.

Although size and cost predominantly determine what constitutes a Tiny House (TH), there is considerable variety within the category. Most are under 400 square feet, with precise dimensions dictated by the wheeled trailers upon which they often rest.[4] A Tiny House on wheels is likely to be just 8.5 ft wide with lengths up to 40 ft, although they can be smaller. Those built on fixed foundations, such as Gladys's in Detroit, may be wider but generally are still the width of a single room. Ranging in style from rustic to modernist, their exteriors mimic traditional residential architecture. Interiors may feature a lofted bed but are usually single-storey open plan spaces. While blueprints for constructions are readily available for purchase online, fully built wheeled-THs can be ordered at prices ranging from $20,000 for unfinished shells to $200,000 for customized models. Even at the higher end, they appear feasible in a challenging housing market.

In the United States alone, Tiny House builds are now the subject of multiple documentaries, television programmes, vlogs, blogs, books (including memoirs, how-to books, children's books and a romance novel), conferences and associations. Tiny House media (henceforth, THM) is a booming industry, even before adding related alternative housing forms with dedicated followings, such as converted vans and modernist container homes. Enthusiasts speak of a Tiny House movement emerging in the late 1990s and expanding to mainstream awareness in the 2010s. A Wikipedia entry stated, 'The tiny-house movement promotes financial prudence, economically safe, shared community experiences, and a shift in consumerism-driven mindsets.'[5] That shift in mindset can also be described as voluntary simplicity, 'choosing lower-cost but visible consumer goods that enable one to signal that one has chosen, rather than been coerced into, a less affluent lifestyle'.[6] According to Tiny House guru and founder of Tumbleweed Tiny House Company Jay Shafer, when he built his first house in the late 1990s there were few places to turn to for advice: 'I didn't actually believe there was a small house movement … These days you Google "tiny house" or "small houses", you could never get through the list of things that pop up'.[7] The TH has become an architectural fetish object, eliciting far more curiosity than other housing options that might provide comparable benefits.

Given the ubiquity of Tiny Houses in popular culture, and recognizing that they may be more a media phenomenon than an actual housing market shift, I employ a media studies approach to investigate what the celebration of TH signals about contemporary social conditions and concerns around housing (in)security.[8] I take a broad overview of the THM landscape but focus in particular on the independently produced documentaries *TINY: A Story about Living Small* (2013) and *We the Tiny House People* (2012), and the cable television series *Tiny House Nation* and *Tiny House Hunting* (not to be confused with *Tiny House Hunters*; all three of which debuted in 2014). These texts are situated alongside newspaper coverage of efforts, such as the one in Detroit, which position TH as a novel solution to combat homelessness. I argue that by miniaturizing the single-family house, the trials and tribulations of attaining the American Dream of home ownership can be acknowledged without being seriously questioned as a goal. By upgrading downsizing, Tiny Houses both mask and reveal precariousness.

Housing anxieties

More than a decade after the 2008 Global Financial Crisis (GFC) and the burst housing bubble in the United States, single-family home ownership remains elusive for many. After the millennial housing boom that was characterized by real estate 'flipping', McMansions and sprawling residential developments, the subprime mortgage crisis following the GFC spurred nationwide handwringing over predatory lending practices, the financialization of real estate and 'bigger is better' mentalities. Headlines like 'Is the McMansion dead?' and 'The case against home ownership' suggested a mood of re-evaluation.[9] Yet, perhaps surprisingly, the resolve for home ownership has strengthened. In 2009, a Pew Research survey found that despite 'the current national housing funk – or maybe as a refuge from it – owners in all the major demographic groups overwhelmingly say they view their home as a comfort. There are no differences by gender, race, age, income or education.'[10]

Such attitudes may be one reason the housing market has been largely revived, even amid the COVID-19 pandemic. In 2020, the rate of home ownership in the US was 65.8 per cent. Although trailing behind the pre-GFC peak of 69.2 per cent, it indicated a strong upward trend that was characterized by Pew as a 'homebuying spree'. It is important to note that the growth is uneven – rates have increased faster and are overall higher for white homebuyers than other racial/ethnic demographics. For example, 74.5 per cent of white households owned their own home compared to 44.1 per cent of Black households in 2020.[11]

While the dearth of cost-effective housing across the country is driven by many complex factors, researchers at Harvard's Joint Center for Housing Studies point out that new construction favours larger, more expensive houses: 'The relative lack of smaller, more affordable new homes suggests that the rising costs of labor, land, and materials make it unprofitable to build for the middle market', they surmise.[12] As a result, median prices are out of reach for many and the average house may far exceed what buyers require. In 2018, the median size of a new single-family home was 2,386 sq. ft with a median sale price of $326,400. More than half sold that year were 2,400 sq. ft or larger. Just 3 per cent were sized under 1,400 sq. ft, which is still more than triple the size of what is usually regarded as 'tiny'.[13] These numbers emphasize the steadfast preference for spacious, detached single-family homes that are prohibitive to lower-income households and multifamily units.

Millennials – a racially and ethnically diverse group born between 1984 and 2005, and who came of age amid a recession – have been especially discouraged from entering the property market. Several years after the housing bubble collapse, journalist Derek Thompson noted the shift: 'If you guessed that young people are staying out of the housing market, you'd be very right. They're low on jobs, high on student debt, and freaked out by the crash.'[14] Alongside other cultural factors, he identifies 'the vicissitudes of the labor market' as playing a part in dampening millennials' interest in home ownership. As they seek jobs in tech-boom cities, they will likely find that reasonably priced housing is scarce. Calling the trend 'The Great Affordability Crisis', Annie Lowrey avers:

> In metro areas such as the Bay Area, Seattle, and Boston, severe supply shortages have led to soaring prices – millions of low- and middle-income families are no longer able to purchase centrally located homes. The median asking price for a single-family home in San Francisco has reached $1.6 million; even with today's low interest rates, that would require a monthly mortgage payment of roughly $6,000, assuming that a family puts down the standard 20 percent.[15]

This has led record numbers of young people to move back in with their parents or persist in the rental market. It is a backward step that stymies 'wealth accumulation, thus consigning them to worse net-worth trajectories for the rest of their lives'.[16]

The Great Affordability Crisis is not only affecting millennials, of course. Approximately one-third of working Americans are considered 'financially fragile', meaning they 'could not cover the cost of a midsize budget shock, such as a car or house repair, a medical bill or a legal expense, within a month'.[17] Education debt, underemployment and lack of insurance are major factors that have compounded the nation's housing crisis. According to a 2019 report, financial fragility measures roughly tracked with the proportion of 'cost-burdened' households who spent more than 30 per cent of their income on housing costs.[18] With overstretched homeowners risking foreclosure and cash-strapped renters facing looming evictions, both groups can and do slip into homelessness. In 2019 and 2020, homelessness was on the rise nationally.[19]

Debt-burdened millennials, wary of unstable work conditions, and older generations facing housing insecurity may not see themselves as part of the same cohort, but their interests overlap. They may be considered part of what Guy Standing terms the precariat, a *'class-in-the-making'*, distinguished by attitudes of mistrust and the absence of a traditional 'security in exchange for subordination' bargain that characterized industrial class structures in welfare states.[20] Members of the precariat are less likely to define themselves by their careers and may have diminished community support structures and insufficient financial reserves. The demographically diverse group 'all share a sense that their labour is instrumental (to live), opportunistic (taking what comes) and precarious (insecure)'.[21] Some experience what Standing calls the four As: anger, anomie, anxiety and alienation. Yet they may also be painted as heroes, 'rejecting [traditional] institutions in a concerted act of intellectual and emotional defiance' and demonstrating a 'free-spirited defiance and nonconformity'.[22]

The Tiny House movement could well be seen as a symbol of that free-spirited defiance in the face of uncertainty.[23] As Standing argues, 'Symbols matter. They help unite groups into something more than a multitude of strangers. They help in forging a class and building identity, fostering an awareness of commonality and a basis for solidarity or *fraternité*.'[24] Setting aside the range of reasons for TH living, the movement could potentially hasten a re-evaluation of zoning codes and mortgage-lending policies, or provide cities a way to address the affordable housing crunch. Clustered TH developments could create inviting public spaces, centralized social services and promote cross-class solidarity. This vision of community might provide one small part of 'a new politics of paradise that is mildly utopian and proudly so'.[25]

The utopian TH village stands against its symbolic foil – the mobile home park, a contrast sociologist Esther Sullivan dramatizes at the beginning of a 2017 TedX talk. Promising to reveal the secret path to affordable home ownership that eighteen million Americans have discovered, she teases the audience, 'You're totally hoping I'm going to say "tiny home"'. Her audience, conscious of the media buzz surrounding TH, laughs knowingly.[26] In fact, Sullivan was talking about the similarly sized and sometimes comparably priced mobile/trailer home, but the key to her joke is that TH are a more palatable option for living within one's means. They carry no stigma and can be marketed as luxury goods. As the slogan of HGTV's *Tiny Luxury* puts it, 'Don't downgrade when you can simply downsize!'

The mobile home is widely seen as a downgrade from standard housing. In an essay for the shelter website *Curbed*, Roxane Gay explains that the negative associations stem not only from 'impermanence or questionable quality but because these homes reveal that sometimes, compromises must be made when it comes to the American dream. Sometimes, a mobile home is all a family can afford.'[27] Sullivan acknowledges the low cultural status of mobile home parks, but through detailed ethnography documents the affection that many residents feel for their houses and close-knit communities.[28] Yet these proud owners of small, well-kept, manufactured abodes may come to recognize that they are only 'halfway homeowners' because although they own their trailer, they do not own the land on which it sits. Increasingly subjected to mass evictions and displacement as mobile home parks are redeveloped for more fashionable uses, many suffer a further blow when they discover that their *mobile* homes are not so mobile after all. Most trailers are not able to withstand transportation and their wheels are rotted from years of disuse, revealing 'the central tension between mobility and rootedness that lies at the heart of the mobile home.'[29]

The class-based disparity between Tiny House and mobile home owners is illustrated by their different experiences and views of relocation. Many TH are designed to maximize mobility; they can be readily towed by their owners using nothing more than a standard pickup truck and without any special permits. Even though TH owners, too, are frequently 'halfway homeowners' – hemmed in by municipal codes that restrict where they can park and even whether their dwellings are legal housing units – these anxieties are rendered invisible in THM, eclipsed by the touted perks of freedom and flexibility. By refusing a fixed location in the first place, TH owners resist the threat of displacement by claiming that they never wanted to stay in one place for too long anyway. Precarity is reframed as mobility.

Both Gay and Sullivan understand the fundamental conceit of Tiny Houses – that their cuteness and novelty allows a mainstream embrace rarely extended to other small-scale housing alternatives. The same can be said for their use as a substitute for homeless shelters, tent cities or tenements. To battle the seemingly intractable challenge of homelessness, tiny individual houses offer an attractive response to crisis. Their aesthetics make them prime fodder for television and documentary producers seeking new material for a thriving landscape of property-themed media.

Property TV: A not-so-tiny media landscape

In the USA, home improvement and property TV programmes proliferated alongside the housing boom, accelerated by the explosion in cable and digital cable/satellite channels during the 1990s and the 2000s, including HGTV, Discovery, FYI, A&E and TLC.[30] Part of a broader genre of lifestyle television, these shows tend toward discourses of personal responsibility and appropriate consumption (in fashion, diet, interior décor and beyond), with didactic wisdom from a cultural intermediary leading to a dramatic transformation at the finale of each episode – a moment known as 'the reveal'.[31] Class mobility is an unspoken animating concern in which 'good taste recommended by the genre becomes a badge of belonging for those feeling uncertain of their place in our social order'.[32] Tiny House programmes, whether or not they feature experts and scenes of intervention, similarly negotiate class anxieties and conclude with a reveal as the new homeowner sees their fully realized 'tiny' for the first time or the audience sees the end result of the owner's labour.

Property TV programmes are economically efficient to produce, endlessly repeatable and formulaic while at the same time admirably malleable, having weathered the 2008–2009 housing market crisis with deft shifts in theme. In relation to British property shows in this post-crash landscape, Ruth McElroy highlights how they echoed or amplified a nationalist discourse of austerity that was encapsulated in the 'Keep calm and carry on' slogan.[33] Despite this new tone, the genre maintained 'the commitment to property as the defining marker of the self's economic accomplishment and the very grounds upon which the rights of good citizenship can be earned'.[34] Formats that were deemed as being too occupied with the financial benefits of home ownership were phased out and replaced with those geared more towards helping people tackle home improvement problems or navigate the real estate market. The shows reinforced home ownership as an unshaken goal, glossing over or avoiding the challenges to its attainment.[35]

Property formats on US cable television convey real estate shopping as a relaxing pastime. As Shawn Shimpach writes, property TV 'offers safe harbor from even the very risks inherent to its apparently straightforward subject matter'.[36] In addition to eschewing talk of mortgages and access to credit, the programmes extend that sense of safety via banal production choices (for example, camerawork and editing) and the predictability of expert advice. Viewers may find comforting familiarity (or stultifying repetition) in the recurring themes, rhythms and production values. Experts rehearse 'the habits and *habitus* of domestic space making' as audiences will come to expect that buyers will request class-coded features – 'open floor plans, granite counter tops, stainless steel appliances, and double vanities in the master bath' – and couples will bicker good-naturedly about housekeeping standards and domestic gender roles but ultimately find happiness in a well-appointed house.[37] Thus, although actual house hunting and homemaking can be sources of stress, the world of property TV presents instead a soothing space for imagining the meaning of house and home. The house is portrayed not just as an investment, but furthermore a source of joy, an expression of self, a sanctuary, a source of stability.

Tiny House-themed programming follows the majority of the aforementioned patterns and omits its more radical potential or utopian communal spirit proposed by some advocates. TH shows, documentaries and web content are strikingly similar, such that, 'To describe any episode … is to describe a typical episode, as there is room for very little variation in the formula'.[38] While there are minor modifications (host or no host; real estate transaction or DIY construction diary), individual episodes stick to their established formulas, replacing only the homeowner in the spotlight. In THM, as in other property television, homeowners and would-be homeowners represent a range of ages, family structures, geographic locations and career paths.[39] Participants' budgets and preferred architectural styles may vary, but all are able to find the home that is right for them. This affirms a pattern Mimi White has identified in *House Hunters*, namely that the relative diversity of participants and the 'numbingly repetitive structure of the show' are not unrelated facets – one validates the other. 'The inclusiveness embraced by the show is based in the affinitive appeal of home ownership, assembling participants and viewers in a common, projected vision of national diversity through the accumulation of disparate, local real estate transactions', she writes.[40] While the set-up is consistent, the narrative underpinning is that home buying is not a one-size-fits-all affair, although it is, in some ways, equally available to everyone.

Across the texts discussed in this chapter, the outcome of everyone realizing their dream of (tiny) home ownership is constant. TH living is rhetorically constructed as superior to other pared-down housing solutions, and whatever their circumstances the homeowners are overwhelmingly depicted as *opting*, not *needing*, to downsize. The very conditions that may have led them to consider this type of living (financial fragility, contingent employment, etc.) are narratively overcome and sometimes refashioned as benefits. Downsizing is upgraded by fixating on the conscious decisions of TH homeowners – of location, lifestyle and custom finishes – that present them as active agents, not victims.

Location

THM focuses on the upsides of mobility-as-freedom, rather than seeing displacement as an effect of living precariously. Building or buying a house on wheels is fashioned as a smart strategy to chase opportunities or adapt to changing circumstances. The young Texan couple with the Hawaiian-inspired TH mentioned at the beginning of this chapter exemplify the optimistic view toward lifestyles that are contingent and mobile, rather than rooted. Their plans to travel are facilitated by their entrepreneurial careers as online marketers. Other would-be downsizers say they are drawn to the ease of pulling up stakes, for example, to complete a three-year medical residency or a four-year graduate degree. Many seem to have work-from-home careers or are self-employed, with the TH lifestyle maximizing these impermanent working conditions and promising the reward of choosing your preferred location. This sort of strategic mobility, though framed as a bonus, may be necessary as it can be difficult to find legal sites to permanently locate a Tiny House. Their tenuous legal standing is seldom broached in THM and can be difficult for the uninitiated to discern given the patchwork of obscure regulations and classifications that pertain to non-standard dwellings.

Building a TH on privately owned rural land is the far safer bet, although the class privilege needed to purchase land is little addressed in THM. A rare exception can be seen in *We the Tiny House People* which features Jenine Alexander, a puppeteer building her own TH, who explains that for now, she has parked in a friend's driveway: 'I don't own any land yet. Land is so expensive around here. I don't have access to that opportunity.'[41] The subject of *TINY: A Story about Living Small* (hereafter referred to as *TINY*), Christopher Smith, does own land: 'For most of my life, I've travelled, but a few months before my thirtieth birthday, I decided to buy a plot of land in Hartsel, Colorado.' Stunning aerial photography of the Colorado countryside accompanies his reflections. Christopher's story suggests that the TH will give him the constancy he has never had, following a childhood of frequent cross-country moves, while also allowing him to avoid a lengthy mortgage or the need to maintain full-time employment in a rural community. Despite the fact that it is on wheels, the TH will ground him in this place. In the concluding voiceover, Christopher calls his Tiny House 'one point of orientation in a world of possibility'.

A similar savvy compromise is expressed by those who choose tiny in order to live in locations that would otherwise be beyond their means, from bustling cities and beachside retreats to mountain resorts. As one couple on *Tiny House*

Hunting explains of their search for a TH in the sought-after skiing destination of Jackson Hole, Wyoming, 'We're living tiny down there so we can live big up here.'[42] As with the well-known *House Hunters*, the nearly identical series *Tiny House Hunters* and *Tiny House Hunting* follow homebuyers as they tour three properties and purportedly decide which one to purchase. When these shows are set in desirable, expensive cities, THM names, but quickly resolves, the urban problem of affordable housing shortages. The TH's lower price point is an antidote to feeling priced out of the market, but not all episodes repeat this 'priced-out' narrative. Episodes are equally as likely to feature successful, established professionals seeking a second home. In this way, the public-school teacher unable to buy a Seattle condominium has the same purchasing power to choose as the elite executive couple from Boston in pursuit of a vacation home in rural Wisconsin. By portraying their searches almost identically, this reinforces the TH lifestyle as universally appealing.

Lifestyle

Accentuating lifestyle choices in THM works to foreground the active agency of TH occupants. The voiceover in the opening titles of *Tiny House Nation* says, 'Whether they're after financial independence or desire to live with less, inspired homeowners are starting to think outside the blueprints of everyday building'. The opening voiceover for *Tiny House Hunting* echoes this, reassuring that 'when ingenuity rules, freedom follows'. From the outset, then, these series applaud the creativity and forward-thinking of their participants who are neither buffeted by extreme circumstances nor beaten back by market forces. For Deek Diedricksen, a builder of quirky, eco-friendly shacks, in having 'less to heat, less to maintain, less to pay for, no mortgage in certain cases ... you're kind of beating the system'.[43] The creative choice contributes to the search for the good life, an idea clearly articulated by a TH dweller named Catherine interviewed outside her 176 sq. ft house in *TINY*, 'This isn't my consolation prize. This is exactly what I wanted.'

One popular strategy for validating downsizing has been to reference America's foremost proponent of voluntary simplicity as a path to enlightenment: transcendentalist philosopher Henry David Thoreau. As Thoreau moved to a one-room cabin in the woods near Walden Pond in Concord, Massachusetts, in 1845 – to 'live so sturdily and Spartan-like as to put to rout all that was not life' – some in the TH movement style their own housing decisions as noble experiments in self-understanding.[44] Two minutes into *TINY*, the protagonist Christopher reflects on commencing construction of his planned tiny home,

'Thoreau has always been a hero of mine, but I'm not sure what he would think about building a cabin on a trailer.' The documentary intercuts scenes from Thoreau's rustic homestead with Christopher's trailer purchase, lending a sober depth and romanticism to an otherwise mundane transaction.

Thoreau and Walden again are pressed into service in *We the Tiny House People*, first with one tiny loft dweller pointing to a well-thumbed pocket copy of *Walden*, to which she says she turns for inspiration. In the final scene of the film, shot at Walden, director Kirsten Dirksen muses grandiosely in a voiceover that, 'All Americans have a little bit of Thoreau in them.' One interviewee in *TINY*, Tammy Strobel, describes quitting her career in investment management to recalibrate her life, asking, 'Do you really want to spend your time working at a job you hate to buy crap that you can't afford?' The sentiment is identifiably in the same mould of Thoreau, with the small footprint of tiny living itself a declaration of values.

While not everyone will engage in such extensive lifestyle recalibration, THM depicts would-be TH owners as proving themselves up to the challenge of tiny living and self-betterment. This may be done via highlighting arduous DIY construction processes, or via formats with game-like structures. In *Tiny House Nation*, host John Weisbarth and builder Zack Giffin arrive to assist/rescue a homeowner's build already in process. The show stresses that to 'go tiny' is a big commitment. While Giffin jumpstarts stalled construction efforts, Weisbarth administers gimmicky tasks to participants to test their recognition of what living tiny will mean. These have included challenging an engaged couple to spend the day chained together, a husband and wife to endure each other's noisy hobbies of sewing and banjo-picking at close range, and a fashionista to cull her walk-in closet to fit within the baggage allowance of commercial airlines. Befitting the well-established narrative structure, participants chafe at these trials but ultimately pass the test. Viewers would be forgiven for wondering if the lessons will really stick as little other evidence of lifestyle change is on view, but for their (at least short-term) efforts the downsizers are rewarded with a completed custom-designed Tiny House.

Customization

Arguably, the most significant way that THM distinguishes the Tiny House from other small dwellings is by concentrating on customization. Whereas mobile homes are factory-built and largely homogeneous, TH are commonly custom designs. Instead of merely cramming some of the trappings of traditional homes into smaller spaces, TH proponents assert that they are creating a space purpose-built for their needs, with every detail attended to. Since the total scope is only a few hundred square feet, high-end finishes can be used, like natural wood panelling or designer glass tiles, that banish any notion of a diminished lifestyle. Even Shafer concurs, stating, 'I prefer quality over quantity, and I really couldn't afford a large house with the kind of features I have in my small house.'[45] Both cable TV programmes and documentaries fixate on the details in the near universal language of the room tour. Homeowner and viewer are invited to cherish control over minute domestic choices in situations where their other life choices may be constrained.

TH builders are praised for their innovative use of the restricted space, which ironically retains many of the attributes and comforts of a traditional, detached single-family house. Whereas standard housing programmes dedicate screen time to open plan design, walk-in closets and spacious patios, THM substitutes this obsession with detail by showcasing multi-function furniture and ingenious organizational solutions. In *Tiny House Hunting*, would-be homeowners express surprised delight at these innovations. Stairs contain storage drawers, shelves double as sliding doors, narrow console tables fold out to seat four for dinner. On *Tiny House Nation*, the hosts lavish attention on homeowners' specific requests, for instance, a tiny porch for a lapdog or hidden storage for golf clubs or a guitar collection. In these television narratives, with enough artisanal craftsmanship, any material possession or lifestyle activity can be accommodated in a Tiny House. Notwithstanding the gimmicky challenges, TH dwellers are invited to resist fundamental re-evaluations of what a house should contain.

In its mutability, the Tiny House turns neoliberalism's demands for agility and self-sufficiency into luxurious lifestyle choices – it comports itself to your needs. This is in keeping with a neoliberal emphasis on private rather than public solutions. There is little to no discussion of external facilities or supports that may be needed to make possible such a tiny lifestyle, including laundromats, gyms, co-working spaces and off-site storage. The versatile fixtures and furniture aim, in part, to reduce the need for these more public and social outlets. Ultimately, the customized, mobile TH may be less practical than a studio apartment in a building with shared facilities, a modest house of 500–1,000 sq. ft, or more radical arrangements like an intentional co-housing community. Yet the relative absences of these alternatives in mainstream entertainment show how the Tiny House endures in the public's imagination as a miniaturization of the archetypal single-family home and an answer to the national housing crisis.

More than beds in sheds?

Although basically absent in THM, tiny dwellings are being employed to combat homelessness in cities across the United States. Newspaper headlines tell a similar story, conveying cautious optimism for this new approach to a persistent issue ('Could tiny houses help solve Philly's big homelessness problem?', 'Tiny houses multiply amid big issues as communities tackle homelessness').[46] Many articles recount an inspiring, hopeful story with formerly unhoused people now expressing pride of ownership and getting their lives on track without the spectre of urban blight or the unpleasant image of the crowded shelter, tent city or shanty town.[47] Some articles go so far as to explicitly link the luxurious Tiny Houses on cable TV and the more bare-bones variety intended as social service, crediting the former with making the latter more enticing. In one story, a church-sponsored TH project in Salt Lake City, Utah, is 'popular, at least in part, because tiny homes are having a moment right now, according to organizers. Since gaining popularity on shows like HGTV's "Tiny House Hunters," they've emerged as a way to eliminate mortgage debt, generate rental income and expand a city's affordable housing options.'[48]

Befitting these comparisons to HGTV, news coverage of tiny shelters for the homeless tends to focus on architectural details with a sense of wonder that betrays low expectations of affordable housing. In Springfield, Missouri, 'The columned front porches and exteriors are painted in beiges, mint greens and brick reds, among other hues, and solar panels are being installed on the roofs.' The reporter adds that the 'colorful little homes' are sometimes mistaken for 'playthings'.[49] In Detroit, 'One house is canary yellow, with a bright-red front door. Another is a beige mini-Tudor with a stone chimney and steeply pitched roof. The lawns are neatly manicured, and last winter, the homes were outlined in Christmas lights – probably the first holiday decoration in this part of the city in decades.'[50]

Reporters amplify the enthusiastic view that Tiny Houses bring colour and charm to otherwise down-at-heel areas. While these are objectively verifiable details, the disproportionate discussion on them implies an attitude of magnanimity, that is, this attention to detail is better than should be expected. This is captured in the remarks of one Texan developer who involves potential tenants in the design process, 'treating them like they're billionaires' with custom designs such as a pagoda-inspired house that is 'cuter than all get-out'.[51] The stylish designs mitigate some of the 'not in my back yard' (NIMBY) angst of neighbours and town planners. One TH advocate in San Diego is quoted as saying, 'They're cute, painted in attractive colors, and the neighbors seem to like them. ... It looks more like a village than a camp.'[52]

Visual appeal, however, does not exempt TH-as-shelter ventures from legal challenges and other objections. While these can be weathered by high-end builds, zoning concerns here are exacerbated by the threat of crime, drugs or violence purported to accompany low-income housing.[53] Journalists report on contentious city council meetings, obscure zoning ordinances and technicalities. Other oppositions spotlighted in newspapers repeatedly question the sufficiency of TH as homes. Are they too tiny? Too bare bones? In Los Angeles, California, some were decried as 'doghouse-like' and others in Oakland as 'coffinlike sleeping boxes on wheels'.[54] Reported measurements lend weight to some of these critiques. These units, tellingly referred to as huts or 'beds in sheds', are often substantially smaller than the 240 sq. ft and larger variety showcased in THM, and may not include kitchens or bathrooms.

At the centre of these debates, then, is the perceived covetable nature (or lack thereof) of these tiny abodes from the assumed perspective of a relatively privileged reader, rather than the prospective occupants who are homeless or dealing with housing insecurity. This tension is expressed by a Philadelphia nun and leader of a social service agency in the city. A reporter paraphrases her response, 'The key ... will be in the bones of the homes. Will they be cozy cottages with some of the style and clever functional attributes people ogle over on HGTV, or will they look more like wooden tents?'[55] Overall, the trend seems to be something in the middle: a cute exterior with a basic interior. One interior that was described approvingly included 'new white cabinets, recessed lighting and Ikea-style beds'; its charm 'broke down a lot of barriers' with folks who were resistant to the project. The housing advocate interviewed in this news story contrasts this venture with other less desirable sites where what has been built 'bears no resemblance to the tiny homes the public sees featured on HGTV shows and in blogs as a chic way to live a minimalist life'.[56]

While adaptability to contain all that a single-family house *should* is stressed in THM, that impression of expansiveness is not prioritized for TH-as-shelter dwellings. At best, inside they are simple rooms with basic kitchen counters. Some are devoid of indoor plumbing, which is compensated by communal facilities. Several articles quote sources implying that storage is simply not a concern for the intended residents, nor are finishing touches. One organizer in Racine, Wisconsin, said, 'For some people, it's hard to envision living in a space this small. They might wonder how they could fit all their clothes inside. These are people recovering from homelessness. They are going to be coming in here with a duffel bag.'[57] While Tiny House owners on cable TV use their dwellings to pare down their possessions, their TH-as-shelter counterparts are given the opportunity to acquire material possessions as part of their journey toward more permanent, traditional housing.

Whether the TH represents a chance for stability and acquisition or flexibility and minimalism, both of these paths share a fetishizing of the form – it is not just a small(er) home, but a *Tiny House*. The term itself and surrounding discourses underscore cuteness as key to their appeal. Architectural distinctions, even whimsy, and their dollhouse-like qualities are celebrated. What purpose does this preoccupation with cuteness serve, especially in relation to the extreme conditions from which the TH movement arises? Why, in a time of volatility, would such minor details be more rewarding than efficient, scalable mass production of housing solutions?

In *The Aesthetics and Affects of Cuteness*, Joshua Dale et al. do not directly name the Tiny House movement among the trends they study, but their discussion of cute culture has direct application. They connect the rise of cute culture – internet kittens, Japanese mascots, mini-anything – to the socio-political moment in that, 'indulging in and communicating through cuteness provides an important coping strategy for subjects caught up in the precariousness inherent to neoliberal capitalism.'[58] Cuteness offers a 'fantasy of respite' that can 'mollify in the face of disquieting truths.'[59] Cute baby animals, for example, disarm us and call forth a nurturing impulse, and may lead us to ignore or forgive upsetting news and exploitative corporate policies. Arguably, the *cute* house may disarm in similar ways, assuaging anxieties about the housing market and consumerism, or moderating dissatisfaction with urban housing policies and social services.

The cuteness of TH-as-shelter solutions fits this template by replacing the blight that makes apparent the 'disquieting truth' of the failed social safety net. For their residents, the familiar domestic architecture may be reassuring and the unique details can become an outlet for individuality. Few formerly homeless residents are interviewed by reporters, partly because most articles discuss projects still in the planning stages and likely because credentialled expert sources are favoured. Therefore, we cannot know from media reports if the cuteness of these shelters matters at all to their intended occupants. To the housing advocates backing these plans, the compact house is a re-entry point into the American Dream, guaranteeing stability and privacy to people whose mobility in the past has been all too public. Cuteness and attention to detail may mask the fact that these are not housing solutions that can be scaled up or that can fully address the scope of the nation's housing problem. In other words, we may only be helping a small number of people ... but just look at what they get.

Coda

For some, opting to downsize is a step towards more ethical consumption, which could be seen as an unexpected upside of the 2008 financial crisis. The boom in Tiny Houses might not have happened otherwise. However, scholars of consumer culture will point out that the capacity for consumer practices to drive meaningful social change is contentious. Economist Juliet Schor posits that the rejection of consumerism 'has taken place principally at an individual level. It is not associated with a widely accepted intellectual analysis, and an associated critical politics of consumption.'[60] In the Tiny House movement, there is opportunity to unite the interests of deliberate downsizers and the vulnerable poor in need of shelter, realizing the latent power of a growing precariat class. Designing TH villages with the intent of comingling occupants from different income levels and forming some intentional community might encourage the breaking down of class barriers. The TH's visibility itself has sparked broader conversations about cost-effective housing, environmental justice and the advantages of the so-called 'sharing economy'.

Yet, few examples of this nascent solidarity can be found in THM, aside from a few comparisons of shelter tinies to the as-seen-on-TV models. Even TH leaders concede the Tiny House is more a media trend or a curiosity than a widespread phenomenon. Shafer refers to people's fascination as a sort of house porn, voyeuristic titillation provided by beautiful images demanding nothing in return.[61] One suspects that THM is aspirational and instructional for a minority, but for the vast majority it affirms their commitment to traditional housing. To the extent viewers find pleasure in saying 'I could never live like that', such reaction validates their ownership of or longing for the 2,400 sq. ft house and thirty-year mortgage.

If increasingly more people encounter working lives that are contingent and where geographic flexibility is expected, then TH living may be a concept whose time has come. Choosing to downsize may make such conditions far more tolerable. But to harness its socially transformative capability would call for a more thoroughgoing rejection of the ideal of the self-contained single-family house than is typically seen in THM. Giving up floor space could be complemented by demanding more public space and reducing personal possessions with greater investment in communal property. These shifts could result in a more resilient and mobilized precariat, and in some corners of the country TH villages are moving in this direction. Until this becomes the norm, the Tiny House remains a cute façade for a scaled-back version of the American Dream, shrunken down to fit in 240 sq. ft atop a wheeled trailer that can be pulled to greener pastures.

Notes

1   *Tiny House Nation*, '325 sq. ft Texan's take tiny house' (season 4, episode 4), exec. prod. Tennessee Edwards, aired 28 January 2017 on FYI.

2   Eve M. Kahn, 'A roof of one's own, with or without the gingerbread', *The New York Times* (3 October 2019), https://www.nytimes.com/2019/10/01/style/tiny-houses. html.

3   Jim Wilson, 'Tiny houses: affordable living for hipsters and homeless alike', *The New York Times* (13 October 2015), https://cn.nytimes.com/slideshow/20151016/ t16containers-ss/en-us/#1.

4   Putting a Tiny House on wheels not only makes it mobile, but also allows it to skirt zoning laws and building codes that apply to fixed-foundation housing.

5   The site has since been edited and this passage is no longer included. Wikipedia, 'Tiny house movement' (2020), https://en.wikipedia.org/wiki/Tiny_house_ movement.

6   Amitai Etzioni, 'Introduction: voluntary simplicity – psychological implications, societal consequences', in *Voluntary Simplicity: Responding to Consumer Culture*, eds. Daniel Doherty and Amitai Etzioni (Lanham, MD: Rowman and Littlefield, 2003), 18, original emphasis.

7   *TINY: A Story about Living Small*, dir. Merete Mueller and Christopher Smith (First Run Features, New York, 2013). Documentary, 61 min.

8   As there are no government statistics on Tiny House occupancy, it is unclear just how many people are using one as their primary residence.

9   Jenny Sullivan, 'Is the McMansion dead?', *Builder: The Magazine of the National Association of Home Builders* 32, no. 11 (2009): 46–50; Barbara Kiviat, 'The case against home ownership', *Time International (Atlantic Edition)* 176, no. 13 (2010): 39–44.

10   Pew Research Center, 'Even as housing values sink, there's comfort in homeownership' (19 February 2009), https://www.pewresearch.org/ social-trends/2009/02/19/even-as-housing-values-sink-theres-comfort-in- homeownership/.

11   Richard Fry, 'Amid a pandemic and a recession, Americans go on a near-record homebuying spree', Pew Research Center (8 March 2021), https://www.

pewresearch.org/fact-tank/2021/03/08/amid-a-pandemic-and-a-recession-americans-go-on-a-near-record-homebuying-spree/.

12 Joint Center for Housing Studies of Harvard University, 'The state of the nation's housing 2019', President and Fellows of Harvard College, Boston (2020), 2, https://www.jchs.harvard.edu/state-nations-housing-2019.

13 US Census Bureau, 'Characteristics of new housing' (1 June 2020), https://www.census.gov/construction/chars/.

14 Derek Thompson, '"We wish like hell we had never bought": voices from the housing crisis', *The Atlantic* (2 March 2012), https://www.theatlantic.com/business/archive/2012/03/we-wish-like-hell-we-had-never-bought-voices-from-the-housing-crisis/253888/.

15 Annie Lowrey, 'The great affordability crisis breaking America', *The Atlantic* (7 February 2020), https://www.theatlantic.com/ideas/archive/2020/02/great-affordability-crisis-breaking-america/606046/.

16 Lowrey, 'Affordability crisis'.

17 Raveesha Gupta, Andrea Hasler, Annamaria Lusardi and Noemi Oggero, 'Financial fragility in the US: evidence and implications', National Endowment for Financial Education (16 April 2018), https://www.nefe.org/research/research-projects/completed-research/2018/financial-fragility-in-the-us-evidence-and-implications.aspx.

18 Joint Center for Housing Studies, 'Nation's housing', 4–5.

19 US Interagency Council on Homelessness, 'HUD releases 2020 annual homeless assessment report. Part 1' (18 March 2021), https://www.usich.gov/news/hud-releases-2020-annual-homeless-assessment-report-part-1/.

20 Guy Standing, *The Precariat: The New Dangerous Class* (London: Bloomsbury Academic, 2011), 7–8, original emphasis.

21 Standing, *Precariat*, 13–14.

22 Standing, *Precariat*, 2, 9.

23 Not every TH owner would fit Standing's characterization of the precariat. Many others better fit the group he calls 'proficians' or 'those with bundles of skills that they can market, earning high incomes on contract, as consultants or independent own-account workers'. To the extent that these professionals are financially fragile, however, their interests might readily align with the precariat. Standing, *Precariat*, 7–8.

24 Standing, *Precariat*, 3.

25 Standing, *Precariat*, 155.

26 Esther Sullivan, 'America's most invisible communities – mobile home parks', filmed 7 July 2017 at Ellie Caulkins Opera House, Denver, video 14:35, https://www.ted.com/talks/esther_sullivan_america_s_most_invisible_communities_mobile_home_parks.

27 Roxane Gay, '"Tiny House hunters" and the shrinking American dream', *Curbed* (25 October 2017), https://archive.curbed.com/2017/10/25/16526872/tiny-house-hunters-roxane-gay.

28 Esther Sullivan, *Manufactured Insecurity: Mobile Home Parks and Americans' Tenuous Right to Place* (Oakland, CA: University of California Press, 2018), 15.

29 Sullivan, *Manufactured Insecurity*, 12.

30 Madeleine Esch, 'Renovating TV, remodeling gender: home improvement television and gendered domesticities, 1990–2005' (PhD dissertation, University of Colorado, 2009), 10.

31 Gareth Palmer, 'Introduction – the habit of scrutiny', in *Exposing Lifestyle Television: The Big Reveal*, ed. Gareth Palmer (Aldershot: Ashgate, 2008), 1–13.

32 Palmer, 'Habit of scrutiny', 4–5.

33 Ruth McElroy, 'Mediating home in an age of austerity: the values of British property television', *European Journal of Cultural Studies* 20, no. 5 (2017): 525.

34 McElroy, 'Mediating home', 527.

35 The Canadian series *Buy Herself* (2012) was one of few exceptions that tackled the financial realities that may prevent citizens, particularly single women, from buying a home. Perhaps because of this dose of reality, the show was cancelled after one season.

36 Shawn Shimpach, 'Realty reality: HGTV and the subprime crisis', *American Quarterly* 64, no. 3 (2012): 533.

37 Mimi White, 'A house divided', *European Journal of Cultural Studies* 20, no. 5 (2017): 588, 580.

38 Shimpach, 'Realty reality', 528.

39 Not surprisingly, TH shoppers are more likely to be single and childless than is typical in other house-hunting formats, but this is not always the case. Empty-nest couples, divorced parents with part-time child custody and even some families with children also participate in THM. As TH shoppers are predominantly (but not exclusively) white, this makes the subgenre somewhat less diverse than other property shows.

40 Mimi White, 'Gender territories: house hunting on American real estate TV', *Television and New Media* 14, no. 3 (2012): 230.

41 *We the Tiny House People*, dir. Kirsten Dirksen (faircompanies, USA, 2012). Documentary, 81 min.

42 *Tiny House Hunting*, 'Going tiny in the Tetons' (season 1, episode 6), exec. prod. Shawn Witt, aired 5 January 2015 on FYI.

43 *TINY: A Story about Living Small*.

44 Henry David Thoreau, *Walden: 150th Anniversary Edition* (Princeton, NJ: Princeton University Press, 2004), 91.

45 *We the Tiny House People*.

46 Julia Terruso, 'Could tiny houses help solve Philly's big homelessness problem?', *The Philadelphia Inquirer* (13 December 2018), https://www.inquirer.com/news/tiny-houses-homelessness-stephanie-sena-seattle-frankford-poverty-affordable-housing-20181213.html; Mike Plunkett, 'Tiny houses multiply amid big issues as communities tackle homelessness', *The Washington Post* (26 October 2018), https://www.washingtonpost.com/graphics/2018/national/tiny-houses/.

47 Statistically speaking, the number of Tiny Houses being built (perhaps one or two dozen in any locale) pales in comparison to the number of homeless individuals in those areas.

48 Kelsey Dallas, 'Can a tiny house play a role in helping the homeless?', *Deseret News* (30 April 2017), https://www.statesboroherald.com/churches/faith/can-a-tiny-house-play-a-role-in-helping-the-homeless/.

49 Kahn, 'Roof of one's own'.

50 Trevor Bach, 'A Detroit project's spin on helping the homeless: homeownership', *The Washington Post* (26 October 2018), https://www.washingtonpost.com/graphics/2018/national/tiny-houses/#detroit.

51 Kahn, 'Roof of one's own'.

52 John Wilkens, 'Homeless in Seattle: tent encampments seem to be working', *The San Diego Union-Tribune* (15 October 2017), https://www.sandiegouniontribune.com/news/homelessness/sd-me-tents-seattle-20171013-story.html.

53 Donna Littlejohn, 'Tiny houses for homeless rejected by Los Angeles lawmakers; "only legal use … is for dogs"', *The Mercury News* (25 August 2015), https://www.mercurynews.com/2015/08/25/tiny-houses-for-homeless-rejected-by-los-angeles-lawmakers-only-legal-use-is-for-dogs/.

54 Donna Littlejohn, '"Doghouses" for homeless create uproar in Los Angeles', *The Mercury News* (12 August 2015), https://www.mercurynews.com/2015/08/12/doghouses-for-homeless-create-uproar-in-los-angeles/; Sarah Maslin Nir, 'Thinking outside the box by moving into one', *The New York Times* (13 October 2015), https://www.nytimes.com/2015/10/14/us/live-in-boxes-in-oakland-redefine-housing-squeeze.html.

55 Terruso, 'Homelessness problem'.

56 Plunkett, 'Tiny houses multiply'.

57 Cara Spoto, 'Tiny houses for homeless vets – nonprofit envisions veterans village', *The Journal Times* (4 April 2016), https://journaltimes.com/news/local/tiny-houses-for-homeless-vets-nonprofit-envisions-veterans-village/article_77fb1f12-2d7b-509b-b942-a760e8d031a9.html.

58 Joshua Paul Dale, Joyce Goggin, Julia Leyda, Anthony McIntyre and Diane Negra, 'The aesthetics and affects of cuteness', in *The Aesthetics and Affects of Cuteness*, eds. Joshua Paul Dale, Joyce Goggin, Julia Leyda, Anthony McIntyre and Diane Negra (New York: Routledge, 2016), 1–2.

59 Dale et al., 'Cuteness', 8, 28.

60 Juliet Schor, 'The problem of over-consumption: why economists don't get it', in *Voluntary Simplicity: Responding to Consumer Culture*, eds. Daniel Doherty and Amitai Etzioni (Lanham, MD: Rowman and Littlefield, 2003), 66.

61 *We the Tiny House People.*

Thinking Climate Through Precarity

Ben Beitler

To think climate change through precarity is, as feminist scholar Donna Haraway would have it, to tell one story with another.[1] The first is one you have no doubt heard before. The UN's Intergovernmental Panel on Climate Change (IPCC) told this story in detail in its 2022 report, announcing: 'Human-induced climate change, including more frequent and intense extreme events, has caused widespread adverse impacts and related losses and damages to nature and people, beyond natural climate variability.'[2] No matter where you find yourself – I am writing from Berkeley, California – you are involved in the IPCC's climate change story. Your place in it is contingent on many factors: whether you live in a region that will experience the worst of global warming's fallout, for example, or whether you were born in a country that has thrived in the carbon economy. You personally might choose not to identify with any part in this story; for those who tell it, that does not matter.

Stories about precarity are perhaps less familiar. They tend to be about bodies. To tell a story about precarity means to ask which bodies find themselves in environments that are 'fraught with physical danger or insecurity; at risk of falling, collapse, or similar accident; unsound, unsafe', and which bodies are 'dependent on chance or circumstance; uncertain; liable to fail; exposed to risk, hazardous; insecure, unstable'. Thinking about precarity means asking why certain bodies are made more precarious than others within contemporary economies[3] or ecosystems.[4] But if questions of precarity constantly return us to bodies, these are not always easy to see. The philosopher Judith Butler has spent many years investigating how certain forms of bodily precarity become unseeable. Reflecting on the terrorist attacks on the USA in 2001, she argued that 9/11 had laid bare the basic precarity of contemporary life, 'the fragile and necessary dimensions of our interdependency' within a globalized society.[5] America's ensuing War on Terror, meanwhile, was motivated by a desire to violently deny this precarity.

Post-9/11 American culture, Butler wrote in *Precarious Life*, 'shores itself up, seeks to reconstitute its imagined wholeness, but only at the price of denying its own vulnerability, its dependency, its exposure, where it exploits those very features in others, thereby making those features "other to" itself'.[6] Unable to confront its own precarity, American society projected this trait onto non-American bodies in Afghanistan and Iraq, whose suffering came to seem natural and therefore inevitable. For Butler, to tell a story about precarity thus meant asking both which bodies were precarious, and who benefited politically from how their precarity was – or was not – represented.

To tell a climate story through a precarity story could therefore mean asking about bodies in the climate system and how they are constructed in the dominant culture. We might explore how our representations of climate reveal which bodies are put at risk by climate change, even as we wonder how these representations display or conceal their own reliance on bodies. This second question gestures to yet another definition of precarity as that which is 'held or enjoyed by the favour of and at the pleasure of another person; vulnerable to the will or decision of others'.[7] A representation of climate is precarious insofar as it depends, for its formulation, on the 'will and decision' of certain bodies. The IPCC's 'Summary for Policymakers' illustrates this second sort of precarity, being based on the collaboration of myriad individuals and bureaucracies. These various bodies determined the report's particularly elitist representation of the climate, in which global warming becomes meaningful mainly as a problem of global governance.

In this way, a story about precarity almost inevitably becomes about the politics of representation, which is to say what a given culture makes visible, which meanings it makes possible, what parts of the world it allows itself to see. Butler claimed that the occlusion of America's precarity was critical to sanctioning the War on Terror and the regimes that sponsored it. More recently, anthropologist Anna Tsing has explored the consequences of Butler's ideas for ecological thinking, contending that noticing hidden precarity is a first step to a more nuanced understanding of the more-than-human environments in which we are enmeshed, and the forms of power that reign there. 'To live with precarity requires more than railing at those who put us here', writes Tsing. 'We might look around to notice this strange new world, and we might stretch our imaginations to grasp its contours'.[8] Tsing follows Butler in taking precarity to be an instigation to political imagination. For both, noticing precarity where it is suppressed involves acknowledging forms of bodily exposure and vulnerability, human or otherwise, that structure everyday life. Doing so enables us to describe more lucidly the politics of a world where certain bodies have the power to make others precarious. If we follow Butler and Tsing, thinking through precarity can train our attention on the relationship between climate change's representation and our imagination of the politics that are possible in response to it.

This chapter is an attempt at thinking climate through precarity via an exploration of the place of precarious bodies in representations of the climate system. I look at two depictions of rapid environmental change and the scientific observation of these shifts, tracing which sorts of precarity they uncover and which they hide. The first is *Our Planet*, a high-budget nature documentary narrated by the naturalist David Attenborough.[9] Produced in 2019, this eight-episode series portrays the effects of climate change across a wide variety of bioregions. The second is Amitav Ghosh's novel *The Hungry Tide*, first published in 2004, which presents the risks encountered by a group of characters studying river porpoises and their precarious environments.[10] What the first depicts on a global stage, the second limits to a local scene. When thought through precarity, however, these works could not be more different. One hides bodies – and bodies of knowledge – that the other discloses. One incorporates precarity into its very form while the other renders it invisible. By comparing their varying representations of precarity, we can begin to consider what an embodied representation of climate could look like, and the role it might play in environmental politics.

In telling one story with another, do we risk knotting knots with knots? Haraway put the question in these terms while pondering the possibility of 'multispecies storytelling', a practice emerging from precarity or, as she put it, a recognition that 'Ontologically heterogeneous partners become who and what they are in relational material-semiotic worlding'.[11] For Haraway, we cannot tell stories about environmental precarity without becoming precarious ourselves. As bodies limited in what we can perceive of our environment and its history, we must rely on others – be it other humans, other species or other knowledges – to comprehend and cope with the environmental risks we face. This reliance on other bodies for an understanding of our surroundings is one of the forms precarity takes in our current moment. Whatever variety of political ecology we subscribe to, we must account for this sort of precarity as much as we do for the more spectacular kinds that have become all too familiar in an age of climate change.[12]

What a walrus represents

Upon its release in 2019, *Our Planet* seemed to diverge from other nature documentaries. In an article entitled 'Netflix's *Our Planet* says what other nature series have omitted', one reviewer wrote: 'Repeatedly, unambiguously, and urgently, *Our Planet* reminds its viewers that the wonders they are witnessing are imperiled by human action.'[13] *Our Planet* did not only show splendid footage of jungles, ice caps and oceans, but depicted environmental threats as well, explicitly linking these to climate change. In the first episode, stunning footage of life on land and sea reels by as Attenborough explains that wildlife populations have declined by 60 per cent over the last fifty years. This juxtaposition, by which natural beauty becomes poignant in the shadow of its loss, is typical of the show's visual storytelling. Nevertheless, were we to watch the documentary series while thinking with precarity, we might be led to question the seductiveness of its rhetoric and the critical enthusiasm that surrounded the show's release. We might wonder what remained unsaid in this documentary's representation of climate change and its consequences, asking which sorts of dependencies and vulnerabilities this representation omitted, and whose will or desire had brought it into existence in the first place. For whom is the environment best understood as a 'planet'? For whom is this planet 'ours'?

In a certain way, these questions were raised in a controversy that erupted over *Our Planet*'s second episode, 'Frozen Worlds'. I write 'in a certain way' because the participants involved did not understand themselves to be arguing over precarity per se, but rather over scientific facts. Offering an alternative account, I contend that while each side of this debate was interested in precarity, they pursued two separate sets of problems attendant to this concept. One side, that of *Our Planet*'s creators, meant to represent the insecurity of a variety of environments, that is, their exposure to collapse. The other, made up of climate change sceptics, sought to reveal the network of influential bodies whose pleasures and decisions had dominated the production of *Our Planet*. Taking place entirely online shortly after the release of 'Frozen Worlds', the dispute between these two camps was typical of ideologically tinged conflicts in the digital realm, in the sense that neither side seemed invested in learning from or even listening to the other. Here, I will listen to both, as their conflict demonstrates a point made in this chapter's introduction: that tracing which types of precarity a representation of the climate ignores can elucidate its politics. Despite their seeming divisions, the politics of both parties were ultimately quite similar, as neither wanted to confront the intertwined questions of which bodies are to blame for climate change and which bodies are made precarious by it.

'Frozen Worlds' depicts wildlife that inhabit the poles of the planet and the risks they face due to climate change. Audiences are presented with sequences depicting albatross, penguins, orcas, seals and polar bears, all struggling to survive in warming habitats. The debate surrounding the episode had to do with its final sequence, which begins with a shot of walruses gathering on 'the far, northeastern coast of Russia'. Attenborough's narration explains that the large mammals have amassed here 'out of desperation', as the sea ice they would prefer no longer forms near their feeding grounds. This sequence concludes with images of literal precarity. Having scaled a cliff to escape overcrowding on the beach, a group of walruses attempt to return to sea. Instead, victims of their own poor eyesight, they plummet to their deaths. Attenborough's voiceover links these deaths to the larger environmental forces evoked throughout 'Frozen Worlds': 'So the lives of walruses, like those of polar bears and seals, are changing. All are living at the frontier of climate change, and all are suffering as a consequence.' For the creators of 'Frozen Worlds', a walrus teetering on a rocky cliffside gave tangible expression to abstract notions of tipping points and species collapse, concepts that are crucial to understanding risks associated with a changing climate.

Not everyone was ready to accept *Our Planet*'s equation of dead walruses with climate change, however. Not long after the release of 'Frozen Worlds', a zoologist named Susan Crockford challenged the documentary's claim that climate change was behind these deaths.[14] Following her lead, climate sceptics began examining the episode's images, eventually concluding that the show's editors had compiled this sequence out of footage shot at disconnected locations. Sophie Lanfear, director of 'Frozen Worlds', admitted that the sequence had been edited this way.[15] But Lanfear did not corroborate what her critics proposed next. Comparing the cliff face from 'Frozen Worlds' to photos found online, they discovered that the beach where the walruses fell was near the Russian village of Ryrkaypiy.[16] An article from *The Siberian Times* was unearthed detailing how polar bears had menaced this village and driven walruses off a nearby cliff in 2017. From this, Crockford and her collaborators concluded that the documentary's creators had recorded this same incident while knowingly concealing the real cause of the walruses' deaths.[17] They claimed this cover-up was orchestrated by a network of scientists, cultural producers and activist organizations that collaborated in the making of *Our Planet*, all of whom shared the desire to spread alarm about climate change. These sentiments were summed up in an opinion article published by Crockford, entitled, 'Netflix is lying about those falling walruses. It's another "tragedy porn" climate hoax.'[18]

The title of Crockford's article might tempt us to dismiss it as sensationalist. Nevertheless, though I am dubious of Crockford's intentions, I think this conflict allows us to better grasp the connection between politics and the representation of climate precarity. On a basic level, this was a disagreement about representation, since it had to do with what sort of precarity *Our Planet*'s images actually represented. Recall that, to undermine the claims made in 'Frozen Worlds', Crockford and others had recourse to images from the show. Initially, they were used to locate where exactly the walrus deaths had occurred. Later, it was claimed that they did not represent evidence of a population under stress due to climate change. Instead, when studied with the information Crockford and her allies had gathered, the images showed *Our Planet*'s editors to be simplifying facts, even lying. As such, the visuals of dead walruses highlighted the precarity of 'Frozen Worlds' itself, since they represented a whole network of influential organizations and experts to which *Our Planet*'s description of the climate was beholden. It could even be said that, for Crockford, the dying walrus came to represent the precarity of *Our Planet*'s viewer, indexing the extent to which this viewer was exposed to manipulation by the show's creators.

Though they saw themselves as opposed, Lanfear and Crockford were not making their arguments on the same grounds, since each had chosen to address a different aspect of precarity while either ignoring or denying the other. *Our Planet* garnered praise from critics for its answer to the question of how a mainstream documentary might represent environmental precarity associated with climate change. Crockford, meanwhile, engaged an entirely separate set of problems related to precarity, focusing on the question of what sorts of power structures were hidden within *Our Planet*'s images.

What is striking about the 'Frozen Worlds' controversy is the implicit *agreements* shared by both sides, revealed in the kinds of precarity they ignored *together*. Though she worked to prove that the show's producers misled viewers, Crockford did not call into question what is perhaps *Our Planet*'s most dubious claim: that there is something like a collective subject who could take responsibility for the planet and its destruction, an 'us' that could claim the planet to be 'ours'. Historically, the onus for the types of destruction *Our Planet* depicts can be attributed to a relatively small portion of the Earth's population, namely the inhabitants of industrialized nations over the last 200 years. Reporting on the 2021 climate summit in Glasgow, *The New York Times* published this clarifying statistic: 'Rich countries ... account for just 12 percent of the global population today but are responsible for 50 percent of all the planet-warming greenhouse gases released from fossil fuels and industry over the past 170 years.'[19] *Our Planet* fails to mention this inequality. In doing so, it promotes what might be called the *same-boat myth*, which holds that, with regard to environmental destruction, humans are all 'in the same boat'. This idea is mystifying insofar as it obscures the historic role differences of nationality, class and race have played in determining who will suffer climate change's effects.[20]

Had either side of the 'Frozen Worlds' controversy pursued the questions raised around precarity further, they might have arrived at similar conclusions. That they did not indicates that, despite the vitriolic tone of much of Crockford's writing, she shares an important assumption with the creators of *Our Planet*: that any story about the changing climate can be told without commenting on who has benefited from the carbon economy and who stands to suffer its worst consequences. This is a political assumption since it stymies any imagination of environmental justice which, if it is to exist, must allow for an accurate apportioning of responsibility for environmental destruction. As the authors of an early critique of this way of thinking asked, 'Just what kind of politics or morality is this which masquerades in the name of "one worldism" and "high minded internationalism"?'[21]

Midway through this attempt to think climate through precarity, we confront the following questions: what might a representation of climate change look like that dwells on precarity in its myriad forms? And how would this work imagine other possibilities for environmental politics than does a commercial entertainment like *Our Planet*? Such a work would not hesitate to inquire simultaneously into climate change's effects and the sorts of interdependencies required to perceive these. Furthermore, it would do precisely what both *Our Planet* and its opponents failed to do, eschewing the same-boat thesis by making overt links between climate change and the exacerbation of historic inequalities among humans. Combining these efforts, this hypothetical work might come to resemble *The Hungry Tide*.

But where are the bodies?

Ghosh's *The Great Derangement: Climate Change and the Unthinkable* is a non-fiction book which is, among other things, a refutation of the same-boat myth. In this work, Ghosh explores the relationship between environmental destruction and human violence. He explains how western colonial powers blocked the industrialization of their colonies, guaranteeing that the riches generated by industry's emissions and the power accruing to this wealth would be theirs exclusively. According to Ghosh, 'carbon emissions were, from very early on, closely co-related to power in all its aspects: this continues to be a major, although unacknowledged, factor in the politics of contemporary global warming'.[22] This statement encapsulates the story Ghosh wants to tell, a story that is at once about climate and precarity. For him, colonialism enabled colonizers to profit from a developing carbon economy while forcing the colonized to pay its price. Ghosh's most poignant illustrations of this come from India's past. He explains, for example, how a nascent Indian steam economy was strangled in the early nineteenth century by colonial laws enacted to protect the interests of British merchants. Given that its effects increase the precarity of many formerly colonized nations, Ghosh understands climate change to be part of this longer history of inequality in the carbon economy. Regarding the world's poor nations, he states, 'their poverty is itself an effect of the inequities created by the carbon economy; it is the result of systems that were set up by brute force to ensure that poor nations remained always at a disadvantage in terms of both wealth and power'.[23] Clearly, Ghosh is willing to make the connections that *Our Planet* will not. From his perspective, the death of the walrus would represent not only an effect of climate change but, in addition, a legacy of colonial violence.

Ghosh's placement of climate change within the context of colonialism distinguishes him from those who would have us think about climate change without attending to its unequal effects on human bodies, as well as from those who would attribute these effects principally to the expansion of capitalism over the last three centuries.[24] With Ghosh, thinking climate through precarity means first asking how a representation addresses the ways global warming intensifies inequalities – of nation, but also of race, gender and class – understood as the ongoing legacy of a collective colonial past.

Scholars have found a variety of responses to this question in Ghosh's *The Hungry Tide*. This is true even though the novel is not about climate change per se, but rather about the Sundarbans, a region of the Bay of Bengal that was exposed to some of climate change's earliest effects. Still, and perhaps precisely because its story never departs from this location, many of Ghosh's readers have taken the novel as an invitation to consider how a concern for environmental problems transforms when it is articulated from a formerly colonized space. Malcolm Sen thus voices a consensus when he writes that *The Hungry Tide* 'returns us to the location-based survey needed for a deep understanding of the environmental crisis. It challenges some of the deep-seated inconsistencies between the global environmentalist movement and the realities of life faced by postcolonial non-elites.'[25] In short, *The Hungry Tide* returns its reader's gaze to those bodies made precarious by a colonial history of environmental destruction, of which climate change is but one result.

The Hungry Tide's main character, Piya, is an American scientist of Indian descent who has come to the Sundarbans to study the habitat of a disappearing species of river dolphin, the *orcaella brevirostris*. Though Piya studies the environment, she cannot do her work without confronting the harsh realities that order life for this region's poor. In grounding Piya's scientific descriptions of the orcaella's environment in this social context, Ghosh invites us to imagine how her representations might reflect the political arrangements in which they are formulated. His prose can therefore be read in juxtaposition to the images of 'Frozen Worlds', distinguished by its effort to represent the sorts of precarity *Our Planet* passes over in silence.

This effort involves paying attention to bodies. Located on the coastal border of India and Bangladesh, this region is precarious for human bodies in more ways than one. Its waters are filled with crocodiles, its forests with tigers and it is subject to tides and storms that continually reshape the local terrain. These risks appear in Ghosh's story, the climax of which involves a tsunami that nearly kills Piya. At the same time, however, Ghosh is just as interested in which bodies become necessary to represent this precarious terrain. Whereas *Our Planet* hid the network of expert bodies required to construct its representation of climate change, Ghosh places this network at the centre of his story. For example, Piya needs the help of the novel's second protagonist, the fisherman Fokir, to track the orcaella. To convey the precarity of Piya's representation of this environment, the way it requires the support of other bodies and so is exposed to failure, Ghosh attends to Piya's reliance on this non-scientist, and especially on his body of traditional knowledge. Since Piya and Fokir do not share a common language, they must rely on Kanai, an interpreter, to communicate. Kanai is thus added to the network of bodies in which Piya's representation is articulated. This network extends to the non-human, with Fokir's boat, Piya's binoculars and the orcaella themselves all becoming integral to the work of representing the Sundarbans. *The Hungry Tide* comes to seem what Adam Trexler terms a 'mediation' of these different bodies – a record of the ways they act on Piya to assert their existence, and ultimately to shape how she represents this environment.[26]

In making visible the network on which Piya's scientific representation of the Sundarbans depends, *The Hungry Tide* becomes a narrative not just about the precarity of bodies in the region, but also the precarity of her particular representation of this environment. In contrast to 'Frozen Worlds', the novel lets us experience both types of precarity. Ghosh's prose gives sensual form to the networks of bodies on which Piya relies to represent orcaella life through literary techniques of multivocality. Thus, when Piya wants to learn how Fokir came to know the orcaella so intimately, the response recorded combines the fisherman's voice with those of his ancestors, his mother and his translator Kanai. It even incorporates dolphin speech. Speaking through Kanai, Fokir explains to Piya:

> I cannot remember a time when I didn't know about this place. … As for the big *shush*, the dolphins who live in these waters, I knew about them too, even before I came here. These animals were also in my mother's stories: they were Bon Bibi's messengers, she used to say, and they brought her news of the rivers … This secret her own father had told her, and he had told her also that if you could learn to follow the *shush*, then you would always be able to find fish.[27]

As Fokir evokes a world in which dolphins speak to gods, gods to humans and humans to their kin, Kanai is translating Fokir's words into a language that Piya will understand. These acts of transmission, interpretation and translation take form in the way Ghosh transcribes Fokir's speech. Fokir's use of reported speech ('she used to say', 'her own father had told her') meanwhile mixes his speech with that of others. Replying to the question of how he knows what he knows, Fokir gestures to the precarity of his knowledge by giving voice to the network of bodies, human and otherwise, from which it arises.

Ghosh's prose encourages us to wonder how such multivocality, and the precarity it conveys, is made absent in other kinds of representations of the environment. We might suppose, for instance, that the academic paper Piya eventually produces on the Sundarbans' orcaella will omit mention of Bon Bibi, the deity with whom these dolphins communicate. Yet, it will have depended on Bon Bibi, because Fokir did, and Piya depended on Fokir. The conventions of the research paper, for which there is no place for the reporting of phenomena such as speaking dolphins and benevolent gods, will occlude the sort of precarity Fokir's speech reveals. This critique could be extended to other representations of the environment: is not the monologuing of *Our Planet*'s narration a formal means of suppressing the precarity that Ghosh's writing makes hearable?

There is a connection between *The Hungry Tide*'s experimental representation of precarity and Ghosh's stance on the historical inequalities at the heart of climate change. There seems a basic similarity between a desire to show how global warming relates to inequalities among peoples, on the one hand, and an artistic practice that seeks to make precarity feelable, on the other. This similarity lies in how both never allow us to lose sight of bodies. *The Great Derangement* would turn our attention to the bodies that are made precarious by climate change, while *The Hungry Tide* would make apparent the bodies, and the bodies of knowledge, that develop and support our representations of climate change. Taken together, they lead us to ask how you could tell a story about both sorts of climate precarity at the same time: this would be a story about bodies that was itself embodied, and a representation of the climate that presented itself as intimately involved in its effects.

A final passage at the climax of *The Hungry Tide* suggests what the politics of this story might be. Caught in a storm surge, Fokir has lashed himself and Piya to a mangrove tree. The scientist finds herself positioned between the fisherman and the tree such that, when the storm's winds turn, Fokir's body protects her from airborne debris.

> Their bodies were so close, so finely merged, that she could feel the impact of everything hitting him, she could sense the blows raining down on his back. She could feel the bones of his cheeks as if they had been superimposed on her own; it was as if the storm had given them what life could not; it had fused them together and made them one.[28]

This moment encapsulates the intertwining of scientific and non-scientific bodies that Ghosh has been elaborating throughout the novel: the non-scientist is shielding the scientist and, virtually, the knowledge of orcaella life she has gathered but has yet to publish. Intriguingly, this protective gesture actualizes the same-boat myth. Here, an American scientist and an impoverished fisherman will experience environmental precarity together, with Piya made to 'feel' the pain of Fokir's body. Through the 'fused' bodies, Ghosh invites us to consider what sorts of sympathies and knowledges might arise if the same-boat myth were at all true. To do so, he gives us an image of the transmission of feeling between a body responsible for describing environmental precarity and a body subject to it, prompting the reader to query what practices of representing environmental precarity might look like if everyone were equally implicated by this precarity, if everyone felt and sensed the 'impact of everything'. How would Attenborough speak if he felt Fokir's pain? How would Piya communicate her knowledge of the environment if she really felt as precarious as the orcaella? Could she do so and still represent her environment with the scientific rigour of the IPCC report writers? What sort of representation of environmental precarity could communicate in such vivid terms the sorts of precarity from which it arises?

As *The Hungry Tide* ends, Ghosh offers a vision in which Piya's endeavour to represent the effects of climate change is literally enclosed within the effects of the centuries-long conflicts that have made bodies like Fokir's precarious. It suggests the place from which representations of the environment might be formulated, were they themselves engaged in struggles over which bodies will die, and which survive, because of climate change's fallout. This is a very different place from that occupied by *Our Planet*'s camera: it is embodied, and because of this it is itself precarious. It is formulated in relation to other bodies and, with them, other ways of knowing. As Laura White argues, 'through [her] encounters with different ways of knowing', Piya becomes, by the novel's end, an 'embodied knower'.[29] Ghosh's protagonist has learned to see how her scientific knowledge arises from the cooperation of many bodies, and this change in vision corresponds to that of the reader, who has encountered in this novel a representation of intertwined bodies of knowledge. White locates in these moments of recognition elements of a decolonial environmentalism, writing that 'the concluding scenes offer not a sense of environmental and social problems finished and overcome, but a glimpse at how the transformation of vision can serve as one part of ongoing processes of decolonizing knowledge and working toward environmental and social justice'.[30]

This possibility of an embodied representation of climate's effects soon vanishes, however. Fokir is killed in the storm, and with him the chance of any immediate fusion between his and Piya's bodies, or their knowledge. It is left to the reader to contemplate how this vision, briefly opened, might reappear within a more durable politics of environmental representation. For such a politics, embodiment would be what connects a recognition of the precarity of our knowledge of the environment to action on behalf of those made most precarious by environmental degradation. While it is beyond the scope of this chapter (and my insight) to announce what this politics might entail, I will end by evoking the work of sociologist and philosopher Bruno Latour, a theorist who has long dwelt on the fragility of scientific knowledge and its consequences for political life. Rather than a conclusion, we might think of this last section as a knot knotted with a knot – a final twist in the story we are trying to tell about climate change and precarity.

Representing bodies in precarious worlds

Thinking climate through precarity has led us to look for bodies in two differing representations of climate change and its effects. *The Hungry Tide* suggested how a representation of climate change's consequences might dwell on its own precarity, which is to say its dependence on bodies and bodies of knowledge necessary to its formulation. That *Our Planet* made such bodies invisible seemed expressive of a politics acknowledging neither climate change's roots in colonialism nor its role in exacerbating current forms of inequality. The final scenes of *The Hungry Tide* seemed to suggest a mode of representing climate change motivated by a different sort of politics: an embodied telling that would efface any difference between its own precarity and that of the environmental destruction it made present. Giving voice to the network of bodies present in its formulation, this representation would express their basic political interest as well, which is nothing less than survival in a precarious world.

Latour might say that such a representation of the climate was 'down to earth'.[31] For Latour, climate science is part of a down-to-earth politics because it illuminates interdependency, allowing for a clearer understanding of which bodies we rely on to survive – and which threaten our survival. Latour says we live with these other bodies in 'territories', taking these territories to be a unit of political action in 'the new climatic regime'. He states:

> To get back to the common world, and perhaps also to the sense of the common (that is, to common sense!), the solution is not to appeal to Totality, which in any case does not exist, but to learn to represent differently the territory to which one belongs. This would then make it possible to modify what one is claiming to defend in the name of hallowed egotism. It is finally a matter of *internalizing* the countless encroachments of the entities on which we depend – to an extent that we are gradually discovering – for our own subsistence.[32]

In 'gradually discovering' the territories to which we belong, different sciences help us to perceive the networks of bodies that make up these territories, and the extent to which we need them to survive. Identifying with these bodies could 'modify' what is considered one's interest: 'internalizing' these other bodies into one's own leads to a rethinking of one's *body politic* and the interests it expresses. Following Butler and Tsing, Latour assumes that a greater awareness and perceiving of our own precarity would lead to a reassessment of our real interests, and with it a reorientation of politics to 'the common world', the world we share and live in and require to survive. Returning to Haraway, 'it matters what stories make worlds'.[33] Stories of precarity would describe our place in worlds of interconnection and exposure, and the sorts of knowledge needed to go on living in these. *The Hungry Tide* is a more complete story of precarity than *Our Planet's* insofar as it shows the kinds of precarity inherent to life in a changing climate *and* the fragility of our knowledge of this precarity. It dramatizes what Latour theorizes, which is the political effort to combine science with other bodies of knowledge in order to learn about worlds held in common so that these might be defended.

Thinking climate through precarity with Latour returns our attention to bodies, but with a perhaps enlarged sense of what the word 'bodies' refers to. Latour seeks an environmental politics arising out of a recognition of bodily interconnection. This politics would have to confront the histories that concern Ghosh, acknowledging the link between environmental destruction and forms of colonial domination that made colonized bodies precarious for centuries. This politics would moreover mobilize all manner of bodies of knowledge – knowledge like Piya's and Fokir's – to better perceive and communicate the interconnections from which it arises. In doing so, this politics would perhaps move us toward a reconceptualization of the *body politic* by seeking to represent human *and* non-human bodies on which these depend. Hence, this politics would reverse a question on which we started. Instead of what a walrus represents, Latour invites us to ask what represents a walrus. Or: what forms of politics would allow for the representation of the interests of human and non-human alliances?

Surely this would be an environmental politics of precarity, arising from a will to defend the forms of bodily interdependence that hold worlds together.

Notes

1   Donna J. Haraway, *Staying with the Trouble: Making Kin in the Chthulucene* (Durham, NC: Duke University Press, 2016), 12.

2   IPCC, 'Summary for Policymakers', in *Climate Change 2022: Impacts, Adaptation and Vulnerability. Contribution of Working Group II to the Sixth Assessment Report of the Intergovernmental Panel on Climate Change*, eds. H.-O. Pörtner, D.C. Roberts, E.S. Poloczanska, K. Mintenbeck, M. Tignor, A. Alegría, M. Craig, S. Langsdorf, S. Löschke, V. Möller, A. Okem and B. Rama (Cambridge: Cambridge University Press, in press), 11, https://www.ipcc.ch/report/sixth-assessment-report-working-group-ii/.

3   Lauren Berlant, *Cruel Optimism* (Durham, NC: Duke University Press, 2011).

4   Joshua Trey Barnett, 'Thinking ecologically with Judith Butler', *Culture, Theory and Critique* 59, no. 1 (2018): 20–39.

5   Jasbir Puar, 'Precarity talk: a virtual roundtable with Lauren Berlant, Judith Butler, Bojana Cvejić, Isabell Lorey, Jasbir Puar, and Ana Vujanović', *The Drama Review* 56, no. 4 (2012): 170.

6   Judith Butler, *Precarious Life: The Powers of Mourning and Violence* (New York: Verso, 2004), 41.

7   All three definitions are taken from the Oxford English Dictionary. OED, 'precarious, adj.' (2021), www.oed.com/view/Entry/149548.

8   Anna Lowenhaupt Tsing, *The Mushroom at the End of the World: On the Possibility of Life in Capitalist Ruins* (Princeton, NJ: Princeton University Press, 2015), 3.

9   *Our Planet*, prod. Alastair Fothergill and Keith Scholey (UK: Silverback Films, 2019). Documentary series.

10 Amitav Ghosh, *The Hungry Tide* (Boston: Mariner Books, 2006).

11 Haraway, *Staying with the Trouble*, 12–13.

12 See Ramachandra Guha and Juan Martinez-Alier, *Varieties of Environmentalism: Essays North and South* (London: Earthscan, 1997).

13 Ed Yong, 'Netflix's *Our Planet* says what other nature series have omitted', *The Atlantic* (1 April 2019), www.theatlantic.com/science/archive/2019/04/wildlife-series-finally-addresses-elephant-room/586066/.

14 Susan J. Crockford, 'Attenborough's tragedy porn of walruses plunging to their deaths because of climate change is contrived nonsense', *Polar Bear Science* (7 April 2019), https://polarbearscience.com/2019/04/07/attenboroughs-tragedy-porn-of-walruses-plunging-to-their-deaths-because-of-climate-change-is-contrived-nonsense/.

15 Ed Yong, 'The disturbing walrus scene in *Our Planet*', *The Atlantic* (8 April 2019), https://www.theatlantic.com/science/archive/2019/04/why-are-walruses-walking-off-cliffs/586510/.

16 Andrew Montford, 'Has Netflix's *Our Planet* hidden the real cause of walrus deaths?', *The Spectator* (9 April 2019), https://www.spectator.co.uk/article/has-netflix-s-our-planet-hidden-the-real-cause-of-walrus-deaths.

17 Paul Homewood, 'Why Attenborough's walrus claims are fake', *Not A Lot of People Know That* (14 April 2019), https://notalotofpeopleknowthat.wordpress.com/2019/04/14/why-attenboroughs-walrus-claims-are-fake/.

18 Susan J. Crockford, 'Netflix is lying about those falling walruses. It's another "tragedy porn" climate hoax', *Financial Post* (24 April 2019), https://financialpost.com/opinion/netflix-is-lying-about-those-falling-walruses-its-another-tragedy-porn-climate-hoax.

19 Nadja Popovich and Brad Plumer, 'Who has the most historical responsibility for climate change?', *The New York Times* (12 November 2021), www.nytimes.com/interactive/2021/11/12/climate/cop26-emissions-compensation.html.

20   For a detailed and poetically rich deconstruction of the same-boat myth, see Malcom Ferdinand, *Decolonial Ecology: Thinking from the Caribbean World*, trans. Anthony Paul Smith (Cambridge: Polity Press, 2022).

21   Anil Agarwal and Sunita Narain, 'Global warming in an unequal world', in *India in a Warming World*, ed. Navroz K. Dubash (Oxford: Oxford University Press, 2019), 83, original emphasis.

22   Amitav Ghosh, *The Great Derangement: Climate Change and the Unthinkable* (Chicago: University of Chicago Press, 2016), 109.

23   Ghosh, *Great Derangement*, 110.

24   For this latter perspective, see for example Andreas Malm, *Fossil Capital: The Rise of Steam Power and the Roots of Global Warming* (New York: Verso, 2016).

25   Malcolm Sen, 'Spatial justice: the ecological imperative and postcolonial development', *Journal of Postcolonial Writing* 45, no. 4 (2009): 375.

26   Adam Trexler, 'Mediating climate change: ecocriticism, science studies, and *The Hungry Tide*', in *The Oxford Handbook of Ecocriticism*, ed. Greg Garrard (Oxford: Oxford University Press, 2014), 210.

27   Ghosh, *The Hungry Tide*, 254.

28   Ghosh, *The Hungry Tide*, 321.

29   Laura A. White, 'Novel vision: seeing the Sunderbans through Amitav Ghosh's *The Hungry Tide*', *ISLE: Interdisciplinary Studies in Literature and Environment* 20, no. 3 (2013): 528.

30   White, 'Novel vision', 528.

31   Bruno Latour, *Down to Earth: Politics in the New Climatic Regime*, trans. Catherine Porter (Cambridge: Polity Press, 2018).

32   Bruno Latour, *Facing Gaia: Eight Lectures on the New Climatic Regime*, trans. Catherine Porter (Cambridge: Polity Press, 2017), 271–72, original emphasis.

33   Haraway, *Staying with the Trouble*, 12.

Precarity in a Time of Fire and Pandemic

Julie Macken and Sonia M. Tascón

It is midnight in late December 2019 and I (Julie) am standing on the containment line we have created over the last twelve hours. We are at the top of the Grose Valley in New South Wales, Australia where the wild old valley meets suburbia and empties out onto the Bells Line of Road. It is a thoroughfare that takes heavy transport – and fire – straight into the heart of Sydney's suburbia. Deep in the valley we can hear the fire roaring and lumbering toward us – the noise punctuated by the thundering crash of massive gum trees falling to the ground. And above the roar and the crash, closer to all of us, is the nervous twitter of hundreds of birds who should be sleeping and the whinnying of the frantic horses up the hill from our line.

We wait. The blue and red lights from the fire trucks create a macabre light show while we watch our feet to keep an eye on the spiders and snakes that are desperately looking for safer ground. We try to ignore the sounds of larger animals – echidnas, wallabies and slow-moving wombats – as they try to outrun the blaze. They will not make it. The birds will not survive, nor will most of those spiders and snakes.

We check our water pressure again and reassure ourselves and each other that the containment line will hold, the ember attack will be manageable, and we will be safe. Though as the light of the approaching fire appears below, I begin to doubt the wisdom of leaving those terrified horses in the paddock above the escarpment.

There is exhaustion and fury on the fire lines across the east coast of Australia – which includes the states of New South Wales and Victoria – as the old year dies and 2020 emerges. Exhaustion because these fires have been burning since June 2019. Fury because this did not need to happen. Before the last federal election in early 2019, twenty-three former fire and emergency chiefs from across Australia called on the Prime Minister, Scott Morrison, to meet with them to develop a strategy for dealing with what they said would be a disastrous fire season. He refused.[1] In late December 2019, he told *A Current Affair* news programme, when asked why he declined their offer, 'I listen to the fire chiefs that are in their jobs now'.[2]

The statistics generated by these fires are incomprehensible. Thirty-four people were killed and thousands evacuated, over a billion animals burned to death, 25 million acres burned and over two thousand houses were destroyed. The estimated economic cost was over AU\$100 billion.[3] The grief is palpable as we understand – many of us for the first time – that we are undone by each other and our loss.

Precarious life. Over that incendiary summer the numbers of those belonging to the newly manifest class of the precariat grew. As the people of Cobargo, New South Wales dealt with first a demanding and insensitive Prime Minister eager for a photo-op handshake after the village had been engulfed by the flames, and the subsequent media analysis, we watched on as they kicked through the remnants of their historic village. A working-class town, they knew they would be last on a long list of communities needing telecommunications, financial support and drought relief. We witnessed five thousand people huddle on the beach of Mallacoota, Victoria to avoid the worst of the inferno as it devoured everything before it. There would be no Dunkirk moment for these panicked families as they tried to breathe through the smoke and comfort their children.

In this historic moment of fire-ravaged Australia, we are asking ourselves: was it always going to end here? Is this the logical conclusion of thirty years of an increasingly grasping, privatizing, neoliberal agenda? Is this where we – the atomized and precariously positioned – were always going to find ourselves: on the beach gagging for breath and hoping for a miracle? Is precarity at the core of the neoliberal agenda and, if so, as we sift through the charred remains of our precarious lives, could it be that we find the antidote to that same precarity, right here in our fire-ravaged communities?

***

In February 2020 these were valid questions to ask in light of the brutal impact of those fires. Just four weeks later in March we again began to ask a whole new series of seemingly unanswerable questions as the COVID-19 virus spread through cities, communities, cruise ships and retirement homes. Would the collective response to the fires be replicated during the oncoming pandemic? Would Australians be weaker or stronger for having weathered the conflagration on the country's east coast together, or would the social capital accrued during that crisis prove to be just so much small change in the face of this pandemic?

Totemic moments rarely arrive with such clarity or clean demarcation. Looking at the Australian nation state from mid-2019 to mid-2020, two uncontrollable events rolled through the lives of 25 million people, an exhausted landscape and the economy. As the first finally slumped to earth brought down by rain and ash, the other rose and grew like its bio-fire equivalent. It can be argued that the nationwide response to the catastrophic fires represents an exceptional example of what economist Guy Standing refers to as 'commoning' – 'participative, communal activity' – which sees an effective and affective reclamation of our shared work, leisure, space and, critically, entitlement.[4] In the case of the pandemic, this commoning would manifest in other ways that pushed back against and illuminated the breaking point of a neoliberal agenda, especially with regards to the plight of vulnerable workers of the precarious gig economy. We examine the texture of the fires and pandemic and ask whether, despite the growing ranks of the precariat class, these shifts could spell the end of the neoliberal hegemony that has precariousness at its heart.

Ever and always economic everyone

The east coast of Australia burnt for nine months from June 2019 to 3 March 2020 when the last of the fires were extinguished.[5] Images of injured koalas and kangaroos fleeing the flames became nightly news fare. The choking air and explosive firestorms that created their own weather and wind systems forewarned what this year's climate change impacts would look like here in the Great Southern Land. It was clearly a natural disaster – or at least a disaster for nature – but what did this tell us and in what way did this event relate to precarity and neoliberalism?

Neoliberalism is, as political scientist Wendy Brown states, an orientation towards free market values that has affected 'all institutions and social action'.[6] It redirects us to think of ourselves as freely negotiating individuals anchored and authenticated by 'the market' which becomes the ultimate reference point for meaning, identity, sociality and ethical decisions. In effect, neoliberalism reconfigures other forms of social and collective arrangements by fostering an ethos of competition. As Jon Stratton writes, 'In this new order individuals replaced groups of any description as the basis for life within the state'.[7] Linking this orientation to its precursor, Trent Hamann makes the crucial distinction that liberalism posits 'economic man' as a 'man of exchange', whereas 'neoliberalism strives to ensure that individuals are compelled to assume market-based values in *all* of their judgments and practices in order to amass sufficient quantities of "human capital" and thereby become "entrepreneurs of themselves"'.[8] The neoliberal subject is an autonomous 'atom' of self-interest who is fully responsible for navigating the social realm using rational choice and cost-benefit calculation. By this logic, those who fail to thrive under such conditions have no one and nothing to blame but themselves.

As the fires sprang up around previously unburnt parts of the continent it was undeniable that neoliberal ideology had so completely redrawn the national imagination that we entered this catastrophe seeing ourselves merely as private individuals. Indeed, referring to people within the Australian electorate as 'consumers' rather than as voters or even citizens had become standard practice, and we would similarly be framed and frame each other as such. There would be few expectations of the increasingly small state, except in so far as the state provides for a military or legal securitization to allow the market, as a supposed neutral playing-ground, to perform its 'natural' processes.[9] Under the guise of 'small state' the primary regulatory role of that state within neoliberal ideology – and in this it is similar to its earlier, simply Liberal, version – is to enable the workings of the market through the containment of civil unrests (protests), drafting laws and policies that limit the monitoring of corporate activity (e.g. limiting resources for regulatory agencies or requiring only certain types of people to run them) and diversion of limited financial state resources towards enhancement of corporate operations (e.g. tax breaks, road-building in mining areas).

One of the most critical aspects and potent affects of the neoliberal ideology is the way it has changed the way we view our selves, environment, work and communities. In colonizing our public lives, it has impoverished our language of the social and political. In *Undoing the Demos*, Brown lays out her argument for the book as, 'a theoretical consideration of the ways that neoliberalism, a peculiar form of reason that configures all aspects of existence in economic terms, is quietly undoing basic elements of democracy'.[10] Brown contends that one of the many outcomes of the neoliberal agenda has been to transform and empty the dynamic, energetic political spheres into the economic and in the process redefine *homo politicus* as *homo oeconomicus*:

when the domain of the political itself is rendered in economic terms, the foundation vanishes for citizenship concerned with public things and the common good. Here, the problem is not just that public goods are defunded and common ends are devalued by neoliberal reason, although this is so, but that citizenship itself loses its *political* valence and venue. Valence: *homo oeconomicus* approaches everything as a market and knows only market conduct; it cannot think public purposes or common problems in a distinctly political way. Venue: Political life, and the state in particular ... are remade by neoliberal rationality. The replacement of citizenship defined as concern with the public good by citizenship reduced to the citizen as *homo oeconomicus* also eliminates the very idea of a people, a demos asserting its collective political sovereignty.[11]

The success of neoliberalism, and the depth with which it has now penetrated what was once the political and the personal, can be seen in universally accepted use of terms like 'human resource' whereby people are now simply expendable resources to be deployed, or not, as the market sees fit; 'sacrifice zones' that refer to tracts of land or communities laid to waste by mining and extraction; and the now-weaponized word 'efficiency'.

As Brown avers, neoliberalism has not only ensured the largest transfer of what was once public into private ownership, it has also taken language and thought with it. This is evidenced in the rationalizations put forward for the preservation of public assets that are almost without exception argued on the basis of the economic, keeping costs down and jobs safe. Few argued, for instance, that aged care should remain a public good in the public sector to ensure standards are created and maintained, and to prevent private corporations from cutting so much flesh from the bones of their budgets in pursuit of a profit extracted from elderly and vulnerable people; this would prove lethal as COVID-19 infiltrated the nursing homes across Sydney and Melbourne. Justifications leading to the eventual privatization of Sydney's ferry services in 2019 were devoid of non-economic reasoning, such as their nostalgic value, their importance to local identity and pride, and the personal joy of travelling on the ferries that makes us smile with their tubby, clever bodies and their sturdiness in even the heaviest weather. We appear unable to remember or recognize the power of collective ownership. We seem to have forgotten that these public places, spaces and services are already ours and we do not need to sell them; they continue to constitute us as an 'our' and a 'we' that is as formidable as it is undermining of the neoliberal agenda. This collectivity has become almost unthinkable.

Further, the magic of the neoliberal ideology has been to convince us that there is no other way. As Richard Denniss observes, 'Neoliberalism's real power came from convincing us that we had none.'[12] That is, until the fires came. The fires demanded the community read and frame the country in a new light that allowed access to every resource of water and land as if we held it all in common. The very volunteer structure of the Rural Fire Services (RFS), coupled with the sense of urgency and the locally based structure of the strike teams, enabled thousands of volunteers to, at least for a short period, reinhabit the role of citizen and to re-imagine what was once private lands and roads as now public thoroughfares. Cutting boundary fences, emptying private swimming pools and using front gardens as staging areas were all part of the daily firefighting practice.

The size, ferocity and scale of the fires burning across three states – New South Wales, Victoria and South Australia – left those espousing the efficacy of small government, privatization of public goods and the rise of the gig economy mute. They had little to offer because fires on this scale can only be fought with the co-ordinated efforts of volunteers and community members risking everything to protect each other – for free. More than 195,000 Australians volunteer with the nation's six state and two territory bushfire services. The most populous state, New South Wales, has the highest number (71,234). From September 2019 through to January 2020 there were at least 3,700 volunteer firefighters on the ground every day and most nights.[13] The number of those feeding this small army and trying to rescue animals has yet to be counted. This is a dangerous development and time for the neoliberal exponents that have spent the last three decades justifying the rightness of a user-pays world where people are encouraged to see themselves as more a 'brand', a 'human resource', than a person, let alone a member of a community, a fire shed and a democracy.

The early moments of the Prime Minister's misjudgement during the fires in mid-December – when he refused to return from his family holiday in Hawaii because he had 'promised the kids a holiday' – served to illuminate the valour of the non-commercial, self-sacrificing cooperation that stood in high contrast to the self-seeking spin of government officials. At the same time, and in a further example of how marginal the Australian government and the business sector were to this extraordinary effort, people commenced raising money for the firefighters, communities and animals left with nothing. But more than the money and the mobilization of thousands of firefighters and volunteers, it was obvious that by the time the rain came many Australians had begun to see themselves as citizens and active members of their communities, exemplifying – albeit born of desperation – Standing's idea of 'commoning'. This manifestation of 'commoning' and shared community endeavour highlights the essential loneliness and fragility at the core of neoliberal ideology as the fires and pandemic have shown. In the neoliberal hegemony the individual is mediated and accompanied solely by 'The anarchy of the market, of competition, and of unbridled individualism (individual hopes, desires, anxieties, and fears; choices of lifestyle and of sexual habits and orientations; modes of self-expression and behaviours towards others)'.[14] This has ethical consequences as individuals are ultimately held together through the forces and mechanisms of the market, which in the present iteration of neoliberalism is motivated by the production of excess capital, or profit.[15] Connections with others, therefore, occur as a function of competition rather than of care or cooperation.

The reconfiguration of subjectivity in neoliberal ideology has meant that this privatized subject is not required to learn the skills of communality nor do they need to brush up against the essential interdependency that characterizes life. The principles of global capital untether us from the social, where we gain personal benefits of acceptance, belonging and risk-reduction in our precarious lives, and form a framework for analysis of the social forces that position us in terms of power relations. It is not coincidental that the rise of neoliberal ideology has corresponded to the decline of trade-union membership and worker co-operatives globally.[16] The ability to organize collectively increases the agency of the individual worker and imbues them with a sense of solidarity and safety. In a practical sense one of the most important roles played by unions within Australia from the early 1900s onwards was to provide widows funds, care for injured workers' families and food relief when the work dried up. In this way the social and the political were given a place, language and resources. These interlocking aspects of life were a force to be reckoned with. In undoing these entwined connections, neoliberalism detaches us from the political, the sphere where governance occurs. This is particularly pronounced for the precariat who are denied access to this domain of public life. This new social class is defined by an uneven, fragmented and uncertain relationship to labour that results in an interminable state of unpredictability, insecurity and diminishing rights.[17] We would add that the precariat is characterized by powerlessness with little or no connection to networks of political power. As we shall examine later, and as COVID-19 has exposed, shutting out hundreds of thousands of people from public life can have unforeseen consequences.

A critical question that must be asked is how the separation of the social and political was achieved. It is no accident that the neoliberal ideology has driven the argument to privatize much that was once held in public ownership. It is in the shared places, spaces and things that we come into contact with each other as patients and carers in public hospitals, and as frantic volunteer firefighters in the face of a conflagration. We encounter each other as commuters on the buses and trains, eyes peering out from masked faces as smoke or virus make the city a health risk. It is in public forums that we share our grief and outrage, as has become evident in recent times with mass gatherings to protest against war, police brutality, social injustices and environmental destruction. It is the public square that attracts the citizen, just as the shopping mall draws in the consumer. Removing such spaces and places removes the platform for engaging with each other as both social and political creatures. But it does more than that in a pandemic.

During the pandemic the difference between the public and the private soon became one of life and death. In August 2020, in the 126 private nursing homes that were affected by coronavirus nationwide – almost all in Victoria – 1,700 elderly residents and 1,300 staff were infected, contributing to over 328 deaths. This constituted almost half of Australia's COVID-19 fatalities which, at that time, was over 700. Of those fatalities, all were people who contracted the virus in the private aged-care institution in which they lived. In comparison, in the public aged-care institutions there had been no deaths and only five people infected with the virus.[18] Tragically, it is all too clear why the figures are so unbalanced. In Victoria approximately 10 per cent of all aged-care beds are publicly owned and 90 per cent are for-profit. The state-run facilities remain regulated and have mandated nurse-staffing ratios, for example, one nurse to seven residents during the day and one nurse to fifteen residents at night. Privately run centres do not need to abide by the same ratios, so they generally do not. Many have no registered nurses and still others have registered nurses responsible for 100 patients. They are predominantly owned by private equity firms, real estate investment trusts and superannuation funds.[19]

It could be argued that the atomization of people inherent in neoliberalism is in part remedied by the connection made possible by public space and public recognition that things have gone awry. In light of the high death rate of residents in Victoria's private aged-care homes, this is more than just a philosophical question. The very durability and constancy of public things stand in opposition to the just-in-time nature of the neoliberal hegemony. Public things are here when we arrive and hold the promise of outliving us in their materiality, utility and, for some, in the esteem and love in which they are held, whether it is the Sydney Opera House, the state buses, trains and trams, or the now-blighted TAFE system of education.[20] These sites, systems and services do more than just hold and serve us, inspire and enrage us. Crucially, they recall a time when we held them in common – that life was not always a user-pays proposition. The 'commons' undermine the foundational idea of neoliberalism that we are all just atoms of energy seeking to buy and sell our wares in an unhinged and unhoused marketplace. The endurance of public things enables us to create material, social and metaphorical points of reference in our lives, and provides us with shared memories, language and identity. Just like fire engines. No one owns a fire engine because *everyone* owns them, and no one owns a public hospital where anyone with the virus is being treated without regard for status or payment.

Precarity and pandemics

As the fires were finally quenched by rain and people were able to go back and sift through the ash and burnt timbers of their homes to find keepsakes of their previous lives, the corporate sector reinserted itself into the story as the Business Council of Australia rolled into the south-coast town of Mogo to build a pop-up shopping mall to get the economy up and running.[21] The transitory period of irrelevance suffered by the business sector during the fires had seemingly passed and it would be back to business-as-usual with the government and business developing a 'rescue plan' for affected communities. Then people started getting sick and dying. Business-as-usual disappeared as nurses and doctors took centre-stage to manage the COVID-19 crisis. Here we want to briefly trace several impacts of this global pandemic that have a bearing on the development of an expanding precariat class even as they signal the potential collapse of the neoliberal hegemony.

Globalization is central to the neoliberal hegemony and it is globalization that appears to be in a critical condition now. International travel, long supply lines, the smooth flow of material and money across an apparently borderless world, the idea that a handful of nations could become the world's factories were the orthodoxy that dominated the last thirty years. Certainly there were other events when this state of affairs was found wanting. The 2008 Global Financial Crisis caused some to consider the hyper-connected and contingent state of the global markets, but very few senior businesspeople or politicians thought it was possible for the whole edifice to come down. A decade after the GFC, Aaron Klein, policy director at the Center on Regulation and Markets at the Brookings Institution confidently declared, 'Many holes in our financial regulatory system are now plugged'.[22]

An event like COVID-19 presents a visceral challenge to the fantasy of an endlessly robust, self-correcting global economy. Consider this: in 2020, global Gross Domestic Product decreased by 3.4 per cent, while the forecast for 2022 was 2.9 per cent GDP growth. At the time of writing, a World Bank report predicted that the rate of global growth was expected to slow from 5.7 per cent in 2021 to 2.9 per cent in 2022. Unemployment is expected to be higher than during the Great Depression and global trade could fall by 13 to 32 per cent, depending on the depth and duration of the worldwide economic downturn.[23] Supply lines are broken, borders are strengthened and, with a worldwide roll-out of a vaccine now considered to be a five-year operation, it is unknown when the seamless international movement of things and people will resume, let alone when it will gain the momentum necessary to drag the global economy back from the brink. The shuddering within the infrastructure of the global economy has been felt across Australia as the custom of just-in-time-manufacturing revealed the state no longer had the manufacturing capacity to produce masks, ventilators, pharmaceuticals or even hand sanitizers.[24] The government was left casting around trying to explain why it was unable to protect the community. Speaking on a day when the total number of deaths in residential aged care in Australia passed two hundred, the Prime Minister said: 'the sad truth is, some days, we fall short'.[25]

Secondly, the health implications of one of the most prized accomplishments of the neoliberal hegemony is now viewed with extreme caution. The gig economy – a term that refers to economic activity which involves the use of temporary or freelance workers who are not employed as employees but rather as freelance contractors for anything greater than a minute's employment – with its unprotected legion of workers, was underscored to be a major concern when it came to stopping the contagion. The reason for this was simple: in this precarious employment, if people do not work they do not get paid. The Australian Council of Trade Unions claims that even before COVID-19 arrived, 3.3 million Australian workers were without paid leave entitlements.[26] According to *ABC News*, 'Combining the estimated number of self-employed workers with those in casual employment would suggest as many as 4.8 million Australian workers, or 37 per cent of the national workforce, did not have access to paid leave entitlements in the lead-up to the coronavirus outbreak'.[27] This meant those who may have taken time off to recuperate from any illnesses could not do so as they needed to keep working. As many of these occupations are in food delivery, customer service and aged care it should have come as no surprise that these decisions had devastating outcomes. In Victoria, the state hardest hit by the second wave of the contagion, this is exactly what happened (which will be discussed in more detail shortly).

Thirdly, there is the now-tenuous nature of an economy built on consumption that has been transformed and fuelled by a lucrative mining export industry. As jobs disappeared and lockdowns continued, as a community progressively saw itself within the frame of citizen, the previous role of the atomized consumer began to wither. As the Governor of the Reserve Bank, Philip Lowe, noted in a media statement in July 2020, this change has material impacts on investment:

> The Australian economy is going through a very difficult period and is experiencing the biggest contraction since the 1930s. Since March, an unprecedented 800,000 people have lost their jobs, with many others retaining their job only because of government and other support programs. … Uncertainty about the health situation and the future strength of the economy is making many households and businesses cautious, and this is affecting consumption and investment plans.[28]

Losing the nexus between the political and the social creates problems for those who seek relationality and community, but losing the capacity or appetite to consume has had a crippling effect on the economy. According to the Westpac COVID-19 research tracker in July 2020, consumer spending has yet to recover from the lows of the pandemic, despite states and territories opening their borders nationally.[29] Nearly 60 per cent of people had a reduction in their household income due to COVID-19, 33 per cent were struggling to meet their financial commitments and 71 per cent of people had already cut their spending and were not making large purchases.

All of these developments have had, and will continue to have, major repercussions on the global economy and international relations. As the proponents of globalization and neoliberalism wrestle with these implications, new and old ideas about how to live, work and organize are emerging into national conversations. Governments across the world are compelled to consider nationalizing health systems, airlines and other critical industries. In Australia a conservative government has been forced to double the amount paid to unemployed people, to essentially pay businesses to retain their employees, and re-examine the need for more securely attached workers who have access to entitlements such as sick leave – though they have yet to introduce any substantial legislation to that effect.[30] Indeed, the idea of government and democracy is being rethought and road-tested in light of this health and economic catastrophe.

But if the numbers of people joining the precariat class are growing as the ranks of the unemployed swell and hundreds of thousands of people are forced to depend on the largesse of charities and non-governmental organizations for the basics of life, where does this leave them? As discussed earlier, precarity is a defining characteristic, if not foundational principle, of neoliberalism. Standing points to three dimensions of the newly emerged precariat class of workers and communities.[31] The precariat face a distinctive work pattern; they are habituated to a life of unstable labour in the gig economy that is based on casualization, temporary work and body-hire companies for which there are few benefits (e.g. paid holidays); and they have a distinctive relation to the state. Consequently, 'they lack an occupational identity or narrative to give to their lives, or any organizational one'.[32] The group's relation to the state sees them losing rights taken for granted by full citizens. Instead, they are denizens who inhabit a locale without civil, cultural, political, social and economic rights, de facto and de jure. The second wave of infections that rolled through Victoria from mid-2020 tells a story of what life is like for members of the precariat class, and the impact this insecurely attached, politically weak and economically poor workforce can have in an already enfeebled democracy.

It appeared as if the city of Melbourne had dodged the worst of the pandemic with recorded infections dropping to almost nil by mid-2020. In early June 2020, school students were permitted to return to face-to-face classes and the rest of the state of Victoria gradually opened up, with its world-famous cafés and restaurants opening their doors and even the previously fire-ravaged regional towns slowly slipping back into business. While further easing of restrictions was announced for 21 June, new coronavirus cases were steadily, but silently, increasing. Within three weeks the daily numbers of people testing positive to the virus had risen to more than ten-fold those experienced in the first wave. As a result, on 7 July the Victorian government re-introduced a protracted lockdown across the state. Hotel quarantine would be called on to act as a buffer between those infected and the broader community. Concerns had begun to mount around Melbourne's hotel quarantine programme for returning international travellers and media reports surfaced that security guards were breaching hygiene protocols and carpooling to and from work and then going home to their families, taking the virus with them.[33] While those stories focused on the individual failings of the guards, a young whistle-blower stepped forward to describe the system of 'employment' that led to a deadly outbreak in Victoria.

Nineteen-year-old Shayla Shakshi told the *ABC 7.30 Report* current affairs programme that her first contact with this work was a WhatsApp message offering her employment as a quarantine security guard in a Melbourne hotel. She said:

> They actually contacted me and they're like, 'Would you like to work at this place?' And I'm like, I don't know what you guys are, what company, nothing. I just got told that you need to be here at a certain time and you're going to dress in a certain way and this is your pay rate. That's it.[34]

Shakshi stayed long enough to see that hand sanitizers were not provided on all the hotel levels, that workers were expected to provide their own personal protective equipment and there would be no training for the security guards on how to keep an entire floor of travellers safe. She left after one day. 'It was just really scary working there because they didn't care', she said. 'It was really horrible.'

As Standing noted, not caring is just the start. In an interview, he stated that 'the global economy wants a precariat. It wants a large number of people to be flexible, to be adaptable, to be prepared to move between jobs, and so on … They are being habituated to accept a life of unstable labor, temporary jobs, casual in and out work, internships.'[35] This emerging class is experiencing acute and perpetual insecurity, with no tie to work beyond their pay. As Shakshi's account highlights, it is a class of people losing rights to work safety, fair pay, protective uniforms, training and comradery, to name a few. Standing suggests that this is producing a potentially 'dangerous class' because the precariat's uncertainty and unevenness of work patterns result in 'anxiety, alienation, anomie and anger'.[36] More dangerous still is that the precariat's relationship to labour is 'emotionally detached', and thus they are 'less inclined to imagine that jobs are the road to happiness or that job creation is a sign of social progress'.[37] The stabilizing effect of a job-for-life, or at least a coherent career trajectory, with the inherent possibility of home ownership and financial security that flows from that narrative, has been part of the Australian story for a century. It is not at all clear what will happen when a critical mass of people know they will never achieve work security, home ownership or even secure housing through the rental market. When these once-constant narratives fail for perhaps millions of people, new ones will emerge. The experience of the pandemic response in Australia has made this evident, with the valorization of the 'heroes' who kept the country safe – the truckies, shelf stackers, nurses, teachers and doctors – and the vilification that lingers on the edge of their lives. That vilification makes a guest appearance each time there is another breach in hotel quarantine or aged-care centres as talk-back radio callers opine about whether those precariously engaged workers have failed in the execution of their duties.

In the case of the pandemic in Victoria, the fact that the decision was made to deploy private security companies without question (as opposed to the military or the police, both public services) indicated that private companies being used for a social purpose had already become a natural and automatic impulse. The people who were subsequently employed, via social media, unregulated and unprotected, were part of this precariat class. In subsequent weeks, this same group was to exacerbate the state's inability to curb the spread of COVID-19 because many returned to casualized work even after being diagnosed because they had no sick leave or access to other labour provisions provided to permanent workers.[38]

How does this story end?

This moment of deep national and global crises is rich in possibilities. There is no doubt that the lives of many people will end before they should and will become harder and more precarious as COVID-19 destabilizes all before it. However, this moment has also shown the neoliberal hegemony to be inadequate to the task of surviving the impact of the pandemic. It may be that as the neoliberal ideology altered language and separated the political from the social, while privatizing the very spaces and places for the political and social to meet, it had sown its own demise. It could be, as Standing proposes, that the precariat is in the process of developing new narratives and ways of being a class for itself, just as the middle, upper and working classes have found innumerable ways of doing. Imagine a precariat class with unifying narratives, ways of identifying one's own membership and the membership of others, ways of organizing effectively in both political and economic spaces. Those living in the knowledge that stable work will not define them, that they need to live in an ongoing state of flux and flex, may see the precariat transformed into communities tied together through a web of relationships built on cooperation and recognition that it may be you today, and me tomorrow.

The nature of fire is not only to destroy but also to reveal. Tearing through the Australian landscape, the fires laid bare the old bones of the country. As one joker on the containment line said to Julie, 'That's why police love bushfires – when the place is burnt back to the bone, the old skeletons are easy to see.' The fires of 2019–2020 have unveiled more than a state of complete unpreparedness on the part of the political class; they have additionally demonstrated the power of what remains in our collective action. As the pandemic spread through the suburbs and regions of Australia, one of the first things done by numerous neighbourhoods was to drop messages in each other's letter box and exchange phone numbers to ensure that if anyone needed help, help would arrive. The pandemic has done what endless advertising campaigns failed to do, that is, acknowledge that we are intimately dependent on each other for our health, our wholeness, and that we are all in this together. COVID-19 continues to expose the isolating and indiscriminating qualities of neoliberal hegemony and practice. While the precariat class already know they live one mistake and misunderstanding away from disaster, those more securely attached are daily reminded of our interdependence on a shared climate, bus, hospital, café, gym and air. The virus links us through touch and breath. If precarity is to be seen as part of the human condition, and 'certain social and political conditions' produce the possibility of more or less precarity, could we not say that precarity contains the seeds of its own productive possibility?[39] Even in Standing's sense, it has been the imposition of an ideology of aloneness that has led to a skewing towards insecurity of a vulnerability that can be productive if it inclines us to an acceptance of our interconnectedness.

As Australia moves into spring and prepares for the fire season of 2021, news that California and much of the west coast of the United States is ablaze serves as a grim reminder. The virus continues to claim many lives and impact national economies, but climate change is leading to climatic destabilization on an epochal scale. It is against this backdrop of increasing global destabilization that the precariat will need to find a way to be for its own self, and for the interdependency that makes survival possible. It could be that the experience of the fires and pandemic, the glimpse it provided so many Australians, offers the beginning of a narrative of radical interdependency.

Notes

1   'Former fire chiefs "tried to warn Scott Morrison" to bring in more water-bombers ahead of horror bushfire season', *ABC News* (14 November 2019), https://www. abc.net.au/news/2019-11-14/former-fire-chief-calls-out-pm-over-refusal-of-meeting/11705330.

2   Channel Nine, 'Interview by Leila McKinnon, *A Current Affair*', transcript (7 January 2020), https://ministers.treasury.gov.au/ministers/josh-frydenberg-2018/transcripts/interview-leila-mckinnon-current-affair-channel-9.

3   Paul Read and Richard Denniss, 'With costs approaching $100 billion, the fires are Australia's costliest natural disaster', *The Conversation* (17 January 2020), https://

theconversation.com/with-costs-approaching-100-billion-the-fires-are-australias-costliest-natural-disaster-129433.

4   Guy Standing, *Plunder of the Commons: A Manifesto for Sharing Public Wealth* (London: Pelican Books, 2019), 28.

5   During the fires and at the time of writing, both authors lived on the east coast of Australia.

6   Wendy Brown, *Edgework: Critical Essays on Knowledge and Politics* (Princeton, NJ: Princeton University Press, 2005), 39, original emphasis.

7   Jon Stratton, *Uncertain Lives: Culture, Race and Neoliberalism in Australia* (Newcastle upon Tyne: Cambridge Scholars Publishing, 2011), 3.

8   Trent Hamann, 'Neoliberalism, governmentality, and ethics', *Foucault Studies* 6 (2009): 38, original emphasis.

9   Friedrich Hayek, 'The fatal conceit', in *The Collected Works of Friedrich August Hayek: Volume 1*, ed. W.W. Bartley III (London: Routledge, 1988), 66–88.

10 Wendy Brown, *Undoing the Demos: Neoliberalism's Stealth Revolution* (New York: Zone Books, 2015), 17.

11 Brown, *Demos*, 39, original emphasis.

12 Richard Denniss, 'Dead right: how neoliberalism ate itself and what comes next', *Quarterly Essay* 70 (2018): 77.

13 Michelle Cull, 'Value beyond money: Australia's special dependence on volunteer firefighters', *Australian Emergency Services Magazine* (4 February 2020), https://ausemergencyservices.com.au/emergency-disaster-management/value-beyond-money-australias-special-dependence-on-volunteer-firefighters/.

14 David Harvey, *A Brief History of Neoliberalism* (Oxford: Oxford University Press, 2005), 82.

15 Nikolas Rose, *Powers of Freedom: Reframing Political Thought* (Cambridge: Cambridge University Press, 1999).

16 International Labour Office, 'ILO highlights global challenge to trade unions', press release (1997), https://www.ilo.org/global/about-the-ilo/newsroom/news/WCMS_008032.

17 Guy Standing, 'The precariat and class struggle', *RCCS Annual Review* 7, no. 7 (2015): 3–16.

18 Anne Connolly, 'Coronavirus is devastating the aged care sector, and it all feels shockingly familiar', *ABC News* (25 August 2020), https://www.abc.net.au/news/2020-08-25/coronavirus-aged-care-australia-crisis-feels-shockingly-familiar/12592178.

19 Sarah Russell, 'Passing the buck: why Victoria's Covid is raging in private aged care homes', *Michael West Media* (24 July 2020), https://www.michaelwest.com.au/passing-the-buck-why-victorias-covid-is-raging-in-private-aged-care-homes.

20 The TAFE (Technical and Further Education) system – Australia's largest vocational education and training (VET) provider – was opened up to private-sector

competition following VET reforms around 2008. Each state and territory moved toward public/private funding models at different speeds, but by 2015 fees had become prohibitive, courses were scaled back and private operators were collapsing leaving thousands of students out of pocket and unqualified.

21 Luke Costin, 'Pop-up mall for bushfire-ravaged town Mogo', *The Leader* (15 February 2020), https://www.theleader.com.au/story/6632084/pop-up-mall-for-bushfire-ravaged-town-mogo/.

22 Renae Merle, 'A guide to the financial crisis – 10 years later', *The Washington Post* (10 September 2018), https://www.washingtonpost.com/business/economy/a-guide-to-the-financial-crisis--10-years-later/2018/09/10/114b76ba-af10-11e8-a20b-5f4f84429666_story.html.

23 James Jackson, Martin Weiss, Andres Schwarzenberg, Rebecca Nelson, Karen Sutter and Michael Sutherland, 'Global economic effects of COVID-19', Congressional Research Service (last modified 9 July 2020), 2, https://crsreports.congress.gov/product/pdf/R/R46270.

24 Just-in-time manufacturing is a management strategy that minimizes inventory and increases efficiency, but because inventory is always just-in-time it is vulnerable to external shocks in transport and the economy.

25 Scott Morrison, 'Press conference – Australian Parliament House, ACT', transcript (14 August 2020), https://pmtranscripts.pmc.gov.au/release/transcript-42975.

26 RMIT ABC Fact Check, 'COVID-19 has put jobs in danger. How many workers don't have leave entitlements?', *ABC News* (30 March 2020), https://www.abc.net.au/news/2020-03-30/fact-file-casual-employment-paid-leave-entitlements/12089056.

27 RMIT ABC Fact Check, 'COVID-19'.

28 Philip Lowe, 'Statement by Philip Lowe, Governor: monetary policy decision (number 2020–17)', Reserve Bank of Australia press release (7 July 2020), https://www.rba.gov.au/media-releases/2020/mr-20-17.html.

29 BT Insights, 'How has COVID-19 changed Australian consumer spending habits?' (22 July 2020), https://www.bt.com.au/insights/perspectives/2020/australian-consumer-spending-changes.html.

30 In March 2020 the Federal government introduced Job Keeper and Job Seeker. Job Keeper was approximately $700 per week and was paid to employees who would otherwise lose their job. This was to ensure employees remained in contact with their place of employment. Job Seeker, formerly known as Newstart, was doubled to $700 per week. Job Keeper was withdrawn in March 2021 and Job Seeker was reduced back to almost pre-COVID levels by 30 March 2021.

31 Guy Standing, 'Who are "the precariat" and why do they threaten our society?', *Euronews* (2 May 2018), https://www.euronews.com/2018/05/01/who-are-the-precariat-and-why-they-threaten-our-society-view.

32 Standing, 'The precariat'.

33 Ben Schneiders, 'How hotel quarantine let COVID-19 out of the bag in Victoria', *The Age* (3 July 2020), https://www.theage.com.au/national/victoria/how-hotel-quarantine-let-covid-19-out-of-the-bag-in-victoria-20200703-p558og.html.

34 Grace Tobin and Alex McDonald, 'Coronavirus quarantine guards in Melbourne hotels were recruited via WhatsApp, then "told to bring their own masks"', *ABC Online* (21 July 2020), https://www.abc.net.au/news/2020-07-21/coronavirus-quarantine-hotel-security-guards-recruited-whatsapp/12476574.

35 Vinnie Rotondaro, 'The "precariat": stressed out, insecure, alienated and angry', *National Catholic Reporter* (19 August 2015), https://www.ncronline.org/blogs/ncr-today/precariat-stressed-out-insecure-alienated-and-angry.

36 Guy Standing, *A Precariat Charter: From Denizens to Citizens* (London: Bloomsbury, 2014), 31–32.

37 Standing, *Precariat Charter*, 32.

38 RMIT ABC Fact Check, 'COVID-19'.

39 Judith Butler, *Precarious Life: The Powers of Mourning and Violence* (New York: Verso, 2004), 29.

Part Three

Precarious Bodies

The Road to Asylum

Alice Driver

I want to finish elementary school.
> Karla Avelar, 40, founder of the Comcavis Trans Association,
> which advocates for LGBTI rights in El Salvador

'Women, don't be deceived', boomed the weary, yellow-eyed preacher, his sombrero tipped dramatically forward in a manner befitting his bus-ride sermon, one that would last all the way from San Salvador, the capital of El Salvador, to Guatemala City. As he made his way down the aisle of the bus, he stopped to touch women and girls on the head or the arm. 'Don't let men trick you', he shouted, holding his bible up so high its well-worn pages brushed the roof of the bus. He didn't touch Marfil Estrella Pérez Méndoza, 26, whose chosen name translates to Ivory Star. As she rested her round, hopeful face on the bus window, dark eyes peering out into the rainy greyness of early morning, the preacher passed by without laying a hand. 'How do you say asylum in English?' she whispered.

Marfil Estrella was born in Cuscatlán, El Salvador, in a body that never felt like her own. She was assigned male at birth, and at 15, she came out as gay to her family. Their response was to disown her. 'They told me that I brought shame on the family, that I should forget about them, and that I needed to leave', explained Marfil Estrella. Like many members of the LGBTI community in El Salvador, her family forced her onto the street, and her schooling ended abruptly at ninth grade because she had no money to continue. She fled to San Salvador and slept in a park where she met other gay boys. 'I saw a transsexual, and I said, "I want to be like her! I want to be like her!"' she recalled. She lived on the street, grew

An earlier version of this article was published in digital format for *Longreads* (29 June 2018), https://longreads.com/2018/06/29/the-road-to-asylum/.

out her hair, and began to dress in women's clothes, but she had no way to earn a living and consequently became very thin. Eventually she started to do sex work, one of the only options available to trans women in El Salvador to earn money.

Lacking the money and medical care to transition, Marfil Estrella did what many young trans women do: consult with friends on the street. 'I saw that my friends injected hormones, and I asked them how they got breasts', Marfil Estrella explained. At first she didn't have money for hormones, so she grew her hair long and started to dress like a girl. 'I started with girls' trousers. I was between being a girl and a boy and wore men's shirts and girls' trousers. I did it little by little because I feared people. I was quite scared when people were looking at me like I was weird – like I was a weirdo. I was between being and not being, between being a boy or a girl', she explained. Her friends advised her to get injections in her nipple – the substance of the injection unknown – a common, cheap procedure, often performed by friends, that trans women desperately seek to help them feel more at home in their bodies. After the injections, Marfil Estrella experienced cold sweats at night, and she became worried, but her friends assured her that the fever was normal and that soon her breasts would grow. As the days passed and Marfil Estrella didn't see any results, she asked another friend to inject her four more times. 'At night I had a double fever, everything, a headache. I was sweating, and she advised me not to continue because it was very dangerous for my health.' After that experience, Marfil Estrella began to inject what she believed were hormones into her gluteus without a prescription or the help of a doctor, because even though in theory trans people have the right to go to the doctor in El Salvador, in practice doctors routinely refuse to treat them. Marfil Estrella spoke of women who injected oil, silicone and other substances, and described a friend who had injected oil as having breasts that were 'rotting, purple, and oozing white pus'.

Karla Avelar, 40, the founder of Comcavis Trans, an NGO that provides services and support to the LGBTI community in El Salvador, wanted to introduce me to Marfil Estrella. One night, Avelar directed our taxi to several street corners where she thought Marfil Estrella might be working. We cruised by trans women in tube tops and colourful skirts who flitted in and out of the shadows. Eventually we found Marfil Estrella on a corner wearing a black dress cut just above the buttocks and matching platform heels. When we invited her for a coffee, she produced a pair of trousers from her purse and slipped into them.

'I'm leaving on the bus at 3 am', said Marfil Estrella, a thick, jagged white scar on her neck visible under the harsh fluorescent lights of Mister Donut, a popular hangout in San Salvador, 'I hope to have a business, a restaurant, to work. I don't know, something different. I don't want to live the life I lead. I want to study. I want to be someone', she continued. Avelar sat on a stool by her side, a sugared donut between her fingers. Avelar, who has wildly curly hair and radiates empathy, was one of the first trans women in El Salvador to make her HIV status public for political reasons. She has helped trans women like Marfil Estrella prepare all the necessary paperwork to request asylum in the United States. A man with an ice pick had attacked Marfil Estrella one night when she was walking home from work – just one story of violence in a lifetime filled with such stories. 'I thank God that I'm still alive to tell my stories', said Marfil Estrella.

At Mister Donut, I sat across the table from Avelar and asked Marfil Estrella if I could join her on her journey to the United States. Marfil Estrella said my presence would make her feel safer. I agreed to accompany her to Tapachula, Mexico, via bus, where she planned to spend a few months while getting her papers in order to legally pass through Mexico. Avelar remembered that Marfil Estrella had told her when they first met, 'I want to leave here because the streets right now are a time bomb. I don't want to be left lying in the street, as so many have been left. I want to seek freedom. I want to seek peace.'

According to a 2014 study, the average life expectancy of a trans woman in the Americas is 30–35 years. Trans women routinely encounter sexual violence and Avelar's experience had been no different. Avelar understood Marfil Estrella, and she knew how to read her scars like a script. Born in 1978 in Chalatenango, Avelar knew at an early age that she was a girl. Her family was not supportive of her identity. By the time she was ten, she had been raped twice by her cousin. She fled the violence at home for the streets of San Salvador. Avelar survived the first six months in the city by scavenging food from the trash. She found a job doing domestic work that offered her a place to stay, but the son of the woman she worked for also raped her. One day while going about chores in the neighbourhood, some fifteen gang members approached and raped her.

Shortly after that, she befriended a trans woman who showed her the ropes of sex work, which offered a way to make some money and have what she felt was a small measure of control over her body. Of that time, Avelar reflected, 'In spite of all that, I wanted to live, to fight, and that gave me the strength to survive again and again even though people want to make you think that you don't belong, that you are an aberration simply because you have a different sexual orientation and gender identity from the heteronormative.'

As a teen, she survived an attack by a man who fit the description of a notorious serial killer known as the *Matalocas*, who was one of several serial killers in El Salvador in recent years who have focused on exterminating the trans population. The man shot her nine times, and she spent two months in hospital in a coma. When she came out of the coma, the doctor informed her that she was HIV-positive. Four years later, Avelar found herself refusing to pay the extortion that local MS-13 gang members required of all sex workers. Gang members shot her five times. She survived, and around that time, she and another trans friend were attacked by three men who tried to kill them. In the process of defending herself, Avelar stabbed one of the men. For this, Avelar was sentenced to four years in Sensuntepeque men's prison. Avelar believed that the judge, due to his Christian beliefs, was unable or unwilling to recognize the violence a young trans woman like herself would experience at a men's jail. Avelar was particularly afraid because she knew several men at the prison. They were gang members who had previously raped, stoned or tried to murder her.

Avelar says she was raped nearly every day for four years until she was released in 2002. She was also denied medical attention – a common plight for the trans population in prison. 'I left prison weighing 75 pounds – all bones. I had advanced HIV, tuberculosis, syphilis, herpes, hepatitis and a lot of other things that I don't even remember', recounted Avelar, sitting in her office at Comcavis Trans. Her mother, a devout Catholic who hands out cards with photos and quotes from saints to everyone she meets, nursed her back to health. After years of barely communicating, the two became close again.

Over coffee at a local mall, Avelar told me about founding Comcavis Trans in 2008. Initially, its mission was to provide support to trans women with HIV, although it later expanded to provide support for the entire LGBTI community. 'In the end, what made me a human rights defender was the experience of jail. It was there that I truly understood the harsh reality and pain that discrimination can cause and the lack of will and the lack of commitment of the state to guarantee the human rights of all citizens', she explained. Avelar said that as of August 2017, she and her seven colleagues at the NGO had helped 132 members of the LGBTI community. She then abruptly added, 'I think I have cancer'. When I asked her why, she pulled down the collar of her shirt and exposed the scarred and oozing flesh of her breasts – the product of an injection of something she referred to as some type of oil. She stood up and lifted her shirt to expose a thick, cavernous scar running up the middle of her stomach punctuated by the scars left by bullet holes. 'If you don't believe my story, my body says everything.'

At work, Avelar provided Marfil Estrella and other trans women information about what documents they needed to prepare to migrate: a passport application, copies of police and court documents, and a plan for how to cover the costs of migrating to the United States. On the topic of migration, Avelar commented, 'It is not only modern slavery – it is sexual slavery', and went on to discuss the role of human trafficking, which for trans women often means being kidnapped and forced into prostitution. Marfil Estrella had attempted to migrate once before, but due to the sexual violence she experienced, she turned around after reaching Tecún Umán, Guatemala. Avelar, who had heard many stories from trans women migrants, said, 'The violation of human rights does not end when a person leaves her or his country. I believe that it is just beginning, because the migratory route is cruel. When a person is LGBTI, Indigenous, has HIV, is extremely poor or is illiterate, they are subject to sexual exploitation, labour exploitation, unpaid work, torture, kidnapping.' Although LGBTI migrants who reached the United States had greater legal rights, Avelar was worried about the US political stance on LGBTI issues. She explained, 'I don't want to be so emphatic to say that the decisions that Mr Trump has made, for example, condemning and reducing the human rights of LGBTI people, are the sole cause of this situation, but the result is fewer human rights. Other countries could replicate the actions that are currently being undertaken by that official [Trump].'

When I arrived at the San Salvador bus station at 3 am, Marfil Estrella was sitting in a plastic green chair, her face and dangling diamond earrings lit up by the electronic light of her cell phone. She had spent all night doing sex work to have more money for the trip and had not slept. As she boarded the bus that would take her from San Salvador to Guatemala City she looked around, scanning the other people on the bus for signs of danger. It started to rain as the bus drove into the early morning darkness, and Marfil Estrella looked out of the window with tenderness and yearning.

Crossing the border into Guatemala, we had to get off the bus and present our passports. To walk with Marfil Estrella was to feel the skin-prickling third sense that every eye in the territory was on you, with looks that showed evident disgust or desire. Men brushed by Marfil Estrella or approached her and whispered things in her ear. In Guatemala City, the bus abruptly turned into a small parking lot and passengers began filing off. As we exited, currency exchangers, men with fists full of cash, circled us like vultures. None of us had expected to end up at a tiny bus station that offered no connecting bus to Tecún Umán, where we would cross the border into Mexico.

An older woman who had sat near Marfil Estrella on the bus asked if she needed help and offered to accompany her to the next bus station as soon as a friend arrived. As the minutes rolled by, all the passengers disappeared and only the hungry-looking money men remained, staring. A young guy holding

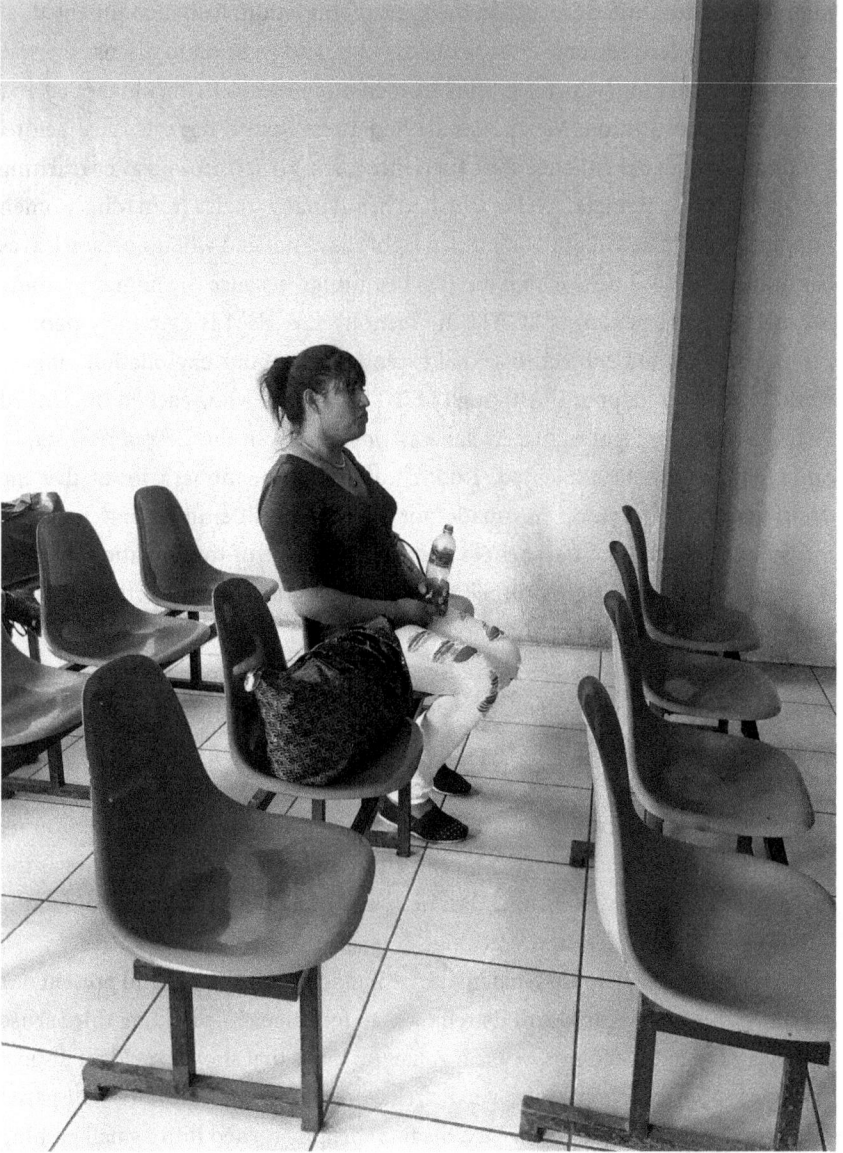

Figure 9.1 Marfil Estrella sits in the waiting room at a bus station in Guatemala City, Guatemala before catching a bus to the Guatemala-Mexico border. Alice Driver, 2018.[1]

up a cell phone in Marfil Estrella's direction sat down and slouched in a plastic chair. She paced. We became worried. The friendly lady typed on her phone, presumably texting her friend. When the friend arrived, Marfil Estrella looked relieved. We followed the old lady and her friend as they made their way into the crowded streets, where we immediately attracted attention. The friend wanted to go to the metro which was some distance away, but as the scene around us became more hectic, we convinced her that it would be better to take a taxi to the bus station where we could catch our next bus. As I squeezed into the back seat of the taxi with Marfil Estrella, the old lady's friend shouted in my ear, loud enough for everyone to hear, 'Does she believe in God?' pointing to Marfil Estrella.

The taxi entered an underground concrete structure filled with old school buses from the States, and Marfil Estrella worried that none of the buses would have air-conditioning. She was right – and, had our schedule been more flexible, I think she would have tried to go to another bus station in search of air-conditioned buses. It was nearing midday and we were sweating as we settled into our next bus, which had smaller seats and less personal space. The ride would last six hours over which time we would be entertained by a young man walking down the aisle with enlarged photos of different types of stomach parasites. After trying to convince everyone that they had a parasite, he then walked around selling a medicine to kill those parasites. It was an effective campaign. At some point, a man stood up and came to sit by Marfil Estrella. He spoke to her low and very close, and I watched his body language, trying to read it for threatening signs. Eventually he moved. Everyone was sweating in the mid-afternoon heat, and traffic was almost at a standstill as we neared the Guatemala-Mexico border. If we didn't arrive before dusk, that would mean crossing the Suchiate River on an inner tube raft at night, which was dangerous. I crossed the same river from Tapachula to Tecún Umán with migrants during the day just a month and a half earlier. I had no idea I would be back so soon. Gangs controlled both sides of the river, and as traffic slowed and the sun set, having eaten almost nothing during the journey, our mood became grim. 'I'm scared to cross the river because there are a lot of men there, and the last time they started yelling things at me and I was afraid. That's where I feel afraid', said Marfil Estrella.

A young boy pedalling a bicycle taxi, working furiously to get us up the dirt track leading to the river, dropped us on the banks. It was dark and void of people. The last time I had crossed the river, I had been among hundreds of people and dozens of rafts. A man and a boy stepped out of the shadows near an inner tube raft and motioned to us. Marfil Estrella got on the raft first and sat down on the wooden slats covering the inner tube. I followed. The river was quiet except for the sound of the raft moving through the water. Once we reached the bank on the other side, we scrambled off the raft and walked quickly up the hill and through the market that would lead us to the town square in

Ciudad Hidalgo, in Chiapas, where we could catch a ride to Tapachula, forty minutes away. I accompanied Marfil Estrella to her hotel, where she would stay in a dank room with peeling walls, and we hugged each other goodbye. Marfil Estrella would spend the next two months in Tapachula getting her paperwork approved to pass through Mexico legally.

I spent the next two days on buses returning to San Salvador, where I had promised to meet Avelar and three of her friends – Sadira Saldaña, 30; Nicole Rosales, 22; and Amy Jeilyn Beckers, 27 – trans sex workers who lived together. I met them at a local park, and as they walked through the dappled sunlight, Nicole slipped her hand into Sadira's, clasping it tight and close. The three talked about their lives as trans women, and Nicole shyly admitted to being in a relationship with Sadira.

Sadira, who is tall and has wide-set brown eyes and long, wavy hair, told her family at age seven that she wanted to be a girl. 'They wanted to kill me at first, and then they kicked me out of the house', she explained. She started her transition at age 12 and had injections in her breasts on the street. 'The truth is that I didn't know what I was injecting', she admitted. Asked to imagine her ideal future, she said, 'I would study law to become a lawyer or a prosecutor, but right now I survive day-to-day. There are no options for the future.'

Amy wore her hair in a tight bun and periodically shouted at men who stared at her as they walked by, admonishing them for their disrespect. She knew at a young age that she liked wearing skirts and high heels and that she was attracted to boys. First, she came out to her family as gay, then later as trans. A lack of educational opportunities led her to sex work. 'The truth is that I wish that I knew that tomorrow, as a trans person, I could finish my studies and I would have a safe place to do it. But in this society, how is that possible? You can't', she admitted.

Nicole, whose direct gaze and warm brown eyes are framed by thick lashes, decided at 15 that she was a trans woman. Her parents had been imprisoned when she was young, and she had inherited their house. But a local gang threatened to kill her if she didn't leave it, so she ended up homeless. 'According to society we are worthless, right? But there are many transsexuals who have shown society what we are worth', Nicole explained. She had tried to migrate to the United States once but only made it as far as Chiapas before turning back. Like Marfil Estrella, she ran out of money and was afraid of being kidnapped and forced into prostitution. She also worried about gangs like the Zetas in Mexico, who were known to prey on trans women – many of whom had never had access to the surgery necessary to achieve their desired body – to get them working in gang-run prostitution rings. Nicole talked about how the Zetas had tried to recruit her friends by offering to pay for plastic surgery so that they could have their dream bodies. However, they'd be forced into sex work, essentially selling their bodies until they died. Nicole said she wouldn't try to migrate again, and when she and Sadira left the park, they walked away hand in hand.

Sadira, Amy and Nicole, like Marfil Estrella and Avelar, had not had the opportunity to finish high school in a society where trans women are routinely denied equal access to both education and health care. All of them ended up doing sex work to survive while dreaming of another life. Avelar promised to introduce me to Bianka Rodriguez, 24, the trans woman in charge of communications at Comcavis Trans. Rodriguez had attended college, which had afforded her more options in life.

Rodriguez has delicate features, brown eyes flecked with green and is soft-spoken yet assertive. She sat at the boardroom table in the Comcavis Trans office, her hands clasped together as she told me about her childhood. 'I discovered my gender identity when I was five years old', she said. 'I used the gestures of a girl. My mother exercised physical and psychological violence towards me for demonstrating those gestures at an early age. She reproached me for being too feminine and said that these things were an aberration and that she had had a boy, not a girl, and that I had to behave as such.'

In 2009, when Rodriguez was 15, she ran away from home and found a job at a bakery. The owners of the bakery, a couple, promised her that she could live her identity as a woman and offered her a place to stay. However, upon moving in with the couple, she was forced to sleep in the storage room and was essentially enslaved. 'My bed at that time was made of sacks of flour used to make French bread, and the bags of sugar served as my pillow', Rodriguez recalled. Given that she didn't have anywhere else to go, she stayed and worked every day from 4 am to 11 pm for two years. When she managed to escape, she tried to press charges against the couple for never paying her, but they threatened to harm her family, so she relented.

Eventually, with the encouragement of her grandma, Rodriguez pursued an education. When she went to enrol in high school, she was informed that she would have to cut her long blonde hair and dye it dark brown, and she would have to wear trousers. Because she wanted to study, she agreed to the terms. Upon her graduation she enrolled in college, initially in an industrial engineering programme. However, a professor in the engineering department told her that he would not allow a trans woman to graduate, and she was forced to switch majors, which is how she ended up studying communications.

After college, she worked for a literacy programme for seniors in her hometown of Cuscatancingo. 'I supported my community, and I fought to help them, and that is where I discovered my potential to fight for human rights. After that, I signed up to volunteer at Comcavis, and now I am the director of communications', she said. The difference between Rodriguez's life and Marfil Estrella's illustrates the power of education and family support. Marfil Estrella, before migrating to Mexico, had said she had one piece of advice for trans women and girls: study as much as you can. 'I already believe that I have reached an age where if I start studying, I won't finish until I'm sixty', she said. 'I will fight to study because the only way you can get ahead is by studying.'

As Rodriguez was talking, a slight young man with a beard stopped by and introduced himself as Gabriel Escobar. 'Do you want to interview me?' he asked. Gabriel, a 22-year-old trans man, works at Comcavis to help keep track of violence against the LGBTI community in El Salvador. When asked about his experience transitioning from a woman to a man, he said, 'My friends congratulated me. In my house, nobody says anything to me. They do not mention it – it's like, they let it be – and in the neighbourhood nobody says anything. I know that if I were a trans woman, something would have already happened to me. It is easier for us to be trans men because of the very ideology in this country about men and masculinity. If a man wants to be a woman, it is humiliating and degrading, but for us, the change is not.' Rodriguez nodded as Escobar spoke, and added, 'It's different, as Gabriel said. He was congratulated because he changed from the weaker sex to the stronger sex.'

Escobar said he planned to go to university to study psychology 'to be able to support trans girls and boys'. When his parents sent him to a psychologist as a child, the psychologist told him that he was wrong to feel that he was a boy. 'They don't know how to approach you as a trans person, and that's why I want to change that reality', Escobar said. In the future, he said he hoped that the government of El Salvador would provide the trans population with health coverage for hormone treatment and also that the law legislating gender identity be changed to allow trans people to change their names on legal documents. When employers discovered during the recruitment stage that the gender expression of the person didn't match their birth name, the result was usually discrimination. 'I have been lucky because I have never suffered violence and I haven't been discriminated against much either', Escobar added.

Rodriguez, whose face adorns the posters that Comcavis Trans created to advocate that the law legislating gender identity be changed, also hoped that the state would respect and protect her legal rights to live out her identity. Until that time, she, Avelar, Escobar, and other members of the staff would both advocate for legislation to protect their rights and help those members of their community threatened by physical violence to migrate. 'We support LGBTI people who decide to migrate, we don't encourage them to do it. We explain the process and give them advice about what they will face. In many cases their lives are in danger, which is mostly reflected in the cases of trans women who must migrate in order to stay alive', explained Rodriguez.

In order to challenge the law legislating gender identity, Comcavis Trans helped Alessandra Jiménez, a 32-year-old trans woman from Zacatecoluca, El Salvador, prepare a case to be presented at the Supreme Court. Jiménez, who has lived in Milan for eleven years, returned to El Salvador in August 2017 to present her case. Of her childhood she said, 'I remember when I was seven years old in first grade here in El Salvador and I told a girl, "I wish I had been born a woman."' When she was 19, a friend of hers – another trans woman – was murdered. With the support of her family, who she said had always wanted to see her live peacefully, she emigrated to Italy. Jiménez said she wished her fellow Salvadorans would understand that 'we were born into a body that we didn't want, but we are human beings and we have value'.

Avelar, who has helped prepare similar cases to challenge the law, was worried. She knew that the court would submit Jiménez to a degrading doctor's assessment to confirm that she had undergone sexual reassignment surgery. 'Trans women are leaving the country for different reasons – not only because of discrimination from their family but also because of the lack of compliance by the state, including the lack of laws guaranteeing human rights for these populations and the lack of opportunities to study and work', explained Avelar. 'Attempts at assassination, persecution and extortion come from uniformed agents in some cases. Currently gangs are talking about exterminating LGBTQ people.' Avelar knows these threats well – due to an increase in death threats, she requested and recently received asylum in Switzerland.

Three months after leaving El Salvador, Marfil Estrella wrote to me on Facebook. She had arrived in Mexico City, but had run out of money and wanted to know if I could lend her some. I sent her the links of organizations that helped migrants, knowing very well that many of them turned away trans women, but hoping she would find the support to finish her journey. On 19 October 2017, Marfil Estrella crossed the border at the San Ysidro port of entry and requested asylum in the United States. It took me several weeks to confirm that she had been taken to the Otay Mesa Detention Justice Center. Given the Supreme Court's recent ruling denying bail hearings for immigrants, essentially allowing for their indefinite detention, it was unclear how long Marfil Estrella would be held or when her request for asylum would be reviewed.

The only way I could communicate with Marfil Estrella was to write her a letter and hope that she would receive it and call me. The detention centre did not allow calls from outside, so all I could do was wait. On 4 April 2018, my phone rang, and through a crackling line I heard her voice, a soft whisper, and I asked if she was doing OK. She told me that from October to January she had been housed in the men's section of the detention centre, and while detained she had experienced violence. In February, they had moved her to a cell with a trans roommate. 'I don't know when I will get out of here', Marfil Estrella said, her voice so low and sad that I had to strain to catch the last word. Just as I was about to respond, the phone cut out and the line went dead.

In May 2018, Marfil Estrella was granted a court date for her asylum hearing. She stood in front of the judge in prison-issue clothes and bright white tennis shoes and told the story of why she fled El Salvador: 'I knew if I stayed, I could lose my life.' At the end of her testimony, the judge meditated for a moment and responded, 'I grant you asylum because I find your testimony credible. The government was unable or unwilling to protect you from acts of violence in El Salvador.' Marfil Estrella left the courtroom, her long hair flowing and scar faintly visible, a marker of violence survived.

Figure 9.2 Marfil Estrella crosses the street on her way to the grocery store before stopping by the university for her first day of English classes in San Diego.

Update (September 2021): After being granted asylum in the United States, Marfil Estrella officially changed her name to Michelle. She works at a pizza restaurant in San Diego and has moved out of group housing and into her own apartment. She loves seeing same-sex couples in her San Diego neighbourhood walk around holding hands, something that she did not see in El Salvador.

For further information, see:

https://www.alicedriver.com/

Note

1   All images in this photo essay are copyrighted by Alice Driver, 2018.

Grieve-able Lives: Precarity in Residential Aged Care

Helen Fordham

In an unstable, uncertain world in which market forces and institutional and political power frame some lives as marginal, disposable and meaningless, Judith Butler theorized ways to critically challenge this constitution by considering how all lives are precarious. The exclusion of certain groups from the shared imagining of humanity is enabled, in part, by the lack of infrastructures that sustain life, such as food and shelter.[1] Exclusion, however, also occurs through representations that shape what is regarded as normal or acceptable in the public space. These discursive 'mechanisms' of power both constitute the human subject in hegemonic discourse as deserving of protection from aggression, injury and death, and enable the dehumanization of some populations by portraying their suffering as natural and inevitable, thus justifying the denial of their rights and agency.[2]

Butler's inquiry into the political function of precariousness was prompted by the 9/11 terrorist attacks on the USA and the nation's subsequent War on Terror. She argues that America's unveiled vulnerability served to sanction the country's escalated aggression towards (foreign) others, even as the nation portrayed itself as a part of an interdependent global community based on equality, rights and national sovereignty. Precarity, she concluded, is politically and socially constructed in particular contexts and the 'failing social and economic networks of support' of specific populations increases their exposure to violence and marginalization.[3] In this chapter, I apply Butler's argument to a different group – the elderly – whose precariousness is heightened by both systematic deficiencies such as difficulties accessing services, sub-standard care, inadequate funding and lack of aged-care sector leadership; as well as ageism and cultural representations in Australia of the elderly as 'frail non-contributors' to society.[4] These stereotypes promote discrimination, have a negative impact on the social functioning of the elderly, legitimate inequality in policy and funding, and exacerbate intergenerational conflict.[5] All of these outcomes are highly problematic in the broader context of the nation's rapidly aging population,[6] an aged care system in crisis, climbing acute-care medical costs, and anticipated national budget deficits until 2060–2061.[7] In order to think through the ways in which the elderly have been constructed as 'other', I recount my experience of placing my mother into an aged-care facility after a broken leg and diagnosis of dementia. Using an autoethnographic approach, this chapter examines how structures and discourse produce and amplify the precariousness of the elderly.

Precariousness and vulnerability

My mother's transition from retired, independent and highly capable former schoolteacher and social worker to increasingly forgetful resident of an aged-care facility seemed abrupt. Late one Saturday morning in July 2021 I rang Mum to let her know I was coming to visit, and she told me she was still in bed and could not walk. I was at her house within twenty minutes, and concerned at how much pain she was in I took her straight to the local hospital. I knew the facility well since we had visited with growing regularity over the last few years for an assortment of injuries – cuts, an eye injury, a broken toe, a negative reaction to medication and even a dog bite. Initially, I tried to get Mum into the extended hours Hospital General Practice, which always seemed to process patients faster than the perennially overwhelmed emergency room. However, this was not possible because she could not remember how and when she had hurt her leg. She may have injured something else, the receptionist explained, and so the only option was the ER. Four hours later, Mum was finally seen by a doctor. Twenty-four hours later, she was admitted to hospital after waiting all night in an emergency-room bed. Three weeks later, she was transferred from the hospital to a transition care facility. And ten weeks after the fall that caused her broken leg, she arrived in her new forever home; a residential aged-care facility. I was devastated at my sense of failure to keep Mum in her own home, and my mother was distraught that she would never go home again.

In reality, my mother's journey was not fast. Like many aging Australians, she had struggled for years to maintain her independence and, insistent that she would die in her own home, had learned to cloak her failing memory. I actively colluded in this process, ignoring her memory lapses and papering over her word dysmorphia, minimalizing problems, and focusing on what she could do rather than what was deteriorating. I had read that this strengths-based approach reduced the sense of isolation and withdrawal experienced by the person with memory loss, and I did not want my mother – with her insightful observations, kind heart and dry sense of humour – to stop talking with me because she felt embarrassed. So we pretended together that everything was all right. I asked her advice on how to get better outcomes with my students, and she delighted in serving as a sounding board for my research ideas.

Increasingly, however, things were going wrong. Mum would ring me several times a day with no memory that we had had the same conversation. She could no longer work out how to retrieve her phone messages. She could not remember how to turn on the computer to play Solitaire, and she was confused by the frequent phone calls from people trying to sell her things or threatening to prosecute her for tax evasion. Coordinating the elements of a meal became a challenge; food was burned or oversalted or boiled to within an inch of its life. Cleanliness declined and we had several refreshers on how to turn on the vacuum cleaner and empty the dust barrel. Personal appearance became less important as she became more isolated, and my once stylish mother, with her four wardrobes full of clothes, developed a passion for an old grey cardigan with frayed wrists and worn elbows.

A friend who had been through this process with her own parents advised me to get an Aged Care Assessment Team (ACAT) evaluation in order for Mum to qualify for subsidized home services and be processed quickly, in case she suddenly had to go into residential care. I explained to Mum that the assessment would keep her in her own home for as long as possible, an outcome we both wanted, and I was confident that her needs would be apparent. This was not the case. Excited by the arrival of visitors, Mum rallied. During the review she delicately balanced on one foot to show she was not a falls risk and completed advanced calculations in her head about the likely cost of a range of services. As a result she qualified for a cleaner once a fortnight, and for handrails in the bathroom and on the front porch. Mum accepted the handrails, but she did not want the cleaner. Strangers posed an unnecessary risk to her property and her privacy, she told me, and so she went on to cancel the service at every opportunity. I sought to reason with the social worker that my mother needed more support, but she explained that there were many more seniors considerably worse off.

Mum continued to drive but scrapes and dents began to appear on her Corolla, and she was losing her bearings. Returning home from my house one evening, she ended up at a petrol station asking for directions. On another occasion she got lost coming to meet me for coffee. Fortunately, she had the insight to pull over at a children's playground and ask one of the parents to call me. My awareness of the significance of these lapses grew after reading of three high-profile cases in which elderly people had driven off, got lost and been found dead.[8] I started to investigate GPS tracking devices, and in the meantime lavishly praised Mum for limiting her own driving to the local shops and offered to drive her if she had to go further afield.

Mum began to find socializing difficult. She was losing her hearing and could not follow the thread of conversations. Always an active listener, the concentration involved in listening intently to people was becoming too much. Gradually she withdrew, and she could go for days without seeing anyone. She became suspicious of people, and rang me one day in a panic because a strange man had tried to come into her house. It turned out to be an old acquaintance who had shown up unexpectedly. Mum had not recognized him. She became convinced money had gone missing from her account. Even though this thought agitated her so much that she went to the bank frequently to request a statement of her transactions, she refused to allow me to raise the matter with the bank manager. This prompted me to begin to regularly check the mail to make sure correspondence was being attended to, and that insurances, memberships and term deposits were renewed. I convinced Mum to list me as an inquiry person at Centrelink, after they sent several letters threatening adjustments to her pension for failing to supply details of a small annuity. At around the same time, her doctor rang me and suggested that it might be a good idea if someone accompanied her to medical appointments. Mum was coming to see him frequently about the same issues, and he was not sure she was remembering what he was prescribing.

Systems of exclusion

By the time Mum went into residential care after her fall, she was stressed, angry and physically and emotionally vulnerable. She did not believe that she needed full-time care, and she was not the only one in denial. I was so resistant to the idea of putting her into aged care against her wishes – or even accepting that she had dementia – that I consulted three gerontologists. Of course Mum had a bit of memory loss, I reasoned, she was in her nineties, for goodness sake. The experts, though, were unanimous: my mother had dementia and the condition would get progressively worse. The advice was my sister or I could take Mum home but at some point we would have to provide 24/7 care. If we were unable to do so, then it would be better to place her into full-time care now so she could adapt.

My sister and I struggled with this decision. After I contemplated moving back to the family home to take care of Mum, we decided that this might not be ideal given I was working full time in a demanding and increasingly precarious job in the higher education sector. Moreover, it was unlikely a Commonwealth Home Care Package at the appropriate funding level was going to be forthcoming anytime soon. If it was approved, it could take up to eighteen months to activate and we would need to figure out how to manage in the interim. And even if the highest level of package was approved, it would be insufficient to provide for full-time home care. My sister, who had been trying for years to get Mum to come and stay with her, finally conceded that it was no longer possible. In the small country town where she lived, there was minimal to no support for aging Australians. Reluctantly, we agreed that full-time care was our only option.

We had seen the news reports of abuse and violence in aged care, and we resolved that this was not going to happen to our mother. She was going to have the best we could manage. My sister and I attended an aged-care expo in the hope of efficiently navigating what looked like a complex process, but we were overwhelmed by choices. We discovered a huge diversity of facilities: independent living, hostels, not-for-profit and for-profit residential-care facilities. We inspected several homes to get an idea of what was available, and engaged a consultant to obtain further background information around the past performance of specific facilities, and to offer insights into board priorities, management stability and looming industry issues likely to impact upon residential care. We marvelled at the furnishings of some of the newer homes that were like high-end hotels, and compared them to the much older and more dilapidated and affordable institutions. We debated the value of luxury accommodation. As a child of the Depression whose life had been profoundly shaped by frugality, Mum had always been uncomfortable with ostentatious displays of wealth. Yet it was these more lavish places that seemed to offer the best range of services and high levels of care and comfort.

As financing the shift to aged care was complicated, we hired a financial advisor. We carefully scrutinized fee structures, which included either a lump-sum room cost option or a daily room rent; a basic daily fee; an income-tested government fee; and for the for-profit homes club fees that in some places were in excess of $45 a day. The latter covered items like subscription TV services, a choice of meals at every sitting and access to a hairdresser and manicurist once a month. While these all sounded like lovely amenities, I was not sure Mum, who could not remember how to turn on a television, and who had historically gone for the budget haircut, would appreciate them.

In our research we learned that putting a loved one into care did not necessarily reduce their vulnerability. Certainly, in care Mum was less likely to fall, or to burn the house down by leaving the stove on, or to scald herself with hot water, or misapply medication. She was less likely to be susceptible to phone scammers or predatory tradespeople, or get lost driving to the shops. However, the residential-care system exposes individuals to a whole range of other risks. Indeed, this was one of the primary reasons for the 2021 Royal Commission into Aged Care Quality and Safety, which concluded that aged care in Australia systematically fails to meet the needs of the elderly, and it is often unkind, uncaring and neglectful of them. The Commission's dire assessment was that the system had become a 'signifier for loss, abandonment and fear'.[9] We sought to understand not only what would keep Mum physically safe from abuse, neglect and ill-treatment but also what conditions optimized the quality of life for a person with dementia in residential care. What could be done to preserve cognition? How could we give someone as physically mobile and intellectually alert as my mother a sense of purpose, meaning and wellbeing even as her memory slowly failed her? She had lived a life of hard work and service to others, and being useful was fundamental to her identity. Who would she be when she needed care herself?

One of the most critical variables for longevity and survival in aged care is frequency of family visits, which in Butler's terms can be understood as attachment: a social bond vital to survival.[10] On this basis we settled on a for-profit place twelve minutes from my home and open to visitors 24/7 with round-the-clock medical care. Mum would be a part of the general population, which would help preserve her cognition, but there was also a dementia wing depending upon how her illness advanced. The home had a varied activity programme, and my sister and I especially liked that there were visits from school children and a pet programme – at least these had been in place before COVID-19. We moved Mum into her second-floor room with ensuite bathroom overlooking the church next door with its solar panels arranged in a cross. To make the room more familiar and homely, we brought in some of her treasured knick-knacks and created a memory box.

Initially, Mum was very reluctant to be involved in the life of the residential-care community. She objected to the regular feedings across the day, derisively telling me that she felt like a battery-fed chook, and she thought the chair exercises were a waste of time. She was disinterested in the activities programme and she missed her car, her cat and her garden. As an able-bodied and still physically healthy woman, she did not identify with the other residents, many of whom had mobility issues but little sign of dementia. Take me home with you, she would beg. I want to be where you are. By then, the doctors had made it clear that she would be unsafe living with me, and we had already sold her home to cover the expenses of care. There was no going back; not for anyone.

Grieve-ability

Butler's 'reimagining [of] the possibility of community on the basis of vulnerability and loss' was linked to her interest in how 9/11 authorized 'limitless aggression against targets that may or may not be related to the sources of one's own suffering'.[11] Her interrogation of the United States' response became connected to the idea of humanness, and the ways in which lives are constituted within social relations and discourses of power. This is political, she insists, because it determines who is human. Butler explained that even as some lives are valorized as a process of nation-building, others are dehumanized in order to validate the violence done unto them. This dehumanization is achieved not only by the removal of the structures that provide the necessary physical support and social networks for survival, but also the production of discourses that frame some lives as ungrieve-able and therefore outside of humanity. The absence of narratives that foster 'norms of recognition' and identify the grounds upon which a life becomes human and grieve-able are barriers, she argued, to political inclusion, obscuring our 'fundamental dependency and ethical responsibility' to each other.[12]

The experience of putting my mother into care laid bare these barriers. A 2020 survey of community attitudes towards the elderly showed that 90 per cent of Australians believe that the elderly have value to society and that society has an obligation to care for them.[13] Despite this, the elderly continue to be perceived as 'ill, mentally slower, forgetful, bothersome, … unproductive', and 'more of a burden than a benefit'.[14] These negative representations contribute to the discriminatory practices and institutionalized ageism that infects the funding, management and regulation of aged care. Depicting the elderly as frail and a danger to themselves justifies their institutionalization and the removal of their independence and agency. This isolation masks both their suffering and diminishing social and economic networks from the public gaze and reduces the shared public narratives that Butler contends cultivates the norms of recognition necessary to renegotiate our social ties. Viewing elderly Australians as a cost in neoliberal discourses also legitimates their exploitation. The abuses identified by the 2021 Royal Commission can, in part, be traced back to the passage of the Australian government's 1997 Aged Care Act, which imposed market logic on care of the elderly. The government at the time claimed that opening up the aged-care industry to private-sector competition and market forces would lead to greater choice for consumers, improve standards of care and generate the capital necessary to repair rundown facilities. Instead, the effect of this legislation has been to increase the cost of aged care, as well as create the enabling conditions for elder abuse and neglect through the reduction in workers and the replacement of medically trained staff with unskilled casual labour.[15]

The importance of skilled staff in reducing the precariousness of seniors cannot be overstated. The Royal Commission made this point, as have other industry reports. Yet, medically trained employees in this sector earn 30 per cent less than their counterparts in hospitals, and carers in aged care earn 25 per cent less than those in the disability sector.[16] This pay gap makes it difficult to attract and retain skilled staff and to ensure the safety of elderly Australians in care. These deficiencies have been made more visible by the pandemic, which has revealed the extent to which the industry relies on casualized labour and the instability of working conditions. These workers take shifts across multiple homes in order to generate a liveable income. Often earning less than supermarket checkout operators, they are a part of a group described as the 'working poor'.[17] Those from culturally and linguistically diverse backgrounds, part-time workers, women and the unskilled are disproportionately represented in this population, and are generally overworked and prone to exploitation by nursing-home employers.[18]

The lower salaries, inadequate training and job insecurity of aged-care workers have a direct impact on residents' continuity of care, which is crucial to the long-term survival of residents in the last stages of life. Continuity of care is the integration of carers, medical staff, families and administrators into a network of people who have regular contact with the resident and who share information in order to monitor, manage and optimize their health outcomes.[19] Nevertheless, this form of integrated and consistent care is impossible to deliver with a large, constantly changing, variably trained and mobile workforce subject to the demands of the marketplace. These employees often do not have the time or opportunity to build relationships with residents and permanent staff, and they may lack the knowledge and skills to provide for high-needs patients like dementia sufferers who require constant care and extreme patience. As a result, the precarious employment conditions of the aged-care workers amplify the precariousness of the elderly; both are mistreated by economic systems and an already overloaded and precarious ambulance service is often called upon to intervene.

The importance of continuity of care was made apparent to me when Mum was in transition care; where I discovered the little things, if left unattended, could be fatal. The nursing staff, despite being advised multiple times that Mum had not had her flu shot, failed to give her one. She contracted influenza and was required to isolate in her room for a week. At a time when she was confused and distressed, she was left alone; this had a significant impact on her wellbeing. In the same facility, information about Mum's care was routinely not passed onto other staff, medications were mislaid or not dispensed and there were insufficient staff to work intensively with Mum on the rehabilitation of her broken leg.

By the time we came to select Mum's new home, quality and quantity of staff was top of our list. The carers at my mother's residential home seem to be affectionate and caring, and she often tells me that she feels safe and well cared for. Yet, even in this very comfortable home with its 24/7 roster, there are not enough staff to administer the level of individualized care many residents need, such as making sure they have their hearing aids in, or their dentures cleaned, or getting particular types of medication. While these are minor things to the able-bodied and cognitively unimpaired, they can have major impacts on the resident's quality of life. If a resident cannot hear, they can become socially alienated from others. Fragile skin can develop life-threatening sores and abrasions if a resident does not remember to regularly moisturize. An undiagnosed urinary tract infection can cause delirium-like symptoms that can be mistaken for dementia, and an inability to access a toilet in a prompt manner can cause incontinence. Further, residential aged care is the sequestering together of people from all walks of life and backgrounds and medical conditions, so a lack of social integration support can lead to bullying, aggression and the marginalization of some residents.

Invisibility

Standards of aged care have been publicly debated in Australia for the last four decades, with failings in the sector highlighted in a government-commissioned report in 1982.[20] Despite the identification of significant issues and recommendations for reform, people in aged care remain vulnerable. The Royal

Commission findings show that many in aged care have their human rights, dignity, agency and identity ignored, and they do not have a full life.[21] The effort at privatization has failed to uniformly improve standards across the sector. While there has been a growth in for-profit providers, the Commonwealth Aged Care Financing Authority noted that more than 40 per cent of aged-care providers recorded a loss in 2017/2018.[22] That same year, the whole sector recorded a profit margin of just 2.4 per cent.[23] The labour-intensive nature of care work and the medical costs associated with extreme old age means that care of the aged is expensive. For-profit providers, therefore, must find additional ways to generate revenue. In my mother's case this is done through club fees. She is charged for Foxtel (even though she cannot remember how to turn on the television), a glass of wine at a Friday sundowner (even though she does not drink alcohol), a choice of meals (even though she does not like the food), a haircut once a month (even though she does not remember to make a monthly appointment) and access to an aromatherapist (even though Mum does not want a stranger touching her body). Residents' dementia or cognitive decline means that it can be difficult for families to even know if their relatives are using these services. The elderly are often in no condition to engage in either the competition of the free-market economy themselves and move to another home if they are dissatisfied with their care, or to complain that they are paying for services they are not receiving. There is an option for families to re-negotiate club fees during quarterly reviews but often variations to these service fees require clinical assessment by the very organization that profits from the services.

The ongoing tolerance of institutionalized abuse and neglect of the elderly forces us to confront how public discourse renders them not only unseen but also 'unrecognizable'. Driven by distraught families, there is sporadic public outrage at media reports of individual cases, but there continues to be little political will to engage in systematic reform. Part of this can be attributed to history where, in the past, care of the elderly was considered a private family matter and was predominantly women's work, and, therefore, largely invisible, poorly paid and of low status. Part of it is a reflection of the reduced public support for care and other social services in neoliberal governments. However, the dearth of action is also a result of bias and conditioned cultural responses that 'establishes the limits of human intelligibility' of the aged.[24] Those who live in ways unintelligible to others are unmarked, unknowable and unreal. Butler calls this the 'violence of derealization', whereby some lives are 'neither alive nor dead, but interminably spectral'.[25] The fragmented and complex economic and institutional arrangements make aged care largely incomprehensible to those who are not directly impacted by the experience of placing a family member into care. Anxieties around aging and prevailing ageist attitudes also lead to ignorance about the complexity of the aging process and a misreading of the cues that signal the phases of human decline and which require preparation, intervention and advance planning.

Perhaps the single largest factor that renders the aged unintelligible to the general population is dementia, a disease that affects reasoning, memory and impulse control, and in its severe forms can render a sufferer violent and incoherent. Since reasoning and logical thinking are regarded as central to an individual's independence, economic and social success, safety and survival, the onset of dementia is feared by both the elderly and the community as it is seen as a marker of deterioration, weakness and proximity to death.[26] Research into what it is like for those affected with dementia and who are aware of their memory loss and growing vulnerability tells a story of conscious and exhausting efforts to compensate for declining cognition and to avoid making mistakes.[27] Participants in one study reported 'being on edge', panicked and ashamed when they cannot remember something, and described obsessively checking calendars and watches and writing notes. 'I don't remember where I put [the notes]', one participant disclosed, 'and so I have a hard time going back and finding them.'[28]

Conclusion

My mother's abrupt move into residential care forced a confrontation with the precariousness that accompanies old age, failing health and dementia. It revealed how social relations, cultural norms, political discourses and institutional systems and practices create differentiated power effects on the aged, exacerbating their marginalization and vulnerability. Indeed, this vulnerability is evident in the widespread depression reported in aged-care homes and the fact that the average length of stay for permanent residents in care is just under two years (nearly twenty-three months) before death.[29] The lives of the elderly are largely invisible and unintelligible to the public, and expose the need for 'new cultural narratives' that normalize the vulnerability of late old age.[30]

My mother's journey also served to illustrate Butler's theorization of precariousness as an opportunity to reflect upon human interdependency. As humans are always constituted within social relations, the act of perceiving another's vulnerability dislocates us from our individual subject position, and 'allows us to see that community itself requires the recognition that we are all, in different ways, striving for recognition'.[31] This acknowledgement is a 'reciprocal exchange' that shifts us from dependency to interdependency, reworking the bonds that link us and renegotiating ideas of equity.[32] My mother's experience has made visible the fact that care of the aged relies on workers, who face their own precarious conditions, and on family networks that may be waning, damaged or non-existent. The paradox of residential care is that even as it physically separates the elderly from their homes, families and communities and can serve as the site for abuse and exploitation, it also exposes our interdependency on others in later life. I have witnessed on many occasions how the extreme vulnerability of the aged has prompted in care workers what philosopher Michel Foucault describes as an ethical self-fashioning. This is a process by which people choose who they will be in the world in relation to others in spite of the systems and structures that control and exploit them.[33] Thus, even as aged-care workers are underpaid and overworked, they can also become strongly attached to residents and often strive within their limitations to provide the intensive and nurturing care so necessary to a liveable life.

Notes

1   Judith Butler, 'Precarious life, vulnerability, and the ethics of cohabitation', *Journal of Speculative Philosophy* 26, no. 2 (2012): 148.

2   Judith Butler, 'Performativity, precarity and sexual politics', *Revista de Antropología Iberoamericana* 4, no. 3 (2009): ii, iii.

3   Butler, 'Performativity', ii.

4   Hannah Swift and Ben Steeden, 'Exploring representations of old age and ageing: literature review' (London: Centre for Ageing Better, 2020), 31.

5   See Jocelyn Angus and Patricia Reeve, 'Ageism: a threat to "aging well" in the 21st century', *The Journal of Applied Gerontology* 25, no. 2 (2006): 137–52.

6   It is anticipated that by 2058 there will be more than 1.5 million people in Australia aged over 85 who will require support. Royal Commission into Aged Care Quality and Safety, 'Final Report – Volume 1: Summary and Recommendations', Commonwealth of Australia (report) (1 March 2021), 24, https://agedcare. royalcommission.gov.au/publications/final-report-volume-1.

7   Shane Wright, 'Debt, deficit and grey haired: COVID-19 upends economic future', *The Sydney Morning Herald* (27 June 2021), https://www.smh.com.au/politics/ federal/debt-deficit-and-grey-haired-covid-19-upends-economic-future-20210627-p584n3.html.

8   These were the tragic deaths of David Hall (79) in 2021, and Ian Collet (65) and Alexander Henderson (87) both in 2018.

9 Royal Commission into Aged Care Quality and Safety, 'Interim Report: Neglect', Commonwealth of Australia (report) (31 October 2019), 118, https://agedcare. royalcommission.gov.au/publications/interim-report.

10 Judith Butler, 'Violence, mourning, politics', *Studies in Gender and Sexuality* 4, no. 1 (2003): 32.

11 Judith Butler, *Precarious Life: The Powers of Mourning and Violence* (London: Verso, 2004), 20, 4.

12 Butler, *Precarious Life*, 43, 22.

13 Royal Commission into Aged Care Quality and Safety, 'What Australians think of ageing and aged care: research paper 4', Commonwealth of Australia (paper) (13 July 2020), 2, https://agedcare.royalcommission.gov.au/publications/research-paper-4-what-australians-think-ageing-and-aged-care.

14 Xue Bai, 'Images of ageing in society: a literature review', *Journal of Population Ageing* 7, no. 3 (2014): 238; Swift and Steeden, 'Representations', 31.

15 K-lynn Smith, 'Why greater private sector participation has not improved aged care performance', *Health System Sustainability* (28 October 2021), https:// healthsystemsustainability.com.au/why-greater-private-sector-participation-has-not-improved-aged-care-performance/.

16 'The future of aged care', *Amana Living* (28 May 2021), https://www.amanaliving. com.au/about-us/news-and-events/the-future-of-aged-care.

17 Lisa Alcock cited in Robert Fedele, 'Aged care workers underpaid, undervalued and short-staffed, Royal Commission told', *Australian Nursing and Midwifery Journal* (16 October 2019), https://anmj.org.au/aged-care-workers-underpaid-undervalued-and-short-staffed-royal-commission-told/.

18 Department of Health, Australian Government, '2020 Aged Care Workforce Census Report' (2 September 2021), 15, 17, 19, https://www.health.gov.au/ resources/publications/2020-aged-care-workforce-census.

19 Benjamin Long, 'Collaboration and continuity key to good medical support in aged care', University of Wollongong Australia (news) (15 April 2021), https://www.uow. edu.au/media/2021/collaboration-and-continuity-key-to-good-medical-support-in-aged-care.php.

20 Pauline Savy and Suzanne Hodgkin, 'Australian rural community aged care services: precarity and capacity', *Australian Journal of Public Administration* 80, no. 2 (2021): 324.

21 Royal Commission into Aged Care, 'Interim Report', 12.

22 Sarah Martin, 'Australia's aged care sector may not be financially sustainable, Senate committee hears', *The Guardian* (23 October 2019), https://www.theguardian.com/ australia-news/2019/oct/23/australias-aged-care-sector-may-not-be-financially-sustainable-senate-committee-hears.

23 Royal Commission into Aged Care Quality and Safety, 'Report on the profitability and viability of the Australian aged care industry: research paper

12', Commonwealth of Australia (paper) (9 September 2020), 3, https://agedcare.royalcommission.gov.au/publications/research-paper-12-report-profitability-and-viability-australian-aged-care-industry.

24 Butler, *Precarious Life*, 35.

25 Butler, *Precarious Life*, 33–34.

26 Amanda Grenier, Liz Lloyd and Chris Phillipson, 'Precarity in late life: rethinking dementia as a "frailed" old age', in *Ageing, Dementia and the Social Mind*, 2nd edition, eds. Paul Higgs and Chris Gilleard (Hoboken, NJ: Wiley-Blackwell, 2017), 143, 144.

27 See Elena Portacolone, Robert Rubinstein, Kenneth Covinsky, Jodi Halpern and Julene Johnson, 'The precarity of older adults living alone with cognitive impairment', *The Gerontologist* 59, no. 2 (2019): 271–80.

28 Portacolone et al., 'Cognitive impairment', 275.

29 Australian Institute of Health and Welfare, Australian Government, 'People leaving aged care' (last modified 22 June 2021), https://www.gen-agedcaredata.gov.au/Topics/People-leaving-aged-care.

30 Chris Phillipson cited in Grenier, Lloyd and Phillipson, 'Rethinking dementia', 151.

31 Butler, *Precarious Life*, 44.

32 Butler, *Precarious Life*, 44.

33 Michel Foucault argued for a critical ontology of the self in which the individual subject, through an awareness of the structures and discourses that control and limits them, can be free by choosing who they will be in relation to others. Michel Foucault, *Ethics, Subjectivity and Truth: Essential Works of Foucault 1954–1984*, ed. Paul Rabinow, trans. Robert Hurley (New York: New Press, 1997).

The Precarious Lives of Slavery Survivors

Alicia Rana and Kevin Bales

There can be few examples of a precarious life more severe and vulnerable than the lived experience of enslavement – violence, inflicted disability, physical and sexual assault, starvation, torture; any of these can occur at any time. Some forty million people live in slavery today, many in hereditary forms of slavery, with the total control of women in slavery greater than the total control of men. This occurs when the control of women in slavery extends beyond their exterior (for work and other uses) to their interior bodily functions (for sexual exploitation, forced impregnation and the theft of organs).[1] With liberation, the vulnerability and precarity of the enslaved does not end, it simply changes. Freedom from slavery should mean the beginning of safety and stability, but consistently that is not the case across all societies and cultures.

Even in the richest countries with mandated social services, those freed from slavery are often treated as criminals or are required to prove they have been victims of a crime in ways that are rarely expected of a victim of any other violent crime. The theft of years of work and earnings which enslavement entails is not met with an opportunity for restitution, and a lack of protection in freedom can also lead to re-trafficking and re-enslavement. This precarious state is exacerbated by a public perception of survivors of slavery as pathetic victims who should be grateful for the help they are given. Arguably, this support is often designed to meet the emotional and egoistic needs of the public rather than the real needs of survivors.

The antidote to this hubris is to listen to the deep knowledge of slavery survivors. In this chapter we call on the voice and recollections of a survivor of trafficking and slavery in the UK who has given us extensive access to her lived experience both in and out of modern slavery. She is in every way the third author, but for a number of reasons chooses not to be identified. We will denote the specific voice of this key informant through quotations that are set in *italics*. At the same time, the reader should not assume that her only contributions are those quoted in that way. Her deep knowledge of precarity informed the structure, content and conclusions of this chapter. In this chapter, we illuminate the clear patterns and specific problems that create the precarious realities lived by survivors of slavery in the UK, a country that is, by any measure, not the worst place to be a survivor. With the help of the first-hand accounts of our slavery survivor collaborator, we delineate how achieving freedom does not necessarily lead to security, but rather a transition to another, albeit legal and largely unrecognized, precarious life. We hope to demonstrate that understanding the ongoing precarious lived experience of survivors post-freedom is crucial if meaningful change is to occur and full freedom is to be achieved.

The extent and shape of slavery today

Consider this thought experiment: imagine a country where people frequently kill each other but the crime of murder has neither a clear definition in the law nor in the public mind. Homicide has played a pivotal role in the long history of this country, not least in the succession of rulers, but when the word 'murder' comes up in conversation, the response is likely to be 'but what do you *mean* by "murder"?' Even for those with a special interest in the subject – policymakers, police, relatives of victims, the media – the disparate definitions of 'murder' in circulation are contested and are often linked with political or ideological positions. For social scientists, attempts to operationalize the concept immediately spark controversy in the academic literature, the blogosphere and public fora. Poets, novelists and screenplay writers feed on this rich ambiguity to produce works of mystery within mystery – works that both explore and increase the conceptual confusion. In this imagined country there is no sound knowledge of how many people are being murdered, or whether the police are catching murderers. As the definition of the crime is so unclear, there is uncertainty as to what, exactly, is to be counted and acted against. Murder, in this country, defies normal criminological techniques for its measurement. Neither its incidence in reports and arrests, nor the number of cases which never come to light (the 'dark figure') can be calculated or reliably estimated.

Now replace the word 'murder' with another serious and violent crime – enslavement. Returning to the real world, the vignette above now describes the current situation in most developed countries. While the Netherlands, Australia, the UK, Norway and Canada have all begun a process of defining and addressing slavery within their borders, there continues to be a significant lack of consensus about what constitutes the fundamental nature of this crime as well as how to address the after-effects on its survivors. This conceptual confusion is a global problem. According to Andrea Nicholson, Minh Dang and Zoe Trodd, there are at least four competing definitions within the United Nations system alone, a competition that has impeded international cooperation and contributed to a haphazard response in meeting the needs of those who have been enslaved.[2] Likewise, as shown by the Antislavery in Domestic Legislation database, 94 countries (49 per cent of UN member states) appear not to have criminal legislation prohibiting slavery or the slave trade, and a further 170 countries (88 per cent of UN member states) appear not to have criminalized the four institutions and practices listed as similar to slavery in UN instruments.[3] However, two key facts that we do know about contemporary slavery, which have been made clear by survivors, are that, firstly, living precariously is often a gateway to enslavement, and, secondly, that once having been enslaved, if the survivor comes to freedom, precarious living is the most likely outcome.

According to the conservative estimate by the Global Slavery Index 2016, there are 40.3 million people in slavery worldwide.[4] The enslaved are not distributed evenly but at varying densities across virtually all countries. The countries with the highest prevalence of slavery are those that are marked by several interlocking factors that create precarity: extreme poverty (such as India, Central African Republic), conflict and war (for example, Democratic Republic of Congo, Syria, Iraq), environmental destruction and related climate catastrophes (recently, Bangladesh, Haiti), life-threatening beliefs and practices that denigrate and subjugate women (Afghanistan, Yemen) or religious/cultural systems that separate and 'other' sub-populations classifying them as sub-human and thus eligible for enslavement and exploitation (USA, Japan, Thailand, Mauritania, South Sudan).[5] Perhaps the most ubiquitous and powerful predictor of the prevalence across all countries is the level of corruption that country suffers. While enslavement is still not specifically illegal in many countries, it flourishes when the rule of law breaks down.

One of the realities that confuses the popular understanding of enslavement is that this crime takes many different forms; historically this has always been the case. Across the centuries the manifestations of slavery have reflected variations in the cultural, economic, technological and political systems within which they emerged. While those living in western cultures tend to hold in their minds one particular image of slavery – that practised during the period of the trans-Atlantic slavery trade – many other forms existed at that time. The same is true today. There are several forms of hereditary slavery in contemporary societies, as well as different types of 'debt' bondage. There is enslavement within war, including that of child soldiers and forced 'brides'. There are those enslaved into forced labour or commercial sexual exploitation through the procurement and transportation process known as 'human trafficking'. The practice of slavery has also always been based upon varying rationalizations and justifications on the part of slaveholders that extend beyond issues of race to include religion, ethnicity and gender, among others. Indeed, any form of social discrimination and 'othering', at its most extreme, might be taken to two ultimate outcomes: enslavement and/or murder (including genocide).[6]

The cross-cutting intersections that drive slavery are exemplified by the links between conflict, environmental destruction and global supply chains. In a context of conflict, a vicious cycle begins: the rule of law disappears and slavery, brutality and environmental destruction feed into each other. The weapons used to drive this cycle might be paid for by the riches torn from the forests or purchased with profits from the products we all buy. Refugees fleeing devastated environments that can no longer support them are caught up and enslaved, and then forced to carry out even more environmental destruction. It is a trade cycle based on armed conflict that grinds up the natural world and crushes human beings to churn out commodities that we enjoy, such as minerals used for electronics, shrimp and fish, gold, cotton and clothing, and iron and steel. When the focus and analysis of this slave-based trade cycle become global, certain surprising facts emerge.[7] Recent environmental treaties and regulations made vast forests around the equator off-limits to commercial logging but created a market vacuum quickly filled by criminal slaveholders.[8] This has led to a conservative estimate that just under half of all illegal deforestation in the world is slave-based.[9] If that is the case, then criminal slaveholders are responsible for 2.54 billion tons of CO_2 entering the atmosphere each year. Put another way, slaves are being forced to produce more greenhouse gases than any country in the world except China and the USA (the two largest polluters).[10]

Linking slavery to environmental destruction and climate change is just one way to illustrate the ways in which the forces that lead to precarious lives can be bundled together, and the ways in which these forces gather strength across rich and poor economies, drive refugees and unsafe migration, disrupt local communities and destabilize lives. All of these conditions and outcomes further increase vulnerabilities and precarity.

It is important to make clear the interconnectedness between factors that generate precarity and thus increase the likelihood of enslavement. For too long simplistic notions about causation have served to diminish the experiences of those enslaved. This has been especially the case with enslavement into commercial sexual exploitation. Not long ago the concept of 'sex trafficking' was seen as simply an extension of an inevitable market for prostitution. It was often accepted as a victimless pursuit of natural needs and 'entertainment'. 'Happy hookers' serviced men who assumed they were just enjoying a reasonable commercial exchange. Women and girls 'working' in this industry were at times considered unfortunate, but ultimately it was assumed that it was their choice to participate. In opposition to this view was another based on public morals which could also be damaging to those girls, boys, women, men and transgender people being exploited. Especially pervasive in religious groups, this viewpoint casts those in commercial sexual exploitation as damaged people, often hopeless, and certainly pathetic. The responses by anti-prostitution groups have often been to 'rescue' or 'save' the female 'victims' of commercial sexual exploitation. Unfortunately, this process of salvation often fails to address the underlying drivers and the specific needs of those who have been enslaved in commercial sexual exploitation.

Standing behind these common perceptions is a much larger set of pan-cultural suppositions that can be perceived in their invisibility and their expression. The enslavement of people, and especially of women, into commercial sexual exploitation is hidden by the fact that every culture, and the industries that profit economically from it, have a set of euphemisms for this exploitation that help to make it invisible – 'she's on the game', 'child prostitute', 'tart', 'call girl'. Virtually every culture has a religious justification for sexual exploitation – and if it is not official doctrine now, then there are still believers (in whatever faith in whichever place) that still hold to that tenet. Education and the socialization of children still continue to reinforce the concept of inferiority and subservience of women and girls, even in countries seen as progressive and championing equal rights, due to cultural norms regarding gender roles.[11] In most cultures and countries legal responses to sexual exploitation (including rape and enslavement) are thin, poorly enforced and grudgingly applied, resulting in a category of violent crime that has low levels of reporting, scarce official investigation, and rare trials and convictions. Lastly, the deep-seated concept of the proper constitution of a 'family' devalues and controls women – a state of being in which women are inevitably suppressed. This context creates a world in which commercial sexual exploitation of vulnerable people is ubiquitous, and for a significant proportion of those exploited this means enslavement.

The nature of being enslaved

It is crucial to emphasize that slavery is, first and foremost, a lived experience – not a legal definition, an analytical framework or a philosophical construct. 'At the moment it is occurring, slavery is first the experience of an individual person, and second a relationship between at least two people: the slave and the slaveholder', noted one commentator.[12] The cultural, political and social meanings associated with slavery are important to understand if we are to grasp the nature of the precarious lives that might precede and include enslavement. To be enslaved is to be diminished, reduced, deprived of rights and respect. Enslavement carries markers of what Orlando Patterson called 'social death' – referring to the slave's non-existence outside of their master and to their natal alienation – and is locked in a circular reinforcement of control and exploitation based on the attributes that render a person a target for enslavement, be they racial, ethnic, religious, political or centred on gender, gender identity, age and ultimately any form or expression of vulnerability.[13]

There has been a recent conceptual breakthrough in our understanding of the lived experience of slavery. This has been linked to the launch of the Survivor Alliance in 2018 (which shall be discussed in greater detail later in the chapter) and driven by the emergence of survivor scholars. The Survivor Alliance is an NGO established by, and run by and for, survivors of slavery. According to their website, they seek to be:

> the architects of connectivity. We build bridges between survivors and our own potential. We build bridges between survivors of different experiences and backgrounds. We are also building bridges, alongside our fellow survivors, between their lives immediately after enslavement and what the rest of their life can be. And with our allies, we build bridges that link the anti-slavery movement to survivors who want to contribute their lived experience expertise.[14]

The Survivor Alliance, and some scholars, are challenging the fact that virtually all of the histories of slavery, the laws and regulations that enable or proscribe slavery, and the guidelines for the aid and advocacy of those who have been enslaved, have been written by people who have never experienced slavery.

For the first time in human history, and within the current decade, survivors of slavery are systematically addressing and elucidating the nature of being enslaved. This development in advocacy work and academic scholarship has been crucial to demonstrating the complex state of being that occurs in enslavement whereby living, thinking and feeling are fundamentally different to that of a free person. Instead, the shock of extreme violence and the condition of total loss of control and free will require and shape very different psychological responses.[15] Primarily amongst these are what have become known as the states of *atemporality* and *aspatiality*. Both of these are responses to the immediate and intense trauma of violence. Pain focuses the mind into the present, so that the enslaved person learns that the avoidance of pain means existing within an eternal present. The slaveholder prefers the person they control to have no other memory or interest that might conflict with their obedience and use. For the enslaved person this means that thinking or acting in ways that link to the past (before slavery), or future (life post-slavery), will incur pain and punishment. The same dark logic applies to freedom of movement, where the consequence of any physical movement that is not ordered or required by the slaveholder is violence and suffering. In addition to enduring a state of atemporality, for their own protection the enslaved become aspatial, not just avoiding forbidden movement, but driving from their minds the possibility of mobility itself. Their world shrinks to the very small space of their confinement.

Enslaved, a person may be harmed or killed at any moment, may be fed or denied sustenance, locked away or set to work – the enslaved person has no control over any of these outcomes. While the word 'precarious' comes from a Latin root for 'to ask, entreat, pray for', in the seventeenth century it came to mean 'held through the favor of another'.[16] Slavery, however, is hardly granted by 'favour' for it involves a totality of control and denigration of an individual or group. It enacts an othering that separates the enslaved person from their rights and dignities, including the right to life. If there is a form of living that exists far beyond the level of uncertainty and vulnerability that might be described as precarious, it is slavery. Given the atemporality and aspatiality of enslavement, it might be best understood as a void, a nullity of self, in which precarity descends into annihilation. If there is a core experience of slavery, it is the constant state of uncertainty sustained at the personal level.

Areas of uncertainty

There are many areas of uncertainty that survivors encounter during and after they have been caught up in modern slavery. Personal insecurity is paramount, but some uncertainties are bureaucratic while others are cultural and conceptual.

Preconceived ideas about slaves and slavery, as well as assumptions about what it is like to live in freedom, can be key obstructions to recovery. For example, our key informant noted: '*there were many opportunities for the authorities to intervene during the ten years I was trafficked and exploited*'. This was, in large part, because she did not fit the stereotypical image of an 'ideal victim' which is widely understood to be a 'helpless' foreign woman who is abused by 'evil traffickers'. In the UK specifically, this might be someone already in the social care system or known to the authorities as being vulnerable. Our key informant is a British citizen, but was of the same immigrant ethnicity as her traffickers. While she came from an impoverished background, she was not in the care system at the time she was groomed and 'recruited'. We call on her experience to illustrate the uncertainties faced in the precarious life of a person within slavery and as a survivor. While we acknowledge the individual accounts of our informant, they express hardships undergone by many others who have been freed from slavery only to be thrust into new uncertainties.

In some ways our key informant was caught in a paradox. Not fitting the 'ideal victim' profile has damaged her chances of being detected since most people with whom she came into contact did not recognize that British citizens could be trafficked and enslaved as well as foreigners. She was often met with the supposition that trafficking and slavery 'does not happen here'. The police, time and time again, failed to understand why she did not speak out about being trafficked. Both police and social services shared a dangerous lack of insight into issues of honour and shame within her ethnicity and culture. Instead, she was labelled as a nuisance or a liar who took up their limited resources and time. The police often treated her as if she was the criminal, or a sex worker, rather than someone forced into commercial sexual exploitation. Once, when the police found her after she had been badly beaten and dumped naked in the street by her traffickers, they asked 'Are you a prostitute?' On another occasion, they used a warrant to search her home and made racist comments about the problems caused by 'people like you in the area'. It was, finally, a female police officer who believed her, having witnessed some of the slavery the informant had endured. This officer spoke up but was soon removed from the case and accused of becoming 'too attached'. Our informant explains:

> I am Southeast Asian, both my parents are not from the UK. My father comes from India, I come from a family who strongly believe in caste systems, and that if a woman is involved in sex trafficking she will become an untouchable or remain

unmarried. This officer and I had formed a rapport and good relationship, she noticed my bruises and on one occasion the traffickers had even called her to see whom I had been speaking with on my phone. The officer had worked with me for years and had seen the 'evidence', as well as the injuries, and she was there when they had pulled glass out of my wounds. However, she was told by her superiors that she was 'overinvolved' and 'unprofessional'. The officer understood issues of honour, shame and stigma in my ethnic community.

What is little understood, by both the public and many of the officials who encounter someone caught in slavery, is how enslavement can take place within what appears to be a 'normal' lifestyle and in public spaces, from hospitals and bus stations to construction sites and the seemingly banal domestic space.[17] Such unseen crimes are undetected, unadjudicated and go unpunished. As our informant stated:

Having adapted over time to a life of slavery, I was able to function on certain levels and appear 'normal' – such as finishing school and trying to work. Due to my ordeal over a prolonged period I was, however, psychologically scarred and in dire need of help with my trauma. Frustratingly, I did not fit the extensive criteria needed to gain access to mental health support: I was not suicidal. I had not been diagnosed with a mental health issue. Without these indicators, accessing appropriate mental health services in order to deal with my past has been impossible. In fact, I have never received any trauma counselling, despite my ten years of sex trafficking that started when I was a child.

In the case of human trafficking for sexual exploitation, it is commonly thought that when a victim has been identified and 'rescued', taken into a government or non-government organization (NGO) safe house, their freedom has now been achieved. However, being emancipated is a singular event while '(re)building a life in freedom' is a long journey.[18]

For the state, and some NGOs, 'rescue' statistics are celebrated. The term 'rescue' itself is used to indicate that captivity has ceased, shifting the discourse from one of victim to survivor. There is the reductive belief held by the public and most of those in law enforcement and social practice that at this point survivors are free to move rapidly toward independent lives. Conversely, our informant describes the survivor's ongoing precarious existence:

From my personal experience, when I was finally identified as a victim of trafficking it was merely the very start of a long process of achieving freedom with many obstacles still ahead. As a survivor, I have found myself the 'victim' of an ill-equipped health system and other services. This lack of understanding has made the process of freedom incredibly difficult and fraught with challenges that I have found, at times, impossible to navigate.

Exemplifying failure in the system is the UK government's National Referral Mechanism (NRM) which aims to identify and support victims of trafficking. Until very recently, the NRM allowed a 45-day period for 'rest and reflection' for victims upon rescue. In actuality, those 45 days are rarely restful or conducive to reflection as within that time all evidence must be marshalled into a case that verifies the victim's application for support and often to avoid deportation. The healing effects of counselling and physical and medical care are prohibited by the pressure of a ticking clock. This period is simultaneously used by the authorities to make a decision on whether a person has in reality been trafficked or enslaved. This dual usage – rest on one hand, official determination on the other – means there is no time for recovery or rest following the trauma of enslavement. Within this period the survivor is subjected to a series of queries and tests, each creating further levels of uncertainty, to determine whether they are able to prove their victimization. It has to be asked, how many other violent crimes require a person to carry the burden of proof that they are a victim? Within the British legal system it seems modern slavery is one of the few cases. As our informant describes:

After ten years of being raped for profit, being subjected to extreme violence and trauma, how can someone recover from their exploitation in such a short period of time? A person cannot even begin to unpick and 'heal' the wounds of their traumatic past and move on to lead an independent life in just 45 days. In my case, as a result of my trafficking experiences, I have needed multiple surgeries and extensive health care which is still ongoing several years after my rescue. This could not have been done within the 45 days I was given in a government NRM safe house. Many non-British survivors can wait several months for a conclusive grounds decision from the Home Office, during which time they can access support under the NRM system. For British survivors, however, this decision normally comes through very quickly and they are then required to move on after 45 days. When they are moved on, statutory support ceases and many survivors then find themselves in a situation where universal services [such as the National Health Service] are not equipped to meet their complex needs, to aid their recovery or to assist them to reintegrate into society. With a broken body and severe trauma after a magnitude of abuse, I was not ready to unpack years of slavery and exploitation in just six weeks. Once receiving my conclusive grounds decision [as to whether I was a victim of enslavement] it was, however, time for me to move on, despite there being nowhere for me to move on to. A lack of housing services available after the 45 days, coupled with the scarcity of services for survivors of trafficking, meant my support started and ended abruptly after my rescue.

Our informant eventually secured a place in one of the three post-NRM aftercare service facilities in the UK, all three of which are run by charities or churches. Due to inadequate resources and funding, however, the facility she entered was closed down while she was still a resident. Several of the other young women residents fell back into the hands of their traffickers at that time, abruptly ending ongoing treatment for drug addiction instigated by the traffickers.

The precarious nature of the provision of essential services to survivors of enslavement underlines the fact that despite the humanitarian efforts of local community or church-run projects, in the absence of professional oversight these endeavours can inadvertently become dangerous. For example, the volunteer workers at the shelter where our informant stayed, as well as the church that owned the facility, lacked the necessary training and preparedness to deal with the extensive trauma of enslavement and to work with survivors with complex needs. Overwhelmed, as our informant reported, the volunteers often suffered compassion fatigue and burnout, leaving even fewer staff available to support survivors. There are presently no formal policies on how to run post-NRM aftercare facilities, nor does the government provide either guidance or assistance to survivors after the NRM. Recent changes to policy, driven by questions of cost-effectiveness, may improve this situation, but as of the time of writing it is too soon to know. As we were completing edits on this chapter in 2021, we asked our key informant whether there had been any improvement in aftercare for survivors. Her response was unequivocal:

Improvements? No! I am yet to receive counselling and therapy, but for the past three years have been on waiting lists, or advised that I need to go private [medical services outside the National Health Service which require direct payment from the patient], the funds for this are beyond me. My current housing is sharing a house with other survivors who are working and I am still living there. There is one organization called Snow Drop that tries to support survivors post-NRM, but this is only if you are in Sheffield, a long way from where I live. Central government services do not have any guidance or tools to support survivors, and they are then caught in the conflict of each local authority. I am in [Southern England] and there are no support services post-NRM here. When I have attempted to get support, I have been told that I 'function well' (so don't need help) or that I am articulate enough to fill applications, so I do not fit any criteria. There is a lack of understanding about contextual risks, such as returning to an area where there are risks of ethnic or gang-related crimes linked to concepts of 'shaming' people. Even talking about this is dismissed by social services. Being Southeast Asian, at home we do not speak English, the police tried to speak to my family in English – without understanding issues of shame, honour or the fact that my experiences were seen to 'bring shame' or a 'curse', or that I was being 'punished for something that I did in my past life', and that I needed to be saved or 'cleansed by monks'. It is this lack of understanding in the white police system that I felt actually placed me at further risk as my local community perceived me as 'bad luck'. There were threats to marry me back home in a village or send me back to Asia for a cleansing ritual – but the police did not consider this.

What is evident from our informant's recounts is the government's failure in aiding this vulnerable population by passing this responsibility to other sectors.

As can be seen, once the 45-day period of testing and adjudication has passed, slavery survivors then face significant challenges as official support tapers off. If survivors are fortunate enough to be given post-NRM accommodation, they are rarely familiar with the town or city to which they have been moved. They are often placed in communal or shared housing – but sharing with men can be especially difficult for those women still recovering from the serial rape which is the hallmark of enslavement into sexual exploitation. Resources and opportunities for establishing independent lives are limited which hinders seeking and securing employment. Due to this instability and financial hardship, many return to, or are lured back to, their traffickers, while others become homeless. Our informant's experience, though precarious, seems fortunate by comparison. She explains:

I had qualifications, as do many other girls who are rescued from slavery, although for some their qualifications are not accredited in the UK. Despite my qualifications I faced significant hurdles trying to find employment. I had no references and there were gaps in my employment history. When I summoned up the courage to be transparent about my past, I was then seen as a liability due to the need for time off for continuing restorative surgery. There was also a common assumption from potential employers that because of my trafficking experiences I would not be able to function in the workplace. It also seemed to be the case that when I needed support, I would be accused of having a sense of entitlement.

In freedom our informant was approached by anti-slavery organizations and other charitable groups to share her story of being trafficked, and often asked to share the especially 'highly emotive' (sensationalist, heart-wrenching) aspects of her enslavement. In the media, and in the awareness-raising and fundraising materials produced by NGOs, attention focused on particular aspects of her case: underage sex, men of migrant ethnicity, or on the 'violence and evil' of slavery. Little or no recognition was given to her resilience, or her struggles in receiving the aftercare services necessary to her recovery. When those who support and work with survivors fail to listen to survivor viewpoints, they create a situation, however well-meaning, which is fundamentally exploitative. As our informant states:

> I have also discovered that those interviewing me have their own agenda and therefore I am unable, and unwilling, to speak freely. This approach also appears to be embedded in the current legal framework, where attention is focused on underage white victims and 'ethnic men'. Highly emotive stories are published in the media which shape society's understanding of trafficking and further feed into the stereotype of an 'ideal victim' – so much so that I believe many people have physically encountered a victim but do not recognize them as such. This bias leaves gaping holes in the reality of our understanding of trafficking and modern slavery – the idea of who is a victim and who are the men that are involved in sex trafficking.

It can be argued that the history of crimes linked to sexual assault, whether rape or enslavement into commercial sexual exploitation, has two key themes. The first is the long-term denial across many cultures that the crime even exists, namely that the use of physical assault and control for the sexual use of another person is a 'wrong' as opposed to the 'right' of husbands (as seen in the legality of marital rape in many countries) or of any man.[19] The second theme is the denial of normal rules of evidence and proof in cases of sexual assault. This can be seen by the widely held beliefs and assumption that attitude, intention and questions regarding the dress, character and demeanour of the victim constitute relevant factors in determining the guilt of the perpetrator that would never be applied to most felonies, thus shifting the onus of responsibility and the blame onto the victim.[20]

Moving forward – reducing precarity

If there is a clear path to improving the precarious, uncertain and insecure lives of slavery survivors, it leads to listening carefully to their voices, learning from their experiences (beyond accounts of trauma), and engaging them intentionally and systematically in policy, organizations and decision-making processes that impact them.[21] Throughout history, only a few survivors of slavery, such as Frederick Douglass or Harriet Tubman, were able to provide significant insight for anti-slavery efforts, and their legacy continues to do so through their writings and speeches. Today, survivors are creating institutionalized methods for sharing their knowledge and expertise. In 2018 a group of slavery survivors established the Survivor Alliance, an organization that unites and empowers survivors of slavery and human trafficking around the world.[22] Within the Alliance survivors are connected to each other through a secure online digital space. They work to ensure that survivor voices are central to anti-slavery planning and efforts, and they reinforce the development of local survivor networks while connecting existing networks to each other across regions, countries and globally. They are fostering the growth and expansion of survivor-led research in order to ensure that all theoretical, sociological and practitioner-based knowledge of slavery is not solely from the perspective of non-survivors.[23] The research conducted by survivor scholars has opened new vistas in understanding the lived experience of slavery, and survivor-led analysis of that lived experience has led to significant recommendations and improvements in policy and practice.[24] Our survivor/key informant for this chapter is an exemplar of this leadership.

Reducing the precarity faced by slavery survivors also requires fundamental changes in both the justice system and systems of social and medical support. To achieve this, the dearth of evidence-based, effective intervention models for the rehabilitation and reintegration of survivors must be addressed. This lack of evidence and guidance contributes to poor practice and an ill-informed knowledge base amongst NGOs and policymakers, which in turn results in unintended harm to survivors. In the UK, it is critical that post-NRM services be instituted, improved and provided by the government, and should include, at a minimum, financial assistance and accommodation for survivors, access to counselling, trauma therapy and help with securing employment. In many cases this would simply mean extending provisions for compensation, medical care and protection that already exist for victims of other crimes. These simple steps to stability will encourage a transition to survivors making their own way, exercising their own free will, calling on and building their own resilience, and making their own choices. Lives lived in that state of active freedom are crucial to the prevention of re-exploitation.

For reasons that are not legally or politically clear, unlike the victims of other crimes, survivors of slavery in the UK are placed into dramatically different categories of eligibility for support. Some survivors are not eligible to work while claiming asylum. If survivors have qualifications or skills not recognized in the UK, they find themselves in a cycle of unemployment. Survivors need places within further and higher education where they can access courses to gain relevant skills and work experience, currently not provided. It is noticeable that while some seventy UK universities offer scholarships to refugees and asylum seekers, there is no such provision for those who have been brought to the UK and enslaved – nor for those British citizens that have been enslaved.[25] Additionally, there are few prospects for survivors to seek work experience or to volunteer. Clearly, the National Referral Mechanism needs a radical reform as it is not consistent. It does not treat survivors of different nationalities, circumstances or geography equally. For example, a survivor with British citizenship may only remain in a government-provided safe place for 45 days, whereas a survivor from overseas awaiting their conclusive grounds decision may remain supported in a safe house for up to two years.

Finally, the physical and psychological methods used by criminals to coerce and control the enslaved are not well understood, leading to the frustrating question regularly asked by members of the public: 'why don't they just walk away?' This viewpoint is similar to that of the police and judiciary – one that doubts the veracity of survivor testimonies. When crime victims are regularly disbelieved, they fall silent, and when victims cannot be heard, the result is low conviction rates.[26] This demands urgent and critical attention if perpetrators are to be brought to justice.

Within the broader culture, a more nuanced and empathetic understanding of the precarious lives of slavery survivors, during and after enslavement, requires a shift away from the set of misconceptions that survivors are pathetic victims, are illegal migrants, are tainted by their victimhood, have no useful or commercial skills, or are too traumatized to work. Many survivors do, in fact, have the skills and resilience that will help them thrive in a workplace if they can overcome the belittling barriers and assumptions they confront. And for those survivors who do need counselling, surgery or other healthcare, there should be open access to these essential services. To provide these normal levels of support to those who have been enslaved presents no great economic cost, their numbers are few, and the more rapid their recovery, the more likely they are to be active and productive members of society.

For further information, see:

https://www.nottingham.ac.uk/research/beacons-of-excellence/

Notes

1   Kevin Bales and Jody Sarich, 'The paradox of women, children, and slavery', in *Trafficking in Slavery's Wake: Law and the Experience of Women and Children in Africa*, eds. Benjamin N. Lawrance and Richard L. Roberts (Ohio: Ohio University Press, 2012), 241–53.

2 Andrea Nicholson, Minh Dang and Zoe Trodd, 'A full freedom: contemporary survivors' definitions of slavery', *Human Rights Law Review* 18, no. 4 (2018): 689–704.

3 Katarina Schwarz and Jean Allain, *Antislavery in Domestic Legislation: An Empirical Analysis of National Prohibition Globally* (Nottingham: University of Nottingham, 2020), 11, https://antislaverylaw.ac.uk/resources/summary-of-findings/.

4 Global Slavery Index, 'Global slavery index, 2016', *Walk Free Foundation* (2018), 2, https://www.globalslaveryindex.org/.

5 This is, of course, a very partial list. The fundamental power of sexism and the cultural legitimation of the oppression of women provide a sound foundation for suppressing the human rights of women and girls and can be found in all countries.

6 See, for example, the interlinking of slavery and genocide in the establishment of the ISIS 'Caliphate' in Northern Iraq, detailed by Nadia Al-Dayel, Andrew Mumford and Kevin Bales, 'Not yet dead: the establishment and regulation of slavery by the Islamic State', *Studies in Conflict and Terrorism* 45, no. 11 (2020): 929–52, https://doi.org/10.1080/1057610X.2020.1711590.

7 Kevin Bales, *Blood and Earth: Modern Slavery, Ecocide, and the Secret to Saving the World* (New York: Spiegel and Grau, 2016), 98.

8 Bales, *Blood and Earth*, 110.

9 Bales, *Blood and Earth*, 114.

10 Bales, *Blood and Earth*, 115.

11 Kevin Bales, 'The social psychology of modern slavery', *Scientific American* 286, no. 4 (2002): 86–87.

12 Kevin Bales, 'Unlocking the statistics of slavery', *Chance (Journal of the American Statistical Association): The Best of Chance* 32, no. 1 (2019): 23.

13 Orlando Patterson, *Slavery and Social Death: A Comparative Study* (Cambridge, MA: Harvard University Press, 1982), 38.

14 Minh Dang, 'Strategic priorities 2021–2023', *Survivor Alliance* (n.d.), https://www.survivoralliance.org/about.

15 Minh Dang, 'The paradox of survivor leadership', in *Wicked Problems: The Ethics of Action for Peace, Rights, and Justice*, eds. Austin Choi-Fitzpatrick, Douglas Irvin-Erickson and Ernesto Verdeja (Oxford: Oxford University Press, 2022), 68.

16 OED, 'precarious (adj.)', (2001–2022), https://www.etymonline.com/search?q=precarious.

17 See, for example, Kevin Bales and Ron Soodalter's discussion on 'Looking for victims' in *The Slave Next Door: Human Trafficking and Slavery in America Today* (Berkeley, CA: University of California Press, 2009), 255–58.

18 Minh Dang, 'Survivors are speaking. Are we listening?', *Walk Free Foundation* (2018), https://www.globalslaveryindex.org/resources/essays/survivors-are-speaking-are-we-listening.

19 Bales and Sarich, 'Paradox', 241–43.

20 Rebecca Hayes, Katherine Lorenz and Kristin Bell, 'Victim blaming others: rape myth acceptance and the just world belief', *Feminist Criminology* 8, no. 3 (2013): 206–207.

21 Sue Lockyer, 'Beyond inclusion: survivor-leader voice in anti-human trafficking organizations', *Journal of Human Trafficking* 8, no. 2 (2020): 135–56.

22 The Survivor Alliance homepage can be found at https://survivoralliance.org/.

23 Minh Dang, 'Confronting the paradoxes of higher education', in *Building the Field of Higher Education Engagement: Foundational Ideas and Future Directions*, eds. Lorilee Sandmann and Diann Jones (Sterling, VA: Stylus Publishing, 2019), 232–34.

24 See Minh Dang, Monica Anderson, Kimberly Forbess, Ummra Hang, Catie Hart, Amy Rahe, Celia Roberts, Genèvieve Tiangco and alix lutnick, 'Achieving health in freedom: what are we aiming for?', paper presented at the Institute of Mental Health, Nottingham, UK (March 2018); Minh Dang, Ummra Hang and alix lutnick, 'Forging partnerships between the researcher and the researched: a community based anti-trafficking response', paper presented at Society of Social Work and Research Conference, Washington, DC (January 2018).

25 According to the centralized UK Universities and Colleges Admissions Service, there are more than seventy universities and colleges offering places to refugees and asylum seekers. UCAS, 'UK university scholarships for refugees and asylum seekers' (blog post) (last modified 28 June 2021), https://www.ucas.com/connect/blogs/uk-university-scholarships-refugees-and-asylum-seekers.

26 There is a broad literature on the failures of, and barriers to, prosecution in cases of sexual violence, which can include those linked to human trafficking. See Kim Thuy Seelinger, Helene Silverberg and Robin Mejia, *The Investigation and Prosecution of Sexual Violence: A Working Paper of the Sexual Violence and Accountability Project* (Berkeley, CA: University of California, Berkeley, 2011), https://www.usip.org/sites/default/files/missing-peace/seelinger-the-investigation.pdf.

216 Westbound: A Topography of Latent Fear

Shona Illingworth, John Tulloch and Caterina Albano

Shona Illingworth's film *216 Westbound* (2014),[1] made in collaboration with media sociologist John Tulloch, explores how the post-traumatic stress disorder experienced by Tulloch, a survivor of the 7/7 London bombings, can amplify another less visible but powerful effect of the attacks: the mapping of a topography of latent threat and fear onto space.[2] The explosion caused dramatic shifts in Tulloch's sensory perception of time and space. His body was embedded with fragments of glass, his eardrums ruptured and he was unable to look up at the sky. The assault on his body and sense of identity was further exacerbated through the subsequent global media dissemination of a photograph of his injured body which was used to promote then-Prime Minister Tony Blair's proposed 90 days without charge anti-terror bill; a move that Tulloch strenuously opposed.[3]

In *216 Westbound*, images surveying London's skyline and near Edgware Road tube station (where the attack on the 216 Westbound train took place) dissolve into scattered flashes of light to convey Tulloch's feeling of what he described as 'assembling and disassembling' sensations during the explosion. This seventeen-minute single-screen artist film is interspersed with bursts of vivid colour and combines layered sound, fragmented voice and animated text with close-up and panoramic views. The film suggests a discrepancy between Tulloch's lived experience of trauma and its dispersal in the media's collective reconstruction and exploitation, while pointing to the intersection of individual experience with broader geopolitical scenarios of terror. The precariousness caused by the terrorist attack, shock wave and heightened state of alert unravels affectively as sounds and images. Atmospheric pressure, vertigo, acoustic interference and mediatic distortion convey the rupture of trauma as well as the sense of insecurity and uncertainty on which the boundaries of a fractured reality are felt more acutely.

In this chapter, Illingworth and Tulloch, together with writer Caterina Albano, reflect back on *216 Westbound* by examining the effect of the terrorist attack at the level of embodied experience, media reporting and the machinery of state control. It includes the transcript of the film, and is structured around eight still images from the video work and short texts that respond and expand on the themes of *216 Westbound*. These texts have developed over extensive conversations among the authors. They relate dialogically to the film and across the chapter. They also suggest the different positions of the authors: Illingworth as the filmmaker (SI), Tulloch as one of the authors and the subject of the film itself (JT) and Albano as an external commentator (CA). Illingworth's voice emerges from her mapping of the film as it unfolds and discussion of the critical approach of her filmmaking practice. Tulloch reflects on his own experience and its broader implications today. Albano opens up a consideration of the work to other cultural trajectories, such as vertigo as an intimation of precariousness, the politics of recollection and the criticality of affect. Intentionally, the authors have chosen this layered structure to generate readers' dialogical responses to the work and their potential interpretations.

Embodied experience

INCREASED PRESSURE
FORMS ON THE SURFACE OF THE EXPANDING VOLUME OF
THE EXPLODING OBJECT

IT TRAVELS AS THE

BLAST WAVE

SI: John walks towards the entrance to Edgware Road tube station. The image dissolves into a cloudy summer sky. An explosion, compressed and intensified in the underground tunnel deep under the city, sends out a blast wave. The physics of its velocity, mass and destructive energy echo the invidious psychosocial and political impacts of the explosion as people in the train feel its full force and it spreads out across the city, media and institutions of power.[4] Intense formations on the surface of an expanding volume travel faster than the speed of sound. John's own voice reverberates in the memory space as sensation struggles to find form.

Deep yellow

Deep yellow

Deep yellow, orange

Deep yellow

This fragmented imagery is now caught up in a pixellated sky. The air is dense with signals, communications and surveillance data, noise, and an incessant ringing.

We hear John's voice as he recalls the tube train carriage being stretched and pulled, disassembling in slow motion. His world is a dark, unpleasant urine yellow, the saturating colour of the explosion. Multiple temporal frames begin to layer and shatter. The shock wave coursing through the underground tunnel and into the ear canals ruptures John's tympanic membranes, severing image from sound, sound from space. Sensory overload spreads through interconnected complex neural networks – an emotional bomb breaking up memory representation as it is being formed.[5] Traumatic splinters become deeply embedded.

Above ground, the familiar cycle of daily weather reports and early morning transport news gives way to urgent talk of a catastrophic power surge, a network emergency, a major incident, as rising terror presses through the confusion, chaos and layers of institutional containment.[6] Below ground and across the city's internal transport communications networks, tube operators, station staff and emergency services frantically relay disjointed accounts of bodies emerging from tunnels blackened by smoke.

This entanglement of memory, media, body and technology sharpens and intensifies as it spreads through the city. Already the press and the government are assembling to disseminate, to contain, to enforce, to control. The autonomy and agency of every person, different communities and civil society are perilously threatened as the shock wave pushes outwards. And then the void pulls with sudden implosive force, as the blast wind carrying debris, dust and the sounds of injured people and voices rushes back to the site of the explosion.

JT: To me Shona's passage above maps the 'above ground/underground tunnel' geography of these opening images of clouds/explosions, and introduces the analogy of the ear/tunnel (body/material world) interface, as well as its absences. But it also offers one possible *style* of intermeshed writing in this chapter that expresses the far-reaching, interdependent affects of the event; like the perilous

Figure 12.1 *216 Westbound*, commissioned by Animate Projects, digital video still. Shona Illingworth, 2014.[8]

shock waves Shona describes, the threat to the agency of person, community and civil society is challenged by the different velocities, histories, accomplishments and interrogations of three differently placed writers. For instance, the analytical description of her video work includes details from conversations with me while she was in production. This can be seen in her mention of the concept/analogy of 'waves extending outwards' and the association of this with the yellow city and the yellow explosion that produces the composite effect that 'traumatic experience isn't just within the body … but extend[s] to the relationship with the outside world'. There then follows her point about its multifarious affects – 'the internal and emotional level' – registered in all populated social spaces, from the explosion victims to the Control Order victims at the end of the film.[7]

Shona's material about the visually pixellated sky and the spaces above and below ground introduces the coming story of early media resistance and denial; and then my very gradual recognition below and above ground (as well as among media and emergency services) of terrorism. That sky represents a time/space 'full of signals' but offering fragmented narratives. *216 Westbound*'s soundtrack mixes and melds these different spaces, resistances, memories and future experiences.

I can't look straight up at the sky
I get this sense of vertigo

Feeling of falling
Feeling of falling away

Deep yellow
Deep yellow, orange
Deep yellow

Darkish yellow

It will be rather cloudy at times with occasional heavy showers,
sunny intervals developing with a top temperature of 21 degrees
Celsius, 70 Fahrenheit. Now unfortunately for public transport
you've got some major incidents occurring at the moment. Just
had a word with TFL. They are asking that please people avoid the
whole tube network. Tickets are being honoured on several bus
routes

I had an instantaneous impression of colour
It was a horrible urine, sort of nasty urine colour

I've had a report that ...
We've had a report that ...

Black, they just look black, covered in smoke, yeah yeah. They're
being treated for ... I can't tell how many there are, I think
there's probably three or four people on the floor being treated.
It looks like they're moving ...

We're hearing an explosion on a train

Tickets being honoured on bus routes – but a bus will be destroyed by a bomb later!

SI: The explosion blows bodies and worlds apart. Visceral and physical, it creates a violent rupturing of memory while presaging an increasingly violent future. In the film, past trauma fractures and overwhelms the present. Complex neural networks are repeatedly reactivated as John moves through the city years later. He wears a peaked cap to shield his eyes because he can no longer look straight up at the sky without feeling as though he is falling. The vertigo is nauseating: this '*feeling of falling, feeling of falling away*'.

Objects bend, twist, break up, become embedded in flesh. In this dark world there is also feeling, sensation, touch and heat. As John tries to find words for embodied feelings, memory loops back to micro-details to seek anchor in the chaos, and to his attunement to the faint sounds of crying heard through his shattered eardrums. There is confusion, distress, but also a tenderness in his voice, and a sensitivity to the acute precariousness of life and the intimate connectedness to human presences in the dark.

Hearing these very faint sounds
Carnage
I did seem to hear some very faint
crying
A faint wailing sound

Intensely present, memory combines with the desperate attempts to comprehend, to rescue, to care that are also palpable in the recordings of the voices of tube and emergency services workers at the scene. This is an evolving entanglement between past and present. At the human scale, we travel on the arc of the film in a sequence of interconnected entrapments. We move from the 'fullness' of sensorial, emotional pain present in voices and memories of the immediate aftermath of the bombing to the charged, politicized spaces between citizen and state where the media operates at the cynical edge of patriotism and fear. Here the use, without his consent, of a photograph of John's injured body by *The Sun* newspaper to support the proposed 90 days without charge anti-terror bill traces a dangerous line that leads to the clinical dissection of the social, cultural, connected and active body via the imposition and rationalized violence of the Control Orders and the machinery of state control.

JT: Shona, your material here is about me at Edgware Road as 'not a straight chronology'. The film's narrative arc here represents developing time and space as agency ('you are not covered in blood' in the second appearance at the station). This is an 'agency of the individual in relation to the state', as your film interrogates the much-diminished social space between them – which the media seek to fill out with their own closures. This is the arc that the film seeks to carry the viewer across, from the opening to the closing images of Edgware Road station, with me as a tiny figure. But this conveying of the viewer from beginning to end of the work is also via a question. What does this walking isolation of a diminished figure in a much-diminished social space mean for the film? You offer the time/space binary borders of 'synchrony and diachrony: continuous entrapment/agency' as a human-centred, often intimate dramatic action. And in actual time – my own historical time – I also walk away, past that station, among the public (where the film ends) and *into* the British media to offer to this same public an alternative view of 7/7 (as in ITN's two-episode 2006 news item, 'John's Journey', where I walk through the streets again, this time of Beeston, Leeds, to find out more about Mohammed Sidique Khan who detonated the bomb in my train carriage, and his colleagues).

CA: Since the scientist Robert Boyle famously demonstrated the proportional inverse relationship between the volume and pressure of gas in the seventeenth century, thin air became more elastic and malleable. It began to be regarded as matter. As a result it turned thicker with affect. But Boyle's experiments on air were not victimless. To prove that a vacuum could be generated by extracting air with a pump from a bell jar, he would place a bird under the jar that would die for lack of oxygen.[9] As air turned into measurable expandable matter, in other words, vertigo emerged as the side-effect of the pliability of volumes and pressures. At a time when the expansiveness of air was infused with awe, the apprehension of its potential compression or contraction quivered with disquiet. Air was made precarious.

Today, according to Michel Serres, matter has become 'airlike' – 'more informational than material'.[10] Matter is volatile in its informational data-like state, but the density of air itself has intensified, as the concentration of information has turned it from a mere conduit to a receptacle of data – ecological data, surveillance data and data related to traces of contamination and other violations of air. Under these conditions, it is as if the relationship between volume and pressure has been reversed, generating saturated atmospheres of colliding communication and pervading emotional charge. Vertigo is the *affect* of these environments of pressured informational matter, where parameters of orientation are blurred by interference and the obfuscation caused by the implosions of its uses.

If, from this state of vertigo, we consider Boyle's experimentation with vacuum, one question arises: what did the bird experience? Historical sources refer to the scientific explanation of the experiment and to what spectators experienced when witnessing it. But there is no account of what it felt like for the bird to be under the bell jar, to feel the air inside rarefying, and then being unable to breathe until collapsing. These narratives are still missing from today's data-saturated air. Vacuums are still created and perspectives obliterated. Still we find ourselves out of bearing with the making of histories and their precariousness.

JT: Caterina's point is about the human and humane. *216 Westbound* articulates for me and others my own bell jar experience of breathlessness and vertigo from the data-saturated air, as vacuums begin to be filled with empathy and dialogue through intimacy and 'embodied listening'.

SI: A fleeting silence, a pause, time slows, John looks out straight through the screen.

> *No sound*
> *As the explosion was happening I heard no sound*
> *And then everything seemed to be moving around*
> *I just saw this*
> *This carriage being stretched and compressed, assembling and disassembling*
>
> *I was lying in the dark on my back*
> *A lot of glass and smoky stuff and just darkness really*
>
> *That's when my body took over*
>
>
> *We've got reports of walking wounded*
> *Oh my God*
> *Call required to Edgware Road*
> *Yeah Circle and Hammersmith Station in Chapel Street*
> *northwest one*
> *Right I just think we're mobilizing at the moment*
> *Just bear with me*
>
> *Then I saw a lighted train right next to me, these two worlds were not commensurate*
> *One was silhouettes, people alive scrabbling, they seemed to be scrabbling at windows*
> *And then in three dimensions, in brute reality, there were the blood and bodies*

The contrast between the projected screens and surfaces of the media and embodied space is mirrored in the unbridgeable chasm between the 'brute reality' of the destroyed train carriage, the 'blood and bodies' and the lighted window of the train next to it on to which silhouettes, people alive 'scrabbling at windows', are cast. The ruptured tympanic membrane, which separates the inside world of the mind and the outside world, and on whose surface sound waves resonate and become meaning, now echoes this breach.

When people are asked to bear witness, they are predominantly asked to describe what they saw. This requires engagement in distancing strategies that are involved in constructing coherent narratives for events. This detaches people from their own experience, connections with others and an intimacy with the scene. This also introduces a rationalized, formalized and often singular dimension of scale. Working closely with John involved an exploration of memory for embodied experience, sense of space, temperature, touch, disorientation across multiple scales and attentive, embodied listening. As a filmmaker, this form of listening does not just attend to what is being recounted, but also to what is held in the body: the materiality of the voice, the shape of the breath, the rise and fall of emotion, the struggle to access feeling, imagery, sensation, to convey experience that is extremely difficult to share. It is important to me to recognize that in the overwhelming space of trauma, there remain delicate networks of connectedness that hold people, materiality and place together.

This form of listening takes time. It reveals other stories, dimensions and questions, which are so often flattened out and delimited as they are co-opted into the instrumentalizing narratives that underpin institutionalized order and control, such as in the much delayed Coroner's inquest.[11] While the prolonged gathering of evidence may or may not have offered the bereaved and survivors

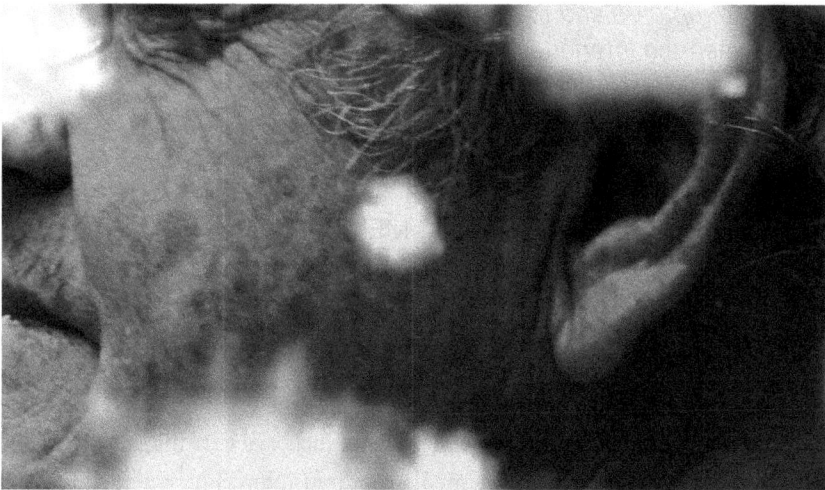

Figure 12.2 *216 Westbound.*

'some memorial closure', it represented 'a monumentalizing opportunity (by the state and the security services in particular) to close down particular narratives around preventability of and accountability for the bombings, as well as other speculative news discourses'.[12] None of this assuaged the rising anxiety and its opaque dispersal within an expanding topography of fear and threat in the personal, domestic, institutional and public spaces of the city and its populations: anxiety that is drawn into well-worn narratives that are used to drive increasingly extensive and pervasive forms of surveillance and disempowerment.

JT: Shona's material on an 'important moment of silence' develops the theme of my entrapment/agency as 'remembering and speaking' via 'a break of silence in the film' where I move 'from being an image to having voice'. This paralleled my own actual moves within the media, as in the 'How *The Sun* stole my voice' *Guardian* article and in the *Newsnight* end-of-2005 programme.[13] But *216 Westbound* operates differently, interfering with *The Sun*'s two-dimensional space, as developed in the ensuing text and in what follows through Shona's emphasis on the intimacy of hands.

> *Both my eardrums had been blown away*
>
> *The blast wave is a pressure wave, a shock front of high pressure, that travels very fast*
> *Faster than the speed of sound*
>
> *They'd ruptured and that was generating this separation between the interior space of my body and any thing outside it*
>
> *Parts of the train became embedded in my body*
> *There was the shrapnel that's still inside my forehead*

> A RUPTURE TO THE TYMPANIC MEMBRANE
> RUPTURES THE BOUNDARY THAT SEPARATES
> THE INSIDE WORLD OF OUR BODY
> FROM THE OUTSIDE WORLD AROUND US

SI: Edgware station entrance appears again, like a ghost. Blurred people move through air thickened by slowed time. Lights flicker across the surface of the screen. This is the site where the media captured John as he emerged bruised and disoriented from the wreckage in the tunnel below.

Media reporting

JT: Shona's visual shift here is from the 'ghostly' space where I was first 'captured' by the media to the 'miasmic yellow' city – the mediasphere. Now my memory is operating differently from when I was underground, as well as in the ghostly space of the triage at Edgware Road. In the mediasphere my image is appropriated 'through echoes', and then reflected back to me, so that I am located but also dislocated. Shona turns towards 'two points of silence [that] are very important, very short but like transitions'. They act as audio-visual *pauses* of questioning and address for the reader before *The Sun* and hands sequence that follows.

CA: The time of remembering is both synchronous and diachronic, as past and present intersect in memories as we create a narrative of the past that resonates for the here and now. Such temporal intersection also relates to the functions of memory that, according to current neuro-psychological understanding, refer to how we use personal but also socially and culturally shared memories to make sense of current situations, to project into the future, and to create social bonds. In memory processes, selectivity plays an important role since it determines what we remember. Put otherwise, unconsciously we choose what memories we use to tell our stories and what memories we supposedly 'forget' since they disturb not only a specific image of the past but also how such an image helps to corroborate ideas about the present.[14] Silencing in remembering also happens when we listen to others selectively recalling past events. Our own individual memories or details in them morph to converge with those that are presented to us. At the same time, mnemonic convergence – the way in which memories of events tend to overlap among groups as a result of how the media or public figures present them, or of how individuals share their recollections – contributes to creating closeness among people. It can also produce authoritative reductive versions of the past – whether about ourselves or as shared accounts within a group or societies at large.

In *216 Westbound*, the two shifts from urban external panoramic views of Edgware Road tube station and the London skyline to John's ear and head are marked by a brief yet noticeable moment of silence. More than internal markers, they are performatively dynamic. In the first instance, conflicting explanations of what might be happening increasingly build tension and imbue the atmospheric space created by the work with fear. This affective space alludes to a site of public memory formation where selectivity begins to define the accepted version of events. The pause that indicates the shift from this external perspective to John's

Figure 12.3 *216 Westbound*, original image in colour (yellow).

intimate recollection of what he experienced underground evokes silences in remembering. Like audio signals whose intensity is lessened or even muted, silenced memories do not disappear. Rather they become inaudible presences in the atmospherics of remembering. They are traces that persist, affecting memory processes. This pause acts as a suspension for the viewers who can turn to themselves and feel the gathering of sensations and emotions that the growing affective charge of Shona's work provokes, and is emphasized by the close focus of the camera lens on John's ear. We hear his voice, and his voice is a trace of his body and of his remembering.

The second pause in *216 Westbound* points again to a transition from an external site of shared recollection to an internal point of view. The underground explosion has happened, and past and present already overlap as memories: who remembers, what is remembered? Sound interference and the yellowish saturated images point to a conflation of perspectives, to the infiltration of politics and the media into the visual and verbal articulations of events, to appropriation and selectivity. This sequence alludes to the space where the 'official' version of the attack is formed and consolidated. Heightened tension is perceptible as the images of clouds condense, before the camera lens moves to John as he turns towards the viewer. The silence that characterizes these frames is unsettling. It can be understood as the internal disturbance that repressed memories cause to remembering. It can also intimate resistance. It invites viewers to contemplate their experience of the work and perhaps allow their own memories of 7/7 to intersect the film's unfolding. Silenced memories, even if they do not reach consciousness, can facilitate the emergence of new memories by generating

Figure 12.4 *216 Westbound.*

associative chains in recollection. We can imagine the frayed fabric of social remembering to potentially renovate itself with an impression of the past that both differs from and complicates official accepted versions. Fleetingly, an interrogation of the past can provide insight and understanding in the present.

When you are as physically threatened as that and injured
The world outside closes in around you
You're fastened in the survival space
And that's now a separated space from the outside world

WE EXPERIENCE SPACE THROUGH ECHOES
IF YOU DON'T HAVE ECHOES
YOU CAN FEEL OPPRESSED
AS THOUGH THERE IS NO SPACE AROUND YOU ANY MORE

SI: The cityscape appears, and it is changing, consumed by a drifting yellow miasma emanating as if from the film itself. John is fastened to the survival space.

When the tympanic membranes are blown, you can no longer hear echoes, and space closes in. It loses its dimensions, flattens out, and you can no longer locate yourself in it in the same way. We orientate ourselves through an ever-changing intricacy of acoustics, frequencies that fill the air within a sensorium that reflects back to us. With it, memory allows us to know and feel space around us and sense our being in the world. The loss of a sense of space signifies a profound vulnerability for self and being, and this aligns with the split-second media-arrest of the photograph of John. The delicate web of almost imperceptible interaction with the world is shattered as he becomes caught in media narratives constructed around this now global iconic image of the attack. It is a form of media violence against being and the physical, social, political, cultural, emotional and psychological dimensions of self.

And again, silence, there is a momentary cut in the sound space of *216 Westbound*. John is isolated close to the surface of the screen in an intimate but airless vacuum. Time is slowed as his eyes turn outwards and break the frame. His thoughts and memory turn inward, remote and inaccessible. A subtle instant of agency in the questioning space that opens out in this gap is followed by John not as a victim but as someone who is being, thinking, remembering, speaking. It is a counterpoint to the politicized image of John's injured body on the front page of *The Sun*, used as a cipher for the phrase 'Tell Tony [Blair] He's Right'. For John, that is a triple loss of agency – personal, social, political.

The broken glass of the train re-emerges from John's body over days, from his forehead, his mouth, from under his tongue. Sound speeds up as though winding in on a coil. In the film, John's voice cuts over the sliding blocks and frames that disassemble his image on the front page of the newspaper, never allowing our eyes to rest or consume it. Across this intricate visual architecture of static and moving parts, John's description of this moment of media entrapment provides a set of coordinates: the fixity of his gaze on his bag, an extension of himself, now dislocated and hanging from the shoulder of an emergency services worker, his bleeding mouth next to the text 'Tell Tony He's Right'.

The glass that for days afterwards was coming out of my body
When I began to feel this nausea most strongly
That's the time when
The photographers were taking the image of me that
Emerged so strongly in the media

The image of the victim that I resisted

It's almost encrusted this blood on my face
Tattered clothes below
My eyes are all unfocused

I'm kind of fixated on the bag, the bag on her shoulder

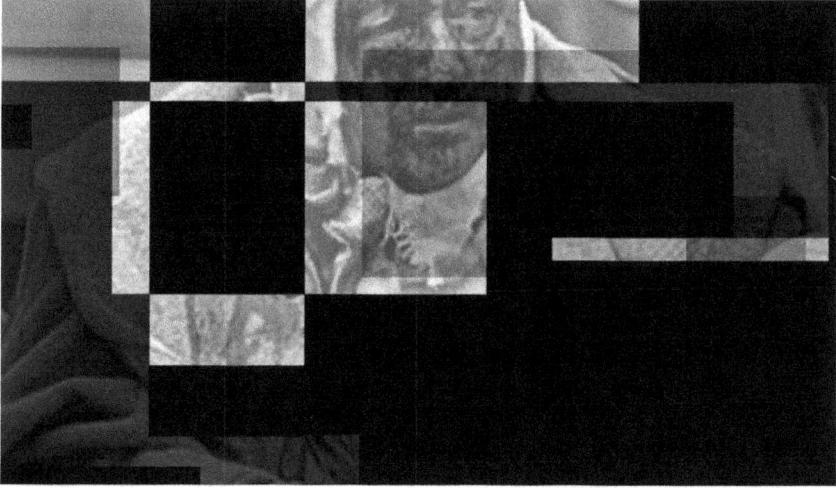

Figure 12.5 *216 Westbound*, original image in colour (red).

This one had to have a mouth
The bleeding mouth
It had next to it, 'Tell Tony He's Right'

The Sun *newspaper using my image*
The words next to the mouth, which said, 'Tell Tony He's Right'
Right next to my mouth

90 days without charge legislation

I totally opposed that legislation

Finally, the sliding frames settle to reveal John's wounded hands, the human touch of a health worker on his arm. Images that emerge almost as if from chemical darkness into the low saturated frequency of red light, poised briefly before human touch fades to black at the edge. In Australia, John's wife Marian sees him on the front page of a newspaper. She cannot recognize his bandaged face, but her eyes fall on his hands. She instinctively recognizes how he holds them, the projective curl of the fingers around the pain in the palms, the taut limpness turning in towards the body, and she knows it is him.

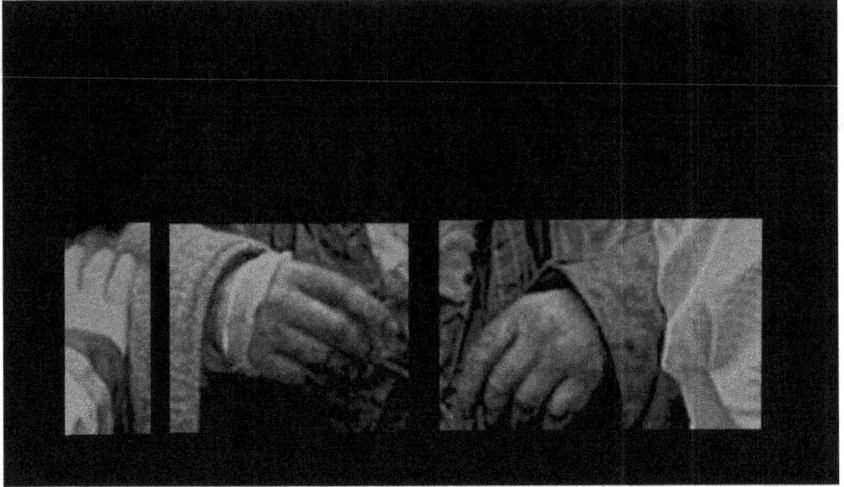

Figure 12.6 *216 Westbound*, original image in colour (red).

When Marian looked at that photograph for the first time, she didn't recognize it was me

She only recognized me by the way I was holding my hands

Disempowerment
Loss of my voice
Use of my image

JT: Contrary to our notion of fetishized images, my fragmented past here becomes a new whole, a moment of intimate discovery, recognition, embodiment and human agency. Something that is shared yet is both new and accustomed. It shimmers against the bombers' yellow and the tabloid's red top as a breach in the two-dimensional reality of terrorist, media and government control.

CA: In the newspaper's photograph, John's hands are both the focal and affective point. In *216 Westbound*, the original photograph is sliced into three frames. The two middle frames show John's hands as they turn towards the body, as if in a pause of movement. They convey restraint and poise, even reluctance and protection. The camera lens meets reservation. As viewers we do not share Marian's insight, her intimate knowledge of those hands. Nonetheless they act as a visual site of utterance. They are *otherwise* eloquent. Rather than the conventional loud emotional appeal that the image of John's bandaged face calls for, those hands mutely draw one's attention. Shona gleans their tacit centrality to subvert the media's instrumentalization and fetishization of this photograph to make us look more carefully, and to allow us as viewer to bring our own understanding of this image – be it emotional and/or intellectual understanding.

All images, as Jacques Rancière reminds us, belong to systems of other images and established modes of representation and, I would add, of bodily postures suffused with affect.[15] Contrary to the media's deployment, the picture of John itself contains a point of resistance. While the photograph is designed to portray 'a victim', John's holding of his hands counteracts such intention. By isolating them, Shona evidences their iconographic resonances with classical statuary and Renaissance painterly compositions where hands visually express the dramatic and narrative tensions within the depiction but can also suggest the internal emotional state and ethical bearing of a figure. Unwittingly, John's hands contradict the attempt of victimization by gathering the energetic composure of the whole body and imbuing it with intensity and disruptive force. They free John's photograph from the instrumentalized emotional investment to which it has been subjected by *The Sun* and open it to a questioning of what we look for and feel when we look at images in the media.

In the third smaller section, on the left-hand side, we see the hand of a health worker lightly touching John's arm that reveals a gesture of care. As viewers, we feel the slight pressure of those anonymous fingers, their haptic reassurance. This detail was cut in the printed version of the photograph, thus removing its empathic association and by extension the possibility of the viewer's identification with such a gesture. Unlike the objectifying intent of that shot, the hand's contact is one of individualization, suggesting an interpersonal exchange and a recognition of pain. If included it would have provided a reflective clue to what the picture showed, raising questions about 'the construction of the victim as an element in a certain distribution of the visible' – in this case, that was effected by the media – and how such distribution 'governs the status of the bodies represented and the kind of attention they merit'.[16] And, we could add, the kind of political exploitation they become subjected to.

JT: That excluded health worker's hand reconstituting my reality was extended after the bombing through new intimacies of the body: the hospital physiotherapist who so carefully wheeled me to my friend's flat, who raised with a wooden frame the most appropriate chair to reduce my vertigo when I sat down or stood up, and who showed me how to protect my damaged ears as she bathed me; the health worker who threw an orange to my left, right and centre – not to catch it, but for me to learn to 'duck and weave' so that I would be able to walk once again on crowded Camden Town streets; the different ladies who helped shower and dry me with their hands each day, and encouraged me in lifting my foot on to the bath edge to stand on one foot while still with vertigo and dry myself once more. These were my professional carers who I wished I could keep as friends. They gave me confidence in the goodness and pleasure of small things.

Machinery of government control

JT: Neoliberalism is the state's yellow, institutionalized. It is *The Sun*'s yellow too, Rupert Murdoch's yellow, seeping through democracy, destroying the commons, privatizing not only the National Health Service but also transport and even poverty itself. Neoliberalism deregulates even as it seeks to impose 90 days without charge. It dehumanizes through Control Orders. Neoliberalism promotes terminal terror to planetary health through fossil fuel. During a pandemic it threatens the vulnerable – always the weak, the poor, the old, the Indigenous, the young people of the future – through its systemic urge to 'reopen the economy'.

SI: In *216 Westbound* I wanted the viewer to read each Control Order as they slide one after another across the cityscape. Each subsequent order identifies and isolates a part of human personal, social and political interaction with the world with brutal efficiency. The dehumanizing and rationalized violence that frames this legal construct is accentuated by its bureaucratic language. It is underpinned by, and a driver of, intensifying forces of fear and threat that spread out, operating below levels of consciousness. This systematic approach, and the forces and histories that underpin it, provide the mechanisms for increasingly sophisticated and invasive use of technological forms of surveillance and control.

The sequence now pauses on the Control Order: 'a requirement on him to allow himself to be photographed.'

90 DAYS DETENTION WITHOUT CHARGE

Figure 12.7 *216 Westbound.*

A PROHIBITION OR RESTRICTION ON HIS POSSESSION OR USE OF SPECIFIED ARTICLES OR SUBSTANCES

A PROHIBITION OR RESTRICTION ON HIS USE OF SPECIFIED SERVICES OR SPECIFIED FACILITIES, OR ON HIS CARRYING ON SPECIFIED ACTIVITIES

A RESTRICTION IN RESPECT OF HIS WORK OR OTHER OCCUPATION, OR IN RESPECT OF HIS BUSINESS

A RESTRICTION ON HIS ASSOCIATION OR COMMUNICATIONS WITH SPECIFIED PERSONS OR WITH OTHER PERSONS GENERALLY

A RESTRICTION IN RESPECT OF HIS PLACE OF RESIDENCE OR ON THE PERSONS TO WHOM HE GIVES ACCESS TO HIS PLACE OF RESIDENCE

A PROHIBITION ON HIS BEING AT SPECIFIED PLACES OR WITHIN A SPECIFIED AREA AT SPECIFIED TIMES OR ON SPECIFIED DAYS

A PROHIBITION OR RESTRICTION ON HIS MOVEMENTS TO, FROM OR WITHIN THE UNITED KINGDOM, A SPECIFIED PART OF THE UNITED KINGDOM OR A SPECIFIED PLACE OR AREA WITHIN THE UNITED KINGDOM

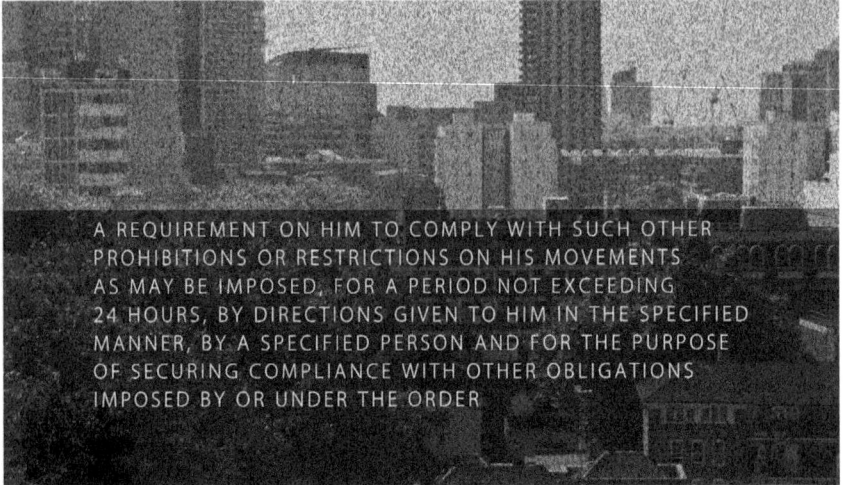

A REQUIREMENT ON HIM TO COMPLY WITH SUCH OTHER PROHIBITIONS OR RESTRICTIONS ON HIS MOVEMENTS AS MAY BE IMPOSED, FOR A PERIOD NOT EXCEEDING 24 HOURS, BY DIRECTIONS GIVEN TO HIM IN THE SPECIFIED MANNER, BY A SPECIFIED PERSON AND FOR THE PURPOSE OF SECURING COMPLIANCE WITH OTHER OBLIGATIONS IMPOSED BY OR UNDER THE ORDER

Figure 12.8 *216 Westbound.*

A REQUIREMENT ON HIM TO SURRENDER HIS PASSPORT, OR ANYTHING IN HIS POSSESSION TO WHICH A PROHIBITION OR RESTRICTION IMPOSED BY THE ORDER RELATES, TO A SPECIFIED PERSON FOR A PERIOD NOT EXCEEDING THE PERIOD FOR WHICH THE ORDER REMAINS IN FORCE

A REQUIREMENT ON HIM TO GIVE ACCESS TO SPECIFIED PERSONS TO HIS PLACE OF RESIDENCE OR TO OTHER PREMISES TO WHICH HE HAS POWER TO GRANT ACCESS

A REQUIREMENT ON HIM TO ALLOW SPECIFIED PERSONS TO SEARCH THAT PLACE OR ANY SUCH PREMISES FOR THE PURPOSE OF ASCERTAINING WHETHER OBLIGATIONS IMPOSED BY OR UNDER THE ORDER HAVE BEEN, ARE BEING OR ARE ABOUT TO BE CONTRAVENED

A REQUIREMENT ON HIM TO ALLOW SPECIFIED PERSONS, EITHER FOR THAT PURPOSE OR FOR THE PURPOSE OF SECURING THAT THE ORDER IS COMPLIED WITH, TO REMOVE ANYTHING FOUND IN THAT PLACE OR ON ANY SUCH PREMISES AND TO SUBJECT IT TO TESTS OR TO RETAIN IT FOR A PERIOD NOT EXCEEDING THE PERIOD FOR WHICH THE ORDER REMAINS IN FORCE

A REQUIREMENT ON HIM TO ALLOW HIMSELF TO BE
PHOTOGRAPHED

A REQUIREMENT ON HIM TO CO-OPERATE WITH SPECIFIED
ARRANGEMENTS FOR ENABLING HIS MOVEMENTS,
COMMUNICATIONS OR OTHER ACTIVITIES TO BE
MONITORED BY ELECTRONIC OR OTHER MEANS

A REQUIREMENT ON HIM TO COMPLY WITH A DEMAND
MADE IN THE SPECIFIED MANNER TO PROVIDE
INFORMATION TO A SPECIFIED PERSON IN ACCORDANCE
WITH THE DEMAND

A REQUIREMENT ON HIM TO REPORT TO A SPECIFIED
PERSON AT SPECIFIED TIMES AND PLACES

JT: Thus is terrorism fixed in place by the neoliberal state, itemized, dissected and specified as commodities of 'terror'. The current pandemic is also underpinned by neoliberalism. Its treatment through private care homes and privatized quarantine has been killing on behalf of the pandemic. And neoliberalism – backed by Murdoch who disbelieves in climate change – is fuelling the new era of Australian mega-bushfires, terrorizing our people, our animals, our common world.

During 2020, facing COVID-19 and three mega-bushfires at the same time on the east coast of Australia, I felt viscerally that I was returning to that tube carriage at Edgware Road. Beyond that 216 Westbound underground train I *recovered* my voice and walked with the populace past the station and through the media. But now the violated personal spaces of bushfire threat or personal lockdown reverberate only with risk, anxiety and frustration. Once more I have no voice, and am disconnected from the echoes that contain me. Where are the membranes of freedom within neoliberal constraint? There is little indeed to be found in government spheres. We are left without social beings beside us. Their body parts – as one victim of 7/7 who lost his legs complained – are itemized for terrorism compensation 'like the Argos catalogue'; or else, in the case of COVID-19, are offered up for often hopelessly mismanaged government inoculation rollouts in separated bursts of vaccination nationalism.

Yet, agency is emerging among the people. The Australian Institute's report in October 2020 shows bushfires as the public's highest of all climate change concerns (82 per cent), and indicates the remarkable shift from 20 per cent to

79 per cent between 2013 and 2020 in Australian belief that climate change is occurring. There is support for the closure of coal-fired power stations (83 per cent), a desire for Australia to become a global leader in climate change (71 per cent), with half believing that fossil fuel producers should pay for climate activity.[17] Rebecca Colvin of the Australian National University, who researches public attitudes to climate change, argues in particular that the recent Institute poll indicates that COVID-19 has not obliterated these climate change concerns, which are now the highest in thirteen years of Institute polling.[18] She says she is surprised by this; but one potential motivator could well be the role of sections of the Australian media. For example, the Australian Broadcasting Corporation ran through October 2020 a series, 'Big Weather (and how to survive it)', which, as well as practical advice regarding further fires and floods similar to the Black Summer of 2020, brought together climate change research by New South Wales and Victorian school students with 'cultural cool burn' traditional technology from Indigenous Australians in Queensland. Both are beginning to receive government and Rural Fire Service notice by way of this media intervention, while traditional custodians and firefighters have been working together for some years with cool burns. Children, First Peoples and volunteer firefighters are now taking climate change leadership across their commonality in the face of government lethargy. My paralysis between terrorism, government ordering and media power after 7/7 could partially be challenged by my own media efforts. The disempowerment was then shockingly restored through the precarity of climate change, but has in turn been interrogated on a much wider media scale by combining these new and ancient powers of young people and First Nations.

SI: In *216 Westbound*, as the final Control Order slides out of view, sound gives way to air and the low city hum, and the camera pans quietly over an almost empty city skyline. At street level, John's head almost fills the frame. It is turned away from us towards the entrance of Edgware Road station, we are in a real-time sound space looking over his shoulder at a world in slow motion. This creates a temporal disjuncture between John and the scene he both inhabits and looks on to. Here the present and memory are folded into one another. We are outside of both, looking in. Nothing happens other than time and thought held in these moments of suspension. Finally, we are returned to the opening view. Again, we see John walking towards the entrance of the tube station. The bag he was so fixated on is now over his shoulder. This time, though, he walks past the entrance to become a small figure in the scene, part of the city, part of the commons.

Notes

1   *216 Westbound*, dir. Shona Illingworth (Animate Projects, London). Artist film, 17 minutes.

2   On 7 July 2005, four co-ordinated terrorist suicide attacks, known as the 7/7 London bombings, targeted travellers on London's public transport system during the morning rush hour. 52 people died and over 700 were injured, of whom more than 100 required hospital treatment.

3   Following the 7/7 London bombings, the UK government proposed a new bill to allow police to hold terrorist suspects for 90 days without charge. The proposed legislation was defeated in the House of Commons on 9 November 2005.

4   From Shona Illingworth's conversations with Tobias Reichenbach, auditory neuroscientist and expert in bomb blast injury at Imperial College London in 2014.

5   For this conceptual connection, see Martin A. Conway's explanation in Shona Illingworth's *The Watch Man Balnakiel* (London: Film and Video Umbrella, 2011), 57.

6   The London Assembly Report of the 7 July Review Committee, 2006, provides a detailed account of the hour following the first bomb explosion at 8.50 am on the Eastbound Circle Line train. The fact that the first three bombs exploded underground and transport communications systems were rendered inoperable contributed to the ensuing chaos, where '[m]ultiple, often conflicting, reports were being made, some to London Underground's Network Control Centre, some to the emergency services, and some to the media'. Meanwhile, the UK government maintained their official line that the disaster was caused by a catastrophic power surge. London Assembly, 'Report of the 7 July Review Committee', Greater London Authority (report) (June 2006), 12, https://www.london.gov.uk.

7   Control Orders were introduced as part of the Prevention of Terrorism Act 2005 and contained 'obligations' considered necessary to prevent or restrict a person's involvement in terrorism-related activity. These far-reaching powers to restrict a person's liberty could be applied without a criminal conviction and last indefinitely. The sixteen main obligations are detailed in *216 Westbound*. The Act was opposed by leading human rights organizations. It was repealed on 15 December 2011.

8   All images in this chapter are copyrighted by Shona Illingworth, 2014.

9   Bruno Latour, 'Air', in *Sensorium: Embodied Experience, Technology, and Contemporary Art*, ed. Caroline A. Jones (Cambridge, MA: MIT Press, 2006), 105–107. See also Isabelle Stengers, *Cosmopolitics I*, trans. Robert Bononno (Minneapolis, MN: University of Minnesota Press, 2010).

10 Michel Serres and Bruno Latour, *Conversations on Science, Culture, and Time*, trans. Roxanne Lapidus (Ann Arbor, MI: University of Michigan Press, 1995), 121.

11 The Coroner's inquest into the 7/7 London bombings led by Coroner Lady Justice Hallett began in October 2010, over five years after the bombing. The Coroner delivered her verdict and series of recommendations on 6 May 2011.

12 Andrew Hoskins, '7/7 and connective memory: interactional trajectories of remembering in post-scarcity culture', *Memory Studies* 4, no. 3 (2011): 270.

13 John Tulloch, *One Day in July: Experiencing 7/7* (London: Little, Brown, 2006); John Tulloch and Warwick Blood, *Icons of War and Terror: Media Images in an Age of International Risk* (London: Routledge, 2012), 175–80.

14 For a broader discussion of memory processes, see William Hirst, Alexandru Cuc and Dana Wohl, 'Of sins and virtues: memory and collective identity', in *Understanding Autobiographical Memory: Theories and Approaches*, eds. Dorthe Berntsen and David C. Rubin (Cambridge: Cambridge University Press, 2012), 141–59; Bernhard Pastötter and Karl-Heinz T. Bäuml, 'Retrieval inhibition in autobiographical memory', in *The Act of Remembering: Toward an Understanding of How We Recall the Past*, ed. John H. Mace (Oxford: Wiley-Blackwell, 2010), 202–27. See also Caterina Albano, *Memory, Forgetting and the Moving Image* (Basingstoke: Palgrave Macmillan, 2016), 132–37.

15 Jacques Rancière, *The Emancipated Spectator*, trans. Gregory Elliott (London: Verso, 2009), 99.

16 Rancière, *Emancipated Spectator*, 99.

17 Audrey Quicke and Ebony Bennett, 'Climate of the Nation 2020', The Australian Institute (report) (27 October 2020), 1, https://australiainstitute.org.au/report/climate-of-the-nation-climate-change-concern-hits-82/.

18 Michael Slezak, 'Climate change worrying more Australians than ever before, Australia Institute report reveals', *ABC News* (27 October 2020), https://www.abc.net.au/news/2020-10-28/australia-institute-2020-climate-change-report-concern-growing/12764874.

Precarious States: Small Explosions in the Time of COVID-19

Alexandra Halkias

The SARS-CoV-2 pandemic took the world by surprise when it surfaced in countries very distant from China, where the virus made its appearance sometime at the end of 2019. Several months later, screens of mobile phones, tablets and computers were flooded with images of the interior of hospitals overflowing with patients and exhausted health services staff. 'Civilized' western countries appeared transformed into warzones, struggling to remain functional in the midst of a peculiar state of siege wherein – without bombs, or other weapons of a national or political enemy – dead human bodies were multiplying beyond the capacities permitted by existing capitalist death industry logistics. Scenes of severe suffering had gone from being a rarity to commonplace, bringing death and its impending proximity to the centre of attention. Precariousness was abruptly writ large. It had become the main fact of life for all.

By the time the World Health Organization announced the pandemic in 2020, Greece was already in the tenth year of a publicly acknowledged sovereign debt crisis. The winding lines of people at ATMs in the summer of 2015 for the initial daily allowance of 60 euros, the lines in the supermarket for food supplies expected to disappear should the country exit the Eurozone (and the European Union), together with the barrage of laws that closed sectors of the public health system and abruptly cut minimum wage limits, public servant salaries and pensions, had all already vividly brought home the insecurity and volatility of everyday life in capitalism. Many were struggling to build their abilities to live 'otherwise', 'to live with precarity'.[1] Precarity, for Anna Lowenhaupt Tsing, is 'life without the promise of stability', 'the condition of being vulnerable to others'

I thank Christina Lee and Susan Leong for their useful comments and insightful suggestions on various drafts of this chapter. I also thank the students who took my classes at Panteion University during the pandemic and helped shape the research I discuss here.

and, as she aptly notes, 'the only reason all this sounds odd is that most of us were raised on dreams of modernization and progress'.[2] This kind of vulnerability had spread in Greece after the sovereign debt crisis to include all but the very wealthy; however, the pandemic would leave no group unaffected. By March 2020, the affluent northern Italian region of Lombardy was in complete lockdown, with the country reporting close to 5,500 fatalities.[3] By July, New York City was being sent refrigerated trucks by the national disaster agency FEMA to store corpses, and 'mass graves' were being dug as a way of handling the overflow of death.[4] Soon, London too seemed to be hurtling towards critical failure.

Notions underpinning so-called normalcy altered with this new global cartography of death. Could this really be Europe? Could that really be the United States? Medical science and several of its material manifestations – hospitals, high-tech emergency rooms, simpler technologies like ventilators and the typically invisible figure of the epidemiologist – became central to the unfolding narrative. Precariousness was no longer 'simply' a latent condition of human life, as suggested by Judith Butler, but had become precarity, since the social and political forces shaping our lives rendered all of us maximally vulnerable to SARS-CoV-2, whatever its origins might be.[5] Less spectacularly perhaps, though equally important, in nations across the globe the power of the state to regulate yet more aspects of human life installed itself as an unquestionable necessity.

Certainly in Greece the newly elected right-wing New Democracy government rose to the occasion. On 11 March 2020, Prime Minister Kyriakos Mitsotakis announced that no public gatherings should occur, worship in churches included, and all educational units, from daycare centres to universities, would close for fourteen days with some remote teaching to take place for students in their final year, to be followed by other grades.[6] Within the week, a law closed all cafes, entertainment venues and shops, except for supermarkets and pharmacies. From the morning of 23 March, from 9 pm to 5 am all but emergency medical visits were forbidden.[7] For the significant migrant population living in Greece without papers, those living in camps were not permitted to exit, while for those living on their own the prospect of being checked by the police at any time meant all mobility was practically eradicated. Many workplaces, meanwhile, including my own at the Department of Sociology, Panteion University of Social and Political Sciences in Athens, began the project of shifting to remote work, with minimal prior practice and problematic infrastructure.

All this should be done, we were told, 'to protect grandparents' and, pointedly, 'for Greece'.[8] This nationalist register was evident in the refrain of the official video campaign for the (first) lockdown, which proclaimed 'we stay home in order to exit it as winners, we stay home, *so Greece shows the world she is a winner*' (my emphasis). On the eve of the national holiday of 25 March, the prime minister again addressed the nation to explain why there would be no parades that year. He declared that 'the enemy now is the pandemic'.[9]

In this chapter, I employ an autoethnographic approach to work with the minute articulations of embodied human precarity within a specific historical moment. As Jacquelyn Allen-Collinson puts it, 'Autoethnography seeks to connect the personal to the cultural and to locate both "self" – however shifting and fragmentary – and others within a social context'.[10] Holding to the need for 'situated knowledges' grounded in social context, I draw on field notes and news media material pertaining to the situation in Athens as it unfolded through three waves of coronavirus transmission and two extensive lockdowns from March 2020 through to April 2021. I approach autoethnography as a gendered process; like the social life it seeks to examine, this approach is inescapably entangled with the social and the stakes of relations of power and yet, too, uniquely positioned to produce knowledge that destabilizes the latter.[11] As Carolyn Ellis notes of her own autoethnographic practice and writing, 'I attempt to integrate physical bodies, feelings, talk, motives, actions, and face-to-face interactions. Though my focus often is on emotionality … I also am interested in how these micro-events play out in and teach us about macro-structures and processes'.[12] Or, as Sarah Wall puts it, 'Autoethnography is an intriguing and promising qualitative method [that] offers a way of giving voice to personal experience to advance sociological understanding'.[13] In my choices therein, I follow Anne Allison's line of thinking that:

> to get a sense of precarity – to survive it and to think through it with social analysis – requires 'arts of noticing' driven by curiosity. The old toolkits no longer work, and we need to see life in different terms to understand the ways it breaks down but also grows anew amidst the blasted ruins of capitalism.[14]

Allison is interested in embodied motivated work. Instead of objective observation or distanced analysis, she calls for fine-grained nuanced accounts of the grit of life in late capitalism which, nonetheless, firmly aim beyond themselves to a discussion, a 'coming to terms' she says, with 'what radical uncertainty implies for the living but also for life itself'.[15]

The rationale for my use of autoethnographic method resides in the goal of a different way of viewing life in precarity, like Allison, but in a way that clarifies both its edges and its potential. My attention here to 'small explosions' in pandemic daily life, and its media representations, is used to enable a vantage point from which to see, and to critically examine, the way a quiet yet broad expansion of the state is actually unfolding around the globe in the time of COVID-19. An eye for new critical relationalities is present but the focus is on the biopower nexus of the pandemic via an unravelling of its micro-sociological articulations in Athens as a site with an already dense interweaving of narratives regarding precarity and the nation, science, danger versus safety, and state power.[16] I am interested in particular in how the management of something as materially objective as a virus and of something as (abruptly) universal as a constitutive precariousness of all human life emerges as a fully social and embodied project which can yield other forms of relationality, challenging prior formations of 'the individual' while actively creating new vistas for state sovereignty. The stories that follow deploy the self, and others, to track how nation-specific representations of a virus and its effects mesh with feelings (such as fear and nationalism) and social practices (such as masking or teleworking). While much of the material comes from my own life in Greece, the result of its processing here gestures towards effects beyond any one nation.

Walking

It was 30 October 2020, about a week before a second lockdown for the wider Athens region (home to close to half of the nation's population of eleven million). During my walk I had felt keenly the change in the urban landscape I was so used to blending in and out of on my daily walks. This was the first day of implementation of a new batch of pandemic measures the prime minister had announced. Just two, this time: restriction of all non-essential movement from midnight to 5 am and mandatory masks in all spaces indoor and outdoor. The measure for the wearing of masks had been through several permutations, here as in the USA from what I read on the *New York Times* website every day. On the quiet side streets of my neighbourhood downtown and then up the busy main avenue, I noted how all humans were now mask-clad. Like myself. Such a strange sight. Such a strange bodily practice; a small piece of cloth, or paper, wrapped in front of the mouth and nose. This hitherto alien practice was on its way to being normalized.

At the local pharmacy, I asked if they had masks and how much they cost. The owner, who I was friendly with, started explaining the different types and prices in some detail. As there were no other customers at that time, he elaborated as I did quick calculations in my head. In the middle of the lockdown, my partner

Petros had just been appointed as a substitute teacher in the public high school system, with hourly class allotments distributed across three different schools. I worried that the simple cloth masks he wore were not adequate protection. The concentration of the virus had grown in Athens. 'What about the mask you are wearing?' I asked Panagiotis, the pharmacy owner, noting the black solid-looking mask on his face. 'These are different', he said, nodding his head thoughtfully, 'they are more expensive, five euros each'. 'Are they one-use only?' He explained, 'I hang today's up, say today is Friday, and then I know I can use it again next Friday. You don't wash them, just hang them somewhere out of the way. I put numbers on them.' 'Oh', I said, 'how many times can you do that?' He paused, 'maybe three or … four?' I decided to buy four of the €4 type and three of this more expensive type. I handed him €50 and he gave me a €10 bill and some coins. As I exited the pharmacy, I re-did the calculations. The total was higher than I had expected. Still, it was right.

This way Petros would have one per day at school; two of the 'heavier' masks for the two days a week he was at a rowdier school with more students crowded into each classroom. I would have two per week of the cheaper, but still better, type, should I need to go into the Sociology Department's main office or anywhere indoors with many people. We would have one of 'the best' kind in reserve for who knows what might come up. I decided I would return another day and buy some for my 82-year-old mother and for her Filipino carer, Ted, whom we had kept on after my father died in 2017. Ted takes the bus on the two days a week he leaves my mother's apartment in a suburb of Athens to go to the small apartment he rents downtown, partly in exchange for cleaning the stairs of that building twice a week.

There were various mask considerations and they were complicated. It was odd to think that at the beginning of the pandemic the wearing of masks was deemed extreme. Many thought it was only hypochondriacs or cowards who wore them routinely. There was a point when authorities in the USA had stated that masks were not necessary. Here too. A few months before, we never would have imagined that events might develop such that any discussion of masks would be part of our daily concerns. Yet, here was downtown Athens densely populated by human animals gingerly going about our business fully mask-clad. This sudden seeming influx of precarity, a realization of the precarity of human existence, was remarkable. Always there for many – like the millions of partly employed or fully unemployed, or those households with a member for whom a physical illness like cancer was a daily reality – it was now an inescapable part of everyone's lives. I headed to the open-air market. Looking down the road at the stands of vegetables, fruit and other wares, the sight encountered seemed to be that of a … mob! People were shoulder-to-shoulder, an almost solid river of humans. Perky noses were peeking out of the top of masks, while several vendors behind the stands had pulled theirs under their chin. No way, I thought to myself, even though it is open-air. *I'm not going to venture there.* The decision was instant: abort mission.

I had learned this lesson several years ago: always be prepared to fully bail on whatever you had decided was the goal. Not willing, but ready. Otherwise, I remain too vulnerable and that may, indeed, jeopardize the larger objective I want to achieve. Walking past the entrance to the flea market, I reminded myself to order more sauerkraut next time we did an online supermarket order, because it is important to have a back-up vegetable for dinner available should we not be able to buy fresh produce. Also, to buy more dried cherries and pineapple from the co-op place where we buy our coffee. For reserve fruit.

I think I learned the lesson of 'always be ready to bail' shortly after the onset of my father's senility and his stroke in 2009, originally diagnosed as Alzheimer's. I decided to sell the apartment I had agreed to buy with pressure from my mother and sister, which had incurred loan payments too heavy for me to shoulder without his assistance. The 'lesson' I am referring to helped me deal with that challenge in ways that eventually left me debt-free and in possession of a sum with which to buy outright a much more reasonably priced, if smaller, apartment later on. Opting not to buy fresh produce now, after my visual assessment of the open-air market in the midst of the COVID-19 pandemic, more than a decade later, was an obvious decision.

This way of moving in space, of negotiating movement, is new. Like wearing the masks, this new state of being had become a sort of second nature. Abilities develop and then become automatic in a short time: the scanning of public places before entering them for things like human density, clearness of pathways and percentage of face coverage on the mask-clad humans populating this terrain, even a conscious gauging of a 'too slight' breeze. I noted the particular angle of the sun at that time as one wherein sunlight was prone to bouncing on my contact lenses, creating small areas of 'blindness' in my field of vision. This pandemic reality has brought the most concrete of evidence for what a lie the common (hetero)sexist retort that 'some things just aren't natural' is, in the form of a little piece of paper or fabric poised so daintily on the face. Just like that. Within days of the prime minister's announcement. My eyes, like everyone else's no doubt, have drastically changed their own 'normal' mode of operation.

Normal is what we choose to accept and ignore. I no longer seem able to turn a blind eye to crowds of maskless humans.

Small explosions

It was 11 pm in mid-April 2020, during Greece's first full national lockdown. I was exhausted from another day of contending with the quirks of the platform Panteion was trying to improve so it might be able to carry all the teaching activities of the university without causing system crashes that would abruptly kick out instructors and/or students. My tiredness was also from the ongoing stress, worry and actual work to help keep friends and family 'safe'. Finally able to lay on the couch, I was talking on the phone with my elderly mother. This was the last chore for the day. 'Not the tomato sauce, dear, the can that has *whole* tomatoes', she said. She was reading out the items I was to e-shop for her. I noted my understanding as to the different canned tomato products. I had no idea this 'whole tomatoes' product existed. Mildly intrigued, I was not sure what recipe it would be helpful for. But I was swamped with work, had been working after dinner and the shopping list dictation was taking longer than I had expected.

As the conversation approached its end, I asked if maybe there was something we had forgotten. Does she have detergent? Soap? 'Oh, yes, dear ... maybe ... a bottle of wine too?' *Wine*, I repeated to myself, curious as to this addition to the bi-weekly pandemic shopping list. 'Any kind, red, a Merlot maybe.' My mother used to drink a bit many years ago, but I had lost track of that aspect of her life in recent years. After my sister and I had insisted that she go to the doctor for a general check-up about five years ago, we found out she had high blood pressure. Should she be drinking with her medication, I wondered? In the middle of a pandemic, I questioned whether policing her liquor consumption was a priority. Maybe it was actually good for her. I proceeded to try to keep things normal. She continued, 'uhm, maybe some pretzels too, dear? Not for me, Ted eats pretzels sometimes.' As I tried to get my mind around these last additions, these seemingly weird and banal requests, I heard myself saying, 'Ok, sounds good.'

Such minutiae. Such grand explosions. This seems to be the way of the present.

In the classroom, located on the computer screen on my desk at home, things were also strange. Here, individuals were proving to be a hard thing to identify. Few students had cameras on. Chat notes told me their microphones did not work or they were connected over mobile phones and their connection could not afford to carry images as well. What I saw as my class were rows of small black boxes with parts of names in white letters. The Zoom windows did not have enough space for most students' full last names.

The net result was an experience of teaching that felt like a radio programme broadcast. I realized that the wealth of information gained by being able to see the bodies of students is immeasurable. Now there was no source of feedback on who might be understanding the lesson, who might like it, who might be angry or bored. I draw from this vital information to run my classes, signalling when to pause, to direct questions or turn my gaze. Suddenly I felt I was in a state of severe impoverishment. Just as my vision was becoming further attuned to details of embodiment, my classroom had become a black box. The individual, at least as we knew it, whether student or professor, no longer seemed to be a salient category of subjecthood. To many of the students too, all of us had been likely relegated to little 'wagging mouth' images on their mobiles or laptops. As one of my master's students put it, it was as though classes were now in the frame of 'entertainment' and our attention becomes the kind we have when 'watching a show'. She added, 'we can drift in and out of our screens somehow'.

In addition to this structural or societal sort of evaporation, a certain spectralization, of the individual, there was at the same time an inner combustion of the individual taking place. We were all emerging as sheer bodies, whether potential patients or potential dead. This was clear from the larger context of public discourse. The official state-delivered daily evening reports on the pandemic, complete with advice to the people, were delivered by a twin male team consisting of the slender, grandfather-like senior epidemiologist Sotiris Tsiodras and the stocky, but fit, middle-aged Vice Minister of Civil Protection Nikos Chardalias, using a particular blend of gentle paternalism with a subtle but discernible nationalist register. To me this performance clearly aimed to soothe and persuade the audience that a caring father-like state was in control, no matter the mess that was unfolding. The Agamben notion of 'bare life', wherein individual humans are reduced to biological dimensions, surfaced between the lines of new state measures and hospitalization and fatality counts being reported.[17] A concept used to underline the unacceptable situation of migrants drowning daily in the Aegean Sea, and more controversially to highlight the biopolitics of Greece's financial crisis, was now eerily close to describing the situation of an 'us' who had heretofore slept more easily. In some respects, this tiny SARS-CoV-2 entity made prior notions of 'the individual' seem quaint.

The unfolding digitalization of life and the spectralizing dematerialization of the transfer to internet space of all educational processes, conducted via viewing on a screen located within tens or hundreds of different residences at the same time, was almost viscerally disorienting. In one case, one of my students turned on her camera to speak and we saw she was sitting in a kitchen just as an older woman entered, clearly irate, and started speaking loudly to her, unaware that the student was in class. 'What are you doing here?' demanded the older woman. Familiar boundaries between private space and workspace were on the brink of collapse. So, too, were some of the students. For the first time in twenty years of teaching at Panteion, I had not one, not two, but three students inform me via email that they were being hospitalized 'for reasons of mental health' and would send me a doctor's report so their class absences could be excused.[18]

Within this chaos, there was an undercurrent of excitement along with discernible examples of some form of pushback. I was surprised, and somehow happy, when a student asked if she might follow our class from the clinic she was in, keeping her camera off. Another notable occurrence in one of my seminars on gender and power was a phenomenon I consider an illustration of the fissures of resistance, of new ways of meaningful relationality created in the otherwise bleak social and technological context of our lives. In this class about half of the students did keep cameras on. Early on in the semester I had received an email complaint from a student stating she felt that the same 'masculinities' kept having more visibility and 'taking the floor'. I responded, noting that I generally am attentive to the need to 'create space' for less assertive students to speak and would continue to try to do so in this technological environment. Meanwhile, feline companions had started making appearances in our class. After ignoring two or three instances of cats coming right up to the students' cameras as I was lecturing, I stopped and commented, 'Ah, looks like this little non-human animal also wants to be part of the show'. We all laughed. From then on we had more of these guest visits, including a kitten that one of the quietest students lifted from her lap and showed to us one day, and greater participation in the discussion part of class time, from the quieter students as well. It crossed my mind that the cats were functioning as props for some in their desire to overcome camera-shyness and become 'part of the show' of our class themselves.

***

I am not sure why these few incidents from my remote teaching during the pandemic seem so telling of the larger historical and social moment. Nor do I understand exactly how this links up with the experience of my mother dictating her shopping list to me over the phone, the experience of my 'abort mission' visit to the open-air market or the peculiar realities of weighing risks and comparison-shopping for face masks. However, what has become evident is that we are constantly in transit between and within interlocking vulnerabilities. While that hones attention towards a strict 'be careful' way of living and moving in space, every step towards some sort of 'safety' – be it by purchasing masks or by undertaking distanced ways of teaching in a vaguely democratic way – also results in the surfacing of new dangers. This state of being seems linked to actual material change in cognitive processes – not just remembering, but also seeing, hearing and interpreting what one sees and hears. There is an intensity of the impact on the self when assorted pre-existing vulnerabilities collide with new ones. The Butlerean suggestion that we distinguish between precariousness as a common state of all human life and precarity as the result of certain social and political forces seems largely mute in this moment. In the case of Greece at least, these meet and mesh at the site of the SARS-CoV-2 pandemic. There is a sensation of dizziness before the cracks that emerge between various seemingly equal, if increasingly virtual, realities. Something of this is familiar. Sara Ahmed says of feminist projects of survival:

> When we say something is precarious, we usually mean it is in a precarious position: if the vase on the mantelpiece were pushed, just a little bit, a little bit, it would topple right over. ... Living on the edge: a life lived as a fragile thread that keeps unraveling; when life becomes an effort to hold on to what keeps unraveling.[19]

Combined with that, there is a stark realization that human animals can become more aggressive when disoriented or feeling weakened. In order to protect what we see as real, there is no hesitation towards barrelling on, even gaslighting others (as I did perhaps in my firm response to my student's request for more visibility in class), whether well-respected, or even loved, as in the case with my mother's shopping list. But there is something else here as well, something that relates to a tenacious creativity in attempting to respond to all this. There is a glimmer of a possibility for a certain shared re-making that follows from the un-making of life as we used to know it to life as we can make it, pushing back together. A glimmer.

On ghosts and earthquakes

Today's mission was to buy cigarette filters from the pharmacy that sells them to me at a substantial discount, and then to go up the road to the open-air market that is set up on Fridays in order to purchase fruit and vegetables for the week. Upon returning home, I disinfected my mobile phone, put my mask in the basin to be washed, changed out of my 'outdoor' clothes and checked on how the kitchen was looking. That was when I heard an odd noise in the front room of our apartment, which doubled as a study and extra bedroom. A low-grade rattle along with a bit of a thumping. Could the dry cleaners three floors below, at the ground level of our apartment building, be causing this rattling? But the sound seemed to be coming from behind the bookshelves ... from the actual wall.

As the sound continued, a thought came to mind. Maybe there is some kind of ghost in this apartment? It was bizarrely reasonable in that moment. I continued to peer at the triple bookshelf.

We bought the apartment several years ago, during the months preceding the implementation of capital controls in Greece in 2015, for a bargain price that was due partly to the fact that it had been vacant for years. Since moving in, I had wondered about a damp spot along part of another wall in the same room. The three plumbers called in to assess this development had no answer. All pipes were checked and seemed fine. One plumber went off to investigate the roof of the building; the dampness was not coming from there. Nor was it from the verandah of the apartment above, another concluded, after a specially arranged visit to our upstairs neighbour's apartment. It could not be from rain against the exterior of the wall, all three agreed. When Petros later connected the geography of the neighbourhood to a phase in the construction of Athens that had involved cementing over the river Ilissos, I developed a theory that perhaps the waterway, somewhere deep below under all those layers of concrete, was somehow *bleeding upwards* and travelling along the concrete to our third-floor wall.

Then, a few years ago, one evening after watching part of an unmemorable television movie, my thoughts went back to the day I received a phone call from a woman in Johannesburg. She identified herself as one of the two former owners of my apartment. Even though she had called to thank me and was clearly pleased to have sold the property, she had sounded sad over the phone. The market was dismal at the time and the economy was deeply in 'the crisis'. Could it be possible that the humid patch on one of our walls was reflecting her sadness somehow, I wondered then. Now, I wondered, might the strange sound emanating from behind the bookshelves be connected to some sort of mournful energy haunting this apartment? No concept of actual ghosts, of course. The rational sociologist in me did not, and does not, believe in such.

And yet, as the sound from behind the bookshelves continued, that vague thought entered the mix. Was there a supernatural presence shaking the bookshelves? It seemed persistent. I pondered the specific books on these bookshelves, a motley array of feminist literature, Greek Far Left, anarchist and queer zines, and Petros's collection of most of Marx's works. Maybe this sound was *mocking* all these books somehow, indicating the futility of the constant micromanagement of time needed to complete the ever-growing pile of work that had been intensified. Or maybe it was reminding me of them.

With that, I abruptly realized the absurdity of entertaining such ideas even fleetingly. Quite simply, it could be an earthquake! Greece has them fairly frequently. We had a big one in Athens, 5.1 on the Richter scale, in July 2019. The most serious one in the Athens area, a 5.9 Richter, occurred in September 1999. That one had caused huge damage to property and 143 deaths.

I double-checked my body. I did not feel like I was shaking or moving in any way. I quickly took two steps back and away from the bookshelves. At that precise moment, the sound stopped. Then, my mobile phone in the living room began to ring. 'Are you ok?' Petros asked over the line. 'Was there an earthquake?' I responded. Petros explained he had not felt it, but the man on the radio programme he was listening to in the car had started exclaiming about how everything in the station was bouncing around. 'Must have been a big one', Petros said.

After I hung up, I sat down at my desk to continue with the mountain of teleworking tasks the pandemic was constantly producing in my job. My brain had become one that was more willing to believe there could be a ghost in our house than to consider the possibility of an earthquake. *My brain.* The unimaginable had become more imaginable than the imaginable. Something has shifted in the boundaries between these two. It has become more plausible that the unimaginable might happen. There is slippery ground emerging here.

The present (tense) of precarity

Perhaps part of the challenge presented by social experiences of the COVID-19 pandemic is to *lean in* to the precarity and to proceed with a certain 'unworlding', in Kathleen Stewart's sense, ahead of time.[20] That is, to reassess the habits, ranging from the local to the global – from modes of life and belief to economic forms and modes of relationality – which together work to create human subjects as beings for whom the completely unimaginable has, in fact, become more imaginable than every human's intrinsic, ever-present raw vulnerability. An almost fully digitalized life appears to many of us at this conjunction as conceivably feasible. As another example, 'zero-COVID' is seriously entertained by some nation-states; as though the fleshy tactile interconnectedness of life in late modernity, with all its vital movements of goods and plants and animals, human and non-human, can somehow be adequately controlled and 'disinfected'. This notion has presently come to seem more real than the messiness of life.

On the idea of 'worlding', Stewart focuses on the affective in individuals' relations to space, time and others that create a world. Stewart writes about how her mother tenaciously reinvents movements, thoughts, the minutiae and the large stuff of her own life in order to be able to live after her husband dies. She says, 'For my mother, my father's death prompted the hard precarity of unworlding'.[21] A certain death of innocence that accompanies living in COVID times can fuel, I suggest, 'this hard precarity of unworlding'. What might it mean to accept that the nation-state, like the father, cannot in fact achieve the protection it claims to afford for *any* of the residents of its territory? More, what might it mean to realize, with the morass of contradictory public discourse and laws, even within any one given nation, concerning mask-wearing or vaccines or quarantine spans, that in fact it/he does not 'know best' although, at the same time, substantial knowledge is certainly present? What might it mean, finally, to understand all this just at the moment when already-present precarity seems to be at its peak?

One thing it might mean is that humans might turn their newly boosted abilities for vigilance in this direction as well; humans might themselves better retain a resistant stance towards allowing further ground to be ceded to *this* entity. One possible pathway to the change required might be glimmering through in the ways in which relationalities tenaciously, if serendipitously, resist surrender to a fully isolated and sterilized, almost ghost-like existence. Here, I turn to what Allison calls 'a new form of commonwealth'. She suggests, 'one can sense, if one senses optimistically, an emergent potential in attempts to humanly and collectively survive precarity: a new form of commonwealth (commonly remaking the wealth of sociality), a biopolitics from below'.[22] While her fieldwork focuses specifically on the 'collapse of mundane everydayness' for many in Japan's capitalism, she also retrieves and presents wisps of gentle belonging and expressions of a collective responsibility in the middle of pockets of capitalist wasteland.[23]

However, COVID-19 brings shared fundamental vulnerability and precarity right in the face of everyone. So-called civilized, western societies have invested a tremendous amount of effort and money in keeping this intrinsic characteristic of human life in the shadows, even as it stands firmly centre stage for people living in 'the Global South', or in the many pockets of 'the third world' within the first. The fetishization of youth, for instance, is a key characteristic of public discourse in many European nations where death and aging is rendered invisible, pushed into less visible spaces. During the pandemic, danger and potential death are everywhere. In this context, the liberal nation-state, too, takes off its gloves, legislating and mandating assorted interventions that direct human bodies and their movements, indeed at the urgent request of many of its own subjects. At this historical juncture, citizens of liberal democratic nation-states around the globe *invite* the nation-state to proceed in maximally aggressive ways to come closer, to control the actual human body. The pandemic works like a dilutant, dissolving the hold of the stories in which our lives are normally embedded.

This chapter uses the self to explore the condition of precarity, with a keen eye turned towards tracing its social potential, along with its visceral iterations and terrifying effects. During the period under examination, the air itself, so invisible and unnoticed prior to the pandemic (pollution levels aside), receives serious and deliberate attention. It has brought the ventilation systems of such disparate things as buildings in Wuhan, cruise boats in the Caribbean and classrooms in Panteion University under scrutiny. Many of us, regardless of social class and cultural, racial and national contexts, have struggled to keep windows open in our various abodes while keeping others firmly closed, as we avoided contact with humans external to our household, all *so as not to breathe the same air*. The very act of breathing, so basic and taken for granted by many, is transformed from an unconscious 'personal' bodily activity to a fundamentally social act of maximum danger.

Yet, with some notable exceptions, these heightened abilities of surveillance and vigilance seem remarkably oblivious to the new intra-psychic territory gained and occupied by the state in many national contexts. Worse, where critical minds are drawn to scrutinize or question the taken-for-granted benevolence of strong-armed state governance, they often do so from the position of denial of the importance of the virus SARS-CoV-2. To lean into the precarity at least involves asking if it is possible to imagine ways of living with COVID-19, or indeed with any kind of precarity, that would shelter our common vulnerability without ceding further power to an already heavy-handed state. What might these look like? Helpful prompts in articulating an answer emerge in two questions posed by Stewart: 'What is the political charge of precarity itself? How does the precarious subject's sensing out of events s/he is in the midst of constitute a political act?'[24] Certainly, the ease with which many of us around the globe turn to disparate states for safety from SARS-CoV-2 does not lend itself as evidence to support the optimism of 'a new form of commonwealth'. How we respond to the challenges the pandemic poses seems to me a vital political and social question. We could all weigh the risk against the benefits and declare 'mission abort', withdraw behind the purported safety of lockdowns and ignore the impossibility of dividing the air we breathe along national lines. Or we could use this moment, when the unimaginable has become more acceptable than the imaginable. The cultural and political tectonic plates holding up our various 'worlds' are shifting.

Notes

1   Elizabeth Povinelli refers to 'the otherwise' as 'forms of life that are at odds with
      dominant, and dominating, modes of being'. She expands on this, suggesting
      'This otherwise may lie in shattering the life-world in which a person finds herself
      situated, but it also might mean maintaining a life-world under constant threat of
      being saturated by the rhythms and meanings of another'. The 'otherwise' is also
      used by Anna Lowenhaupt Tsing to refer to 'the imaginative challenge of living
      without those handrails, which once made us think we knew, collectively, where we
      were going'. Elizabeth Povinelli, 'Routes/worlds', *e-flux Journal* 27 (2011), https://
      www.e-flux.com/journal/27/67991/routes-worlds/; Elizabeth Povinelli, *Economies
      of Abandonment: Social Belonging and Endurance in Late Liberalism* (Durham,
      NC: Duke University Press, 2011), 130; Anna Lowenhaupt Tsing, *The Mushroom
      at the End of the World: On the Possibility of Life in Capitalist Ruins* (Princeton, NJ:
      Princeton University Press, 2015), 2.
2   Tsing, *Mushroom*, 2, 20.
3   Michael Safi, Angela Giuffrida and Martin Farrer, 'Coronavirus: Italy bans any
      movement inside country as toll nears 5500', *The Guardian* (23 March 2020).
4   The news media coverage in Greece, a country that then had less than forty cases
      of COVID-19, evinced a sense of awe with particular details that portrayed 'the
      West' in shambles. Regarding New York, Greek news media reported, 'At the central
      prison of Reeks Island prisoners are being offered $6 an hour to dig thousands
      of new graves on Hart Island'. On 10 April, the front page of several newspapers

sported a large drone picture of the digging of a huge ditch and several people dressed in full PPE. *To Vema* reported that 'group graves are being dug in Nosa Hart, east of the Bronx, New York', while a BBC video-story referred to 'mass graves' operations in New York. Petros Papakonstandinou, 'The week of passions in New York', *Kathimerini* (5 April 2020); 'From the American dream to the American nightmare', *To Vema* (12 April 2020); 'Coronavirus: New York mass graves operations ramp up amid virus', *BBC* (10 April 2020).

5   Taking on US responses to the 9/11 attack, predominantly the ensuing war in Iraq, Judith Butler in *Precarious Life* addresses the precariousness of life as a shared quality whose recognition, however, is distributed unevenly, indeed aggressively so. This uneven recognition occurs, she suggests, even via the media and cultural politics of showing a face to effect its (de)humanization. In *Frames of War*, Butler elaborates on the link between the 'more or less existential conception of "precariousness"' and 'a more specifically political notion of "precarity"'. While these are intersecting concepts, precarity is distinguished as a 'politically induced condition in which certain populations suffer from failing social and economic networks of support and become differentially exposed to injury, violence and death'. Judith Butler, *Precarious Life: The Powers of Mourning and Violence* (London: Verso, 2004), 134–35, 141–42; Judith Butler, *Frames of War: When is Life Grievable?* (London: Verso, 2009), 3, 25.

6   Kyriakos Mitsotakis, 'Address to the nation about the SARS-CoV-2', Hellenic Republic: Prime Minister (11 March 2020), https://primeminister.gr/en/the-prime-minister/the-office.

7   The strict night-time curfew is particularly remarkable for a country where the memory of the Regime of the Colonels or Greek junta that ended in 1974, along with its military-backed restrictions of movement, is still alive. The anniversary of the student uprising leading to its demise remains a key national holiday.

8   Mitsotakis, 'Address'.

9   This resonates with the 'tradition vs. modernity' nationalist politics of the 1990s in the project to manage what was seen as a nation-threatening drop in births. Now, on 25 March 2020, Prime Minister Mitsotakis stated, 'We will not celebrate in streets and town squares … With our flags flying high and our thoughts on our ancestors' fight for Freedom. … The enemy now is the pandemic. Our strength and our unity will parade before it.' See Alexandra Halkias, *The Empty Cradle of Democracy: Sex, Abortion and Nationalism in Modern Greece* (Durham, NC: Duke University Press, 2004), 118, 135–48; 'Mitsotakis on 25 March: our enemy now is the pandemic', *I Efimerida* (25 March 2020).

10 Jacquelyn Allen-Collinson, 'Autoethnography as the engagement of self/other, self/culture, self/politics, and self/futures', in *Handbook of Autoethnography*, eds. Stacy

Holman Jones, Tony Adams and Carolyn Ellis (Walnut Creek, CA: Left Coast Press, 2013), 283.

11 I use a feminist approach to the formation of gender as a social identity that works not only to reproduce social inequalities and hierarchies, but also to shape the individual subjectivities that 'fit' within them. While gender per se is not the explicit focus here, it is part of the new 'normal' and the precarities that this project critically examines. See Sara Ahmed's *Living a Feminist Life* (Durham, NC: Duke University Press, 2017).

12 Carolyn Ellis, *Revision: Autoethnographic Reflections on Life and Work* (Walnut Creek, CA: Left Coast Press, 2009), 8.

13 Sarah Wall, 'Easier said than done: writing an autoethnography', *International Journal of Qualitative Methods* 7, no. 1 (2008): 39.

14 Anne Allison, 'Precarity: commentary from Anne Allison', *Cultural Anthropology*, Curated Collection on Precarity (2016), https://journal.culanth.org/index.php/ca/precarity-commentary-by-anne-allison.

15 Allison, 'Precarity'.

16 Michel Foucault introduces the concept of biopower to refer to the circa seventeenth–eighteenth centuries' 'explosion of numerous and diverse techniques for achieving the subjugation of bodies and the control of populations'. The disciplining and regulation of individual bodies and entire populations during COVID-19 takes the concept to another level. Michel Foucault, *The History of Sexuality, Vol. 1: The Will to Knowledge* (London: Penguin, 1990), 140.

17 Giorgio Agamben, *Homo Sacer: Sovereign Power and Bare Life* (Stanford, CA: Stanford University Press, 1998), 7.

18 COVID-19 prompted a mental health epidemic in nations around the world. One of the first studies of this phenomenon focused on the US and reported that 'depression symptom prevalence was more than 3-fold higher during the COVID-19 pandemic than before'. Catherine Ettman, Salma Abdalla, Gregory Cohen, Laura Sampson, Patrick Vivier and Sandro Galea, 'Prevalence of depression symptoms in US adults before and during the Covid-19 pandemic', *JAMA Network Open* 3, no. 9 (2020): e2019686, https://doi.org/10.1001/jamanetworkopen.2020.19686.

19 Ahmed, *Feminist Life*, 238.

20 Kathleen Stewart, 'Precarity's forms', *Cultural Anthropology* 27, no. 3 (2012): 520.

21 Stewart, 'Precarity's forms', 520.

22 Anne Allison, *Precarious Japan* (Durham, NC: Duke University Press, 2013), 18.

23 Allison, *Precarious Japan*, 2.

24 Quoted in Jennifer Shaw and Darren Byler, 'Precarity: interview with the authors', *Cultural Anthropology*, Curated Collection on Precarity (2016), https://journal.culanth.org/index.php/ca/precarity-interview-with-the-authors.

Coda

Susan Leong and Christina Lee

What is the point of books such as this? As scholars we are painfully aware of the criticisms often levelled at those in academia: that we preach only to the converted, or that we write only for each other. Hence, we deliberately set out to make this a widely accessible book that could offer points of relatability that people could identify with. Wherever possible we made the decision to write and edit in practical, everyday English to appeal to a broader readership. We included a fair number of photographs as they speak louder and more clearly on some issues than words do. If we have succeeded, then this book will have served one of its main purposes.

Further answers to the above question come from the three main findings of this book: (1) that precariousness applies to many more quarters of life than assumed; (2) that we are not alone in our sense of constantly being at a tipping point in life; and (3) that others are coping and, therefore, we may find tactics and strategies for doing so ourselves. If you have read the book's Foreword and Introduction you will already know this. The point is not so much to provide a solution but to present many possible answers that allow others to think on what they come up against. There can be no one definitive answer because our problems and societies are too complex and multifaceted for universal solutions.

Books such as this identify the spaces where critical inquiry, action and review can make precariousness bite less. The range found in the chapters here – including employment, housing, climate change, violations against human rights, migration, aged care, and the outcomes of neoliberal ideology and its agendas of progress – present some areas where embedded precariousness in policies, practices and perceptions need to be urgently addressed. Even so, there is no question that precariousness will continue to be a defining quality of life today. As our authors have shown, few, if any, will be spared the experience of living with precariousness. The migration from metropolitan centres to rural districts, the mass return to self-sufficient homes and the contraction of far-flung ties to familial circles are all responses to the disquiet. Our instinctive reaction is to retreat from threat, but our safe havens are not sustainable over time without others – the more we shrink our circles of contact with the world, the greater the areas of unknowns and vulnerability will grow. Taking shelter until the storm blows over only works if a crisis is short-lived. Yet, a return to life as we knew it is impossible because we have collectively experienced how swiftly life can be upended on a global scale, whether it be from a global pandemic, climate crisis or the shock waves of conflicts occurring far away. How do we go on, then? Can we, dare we, hope for the future? Optimism is only cruel when we enter into it with some confidence and expectation that things will turn out right eventually. Is it possible, then, to act and hope, without expectation of success? We believe we can, and have to, because there is in fact no unfailing surety to be had.

As the authors in this book have demonstrated, the interdependency of human and non-human agents exposes us to precariousness, but it is also these very connections and inter-vulnerabilities that allow us to live with (and through) precariousness. We need not be alone. This book is our stand against shrinking lifeworlds, beyond apathy towards hope for the future. Your reading it means it has at least achieved another of its purposes.

Bibliography

Foreword (Anne Allison)

Abélès, Marc. *The Politics of Survival.* Translated by Julie Kleinman. Durham, NC: Duke University Press, 2010.

Berlant, Lauren. *Cruel Optimism.* Durham, NC: Duke University Press, 2011.

Berlant, Lauren. 'Nearly utopian, nearly normal: post-Fordist affect in *La Promesse* and *Rosetta*'. *Public Culture* 19, no. 2 (2007): 273–301.

Care Collective, The (Andreas Chatzidakis, Jamie Hakim, Jo Littler, Catherine Rottenberg and Lynne Segal). *The Care Manifesto: The Politics of Interdependence.* London: Verso, 2020.

de Spinoza, Benedict. *Ethics*, edited and translated by Edwin Curley. New York: Penguin Books, 1996.

Goldberg, David Theo. *Dread: Facing Futureless Futures.* Cambridge: Polity Press, 2021.

Millar, Kathleen. *Reclaiming the Discarded: Life and Labor on Rio's Garbage Dump.* Durham, NC: Duke University Press, 2018.

Tsing, Anna Lowenhaupt. *The Mushroom at the End of the World: On the Possibility of Life in Capitalist Ruins.* Princeton, NJ: Princeton University Press, 2015.

Introduction: Living with Precariousness (Christina Lee and Susan Leong)

Allison, Anne. *Precarious Japan.* Durham, NC: Duke University Press, 2013.

Beck, Ulrich. 'Incalculable futures: world risk society and its social and political implications'. In *Ulrich Beck: Pioneer in Cosmopolitan Sociology and Risk Society*, edited by Ulrich Beck, 78–89. Heidelberg: Springer, 2014.

Berardi, Franco 'Bifo'. *The Soul at Work: From Alienation to Autonomy.* Los Angeles: Semiotext(e), 2009.

Berlant, Lauren. *Cruel Optimism.* Durham, NC: Duke University Press, 2011.

Butler, Judith. *Precarious Life: The Powers of Mourning and Violence.* London: Verso, 2004.

Chapman, Adam, prod. *Our Planet.* Season 1, episode 1, 'One planet'. Aired 5 April 2019 on Netflix.

Crutzen, Paul J. 'The "Anthropocene"'. In *Earth System Science in the Anthropocene*, edited by Eckart Ehlers and Thomas Krafft, 13–18. Berlin: Springer, 2006.

Douglas, Mary. *Risk and Blame: Essays in Cultural Theory*. London: Routledge, 1992.

Haigh, Susan. 'Chinese immigrant attacked in NYC dies months later'. *Associated Press*, 9 January 2022. https://apnews.com/article/crime-new-york-new-york-city-homicide-hate-crimes-f159287b034a312e060a613aa5644ba7.

Kriegstein, Brittany, and Clayton Guse. '"He is a kind person": anguished wife of Asian man in coma after beating on East Harlem street now fears for her own safety'. *New York Daily News*, 25 April 2021. https://www.nydailynews.com/new-york/ny-asian-man-attack-east-harlem-bottle-collector-20210425-ckg3y4b7lferbjv3cn4hczzxli-story.html.

Neilson, Brett, and Ned Rossiter. 'Precarity as a political concept, or, Fordism as exception'. *Theory, Culture and Society* 25, nos. 7–8 (2008): 51–72.

Spocchia, Gino. 'Chinese immigrant attacked on streets of New York dies'. *Yahoo News*, 9 January 2022. https://sports.yahoo.com/chinese-immigrant-attacked-streets-york-113535042.html.

Standing, Guy. *The Precariat: The New Dangerous Class*. London: Bloomsbury Academic, 2011.

Stewart, Kathleen. 'Precarity's forms'. *Cultural Anthropology* 27, no. 3 (2012): 518–25.

Taylor, Charles. *A Secular Age*. Cambridge, MA: Harvard University Press, 2007.

Weber, Max. *The Vocation Lectures: 'Science as a Vocation', 'Politics as a Vocation'*, edited by David Owen and Tracy Strong. Indianapolis, IN: Hackett Publishing, 2004.

Wittgenstein, Ludwig. *On Certainty*, edited by G. E. M. Anscombe and G. H. von Wright. Oxford: Blackwell, 1969.

Part One: Precarious Conditions

Chapter 1: Banal Precariousness (Susan Leong)

Armstrong, Philip. 'Precarity's prayers'. *Minnesota Review* 85 (2015): 180–88.

Baines, Victoria. *The Rhetoric of Insecurity: The Language of Danger, Fear and Safety in National and International Contexts*. Abingdon: Taylor & Francis, 2021.

Berardi, Franco 'Bifo'. *The Soul at Work: From Alienation to Autonomy*. Los Angeles: Semiotext(e), 2009.

Billig, Michael. *Banal Nationalism*. London: Sage, 1995.

Butler, Judith. *Precarious Life: The Powers of Mourning and Violence*. London: Verso, 2004.

Department of Statistics Malaysia. 'Graduate statistics 2019'. Press release, 16 July 2020. https://www.dosm.gov.my/v1/index.php?r=column/pdfPrev&id=b3ROY1djSVROS2 ZhclZaUWhLUVp5QT09.

Department of Statistics Malaysia. 'Key statistics of labour force in Malaysia'. 2020. https://www.dosm.gov.my/v1/index.php.

Douglas, Mary. *Risk and Blame: Essays in Cultural Theory*. London: Routledge, 1992.

Ettlinger, Nancy. 'Precarity unbound'. *Alternatives: Global, Local, Political* 32, no. 3 (2007): 319–40.

Fromm, Erich. *To Have or To Be?* London: Bloomsbury, 2013.

Gilliver, Peter. 'Precarious'. *Oxford English Dictionary*, 16 August 2012. https://public. oed.com/blog/word-stories-precarious/.

Giorgi, Gabriel. 'Improper selves: cultures of precarity'. *Social Text* 31, no. 2 (2013): 69–81.

Leong, Susan. 'No longer Singaporean'. *Continuum: Journal of Media and Cultural Studies* 25, no. 4 (2011): 559–72.

Lindley, Dennis V. *Understanding Uncertainty.* Hoboken, NJ: John Wiley & Sons, 2006.

Loh, Kah Seng, Thum Ping Tjin and Jack Meng-Tat Chia, eds. *Living with Myths in Singapore*. Singapore: Ethos Books, 2017.

Lorusso, Silvio. *Entreprecariat: Everyone Is an Entrepreneur. Nobody Is Safe.* Eindhoven, Netherlands: Onomatopee, 2019.

Mattoni, Alice, and Markos Vogiatzoglou. 'Italy and Greece, before and after the crisis: between mobilization and resistance against precarity'. *Quaderni* 84 (2014): 57–71.

McCormack, Donna, and Suvi Salmenniemi. 'The biopolitics of precarity and the self'. *European Journal of Cultural Studies* 19, no. 1 (2016): 3–15.

Neilson, Brett, and Ned Rossiter. 'Precarity as a political concept, or, Fordism as exception'. *Theory, Culture and Society* 25, nos. 7–8 (2008): 51–72.

Ngai, Sianne. *Ugly Feelings.* Cambridge, MA: Harvard University Press, 2005.

Oxford Reference. 'Structures of feeling'. 2022. https://www.oxfordreference.com/ view/10.1093/oi/authority.20110803100538488.

Pocket Stats Q3 2021, Malaysia. 'Demographic statistics by states'. 2021. https://cloud. stats.gov.my/index.php/s/x4xSjTYRTuPCo8e.

Rand, Paul. 'Why chasing the good life is holding us back, with Lauren Berlant (ep. 35)'. *University of Chicago News* (podcast), 4 November 2019. https://news.uchicago.edu/ podcasts/big-brains/why-chasing-good-life-holding-us-back-lauren-berlant.

Special Broadcasting Services. 'Revisit Pauline Hanson's infamous maiden speech'. *SBS*. Last modified 1 August 2016. https://www.sbs.com.au/guide/article/2016/07/19/ revisit-pauline-hansons-infamous-maiden-speech.

Special Broadcasting Services. 'The year of record interest rates – 1990'. *SBS News*. Last modified 1 January 2016. https://www.sbs.com.au/news/the-year-of-record-interest-rates-1990.

Standing, Guy. *The Precariat: The New Dangerous Class.* London: Bloomsbury Academic, 2011.

Steffen, Megan. 'Real people: or, how I learned to stop worrying and love housework'. *A Day is a Struggle*, 14 October 2013. https://a-day-is-a-struggle.decasia.org/texts/ real-people.html.

Stewart, Kathleen. 'Precarity's forms'. *Cultural Anthropology* 27, no. 3 (2012): 518–25.

Stewart, Kathleen. 'Writing, life'. *PMLA* 133, no. 1 (2018): 186–89.

Williams, Raymond. 'From *Preface to Film* (UK, 1954)'. In *Film Manifestos and Global Cinema Cultures: A Critical Anthology*, edited by Scott MacKenzie, 607–13. Berkeley, CA: University of California Press, 2014.

Chapter 2: A Life for a Voice: The Work of Journalist James W. Foley Through the Eyes of his Family (Diane Foley)

Oakes, Brian, dir. *Jim: The James Foley Story*. New York: HBO, 2016. Documentary, 109 min.

Chapter 3: Teaching for Buoyancy in the Pre-carious Present for an Evitable Future (Julian C. H. Lee, Anna Branford, Sam Carroll-Bell, Aya Ono and Kaye Quek)

Acaroglu, Leyla. 'Problem solving desperately needs systems thinking'. *Medium*, 3 August 2016. https://medium.com/disruptive-design/problem-solving-desperately-needs-systems-thinking-607d34e4fc80.

Acaroglu, Leyla. 'Toolkits'. *Leyla Acaroglu*, 2021. https://www.leylaacaroglu.com/toolkits.

Bowman, Kimberly, John Chettleborough, Helen Jeans, Jo Rowlands and James Whitehead. 'Systems thinking: an introduction for Oxfam programme staff'. *Oxfam: Policy and Practice*, 2015. https://policy-practice.oxfam.org.uk/publications/systems-thinking-an-introduction-for-oxfam-programme-staff-579896.

Brooker, Ben. 'I'm afraid something might be coming'. *Overland* 230 (2018): 40–47.

Buckle Henning, Pamela, and Wan-Ching Chen. 'Systems thinking: common ground or untapped territory?' *Systems Research and Behavioral Science* 29, no. 5 (2012): 470–83.

Castelloe, Molly S. 'Coming to terms with ecoanxiety'. *Psychology Today*, 9 January 2018. https://www.psychologytoday.com/gb/blog/the-me-in-we/201801/coming-terms-ecoanxiety.

Ceballos, Gerardo, Paul Ehrlich and Rodolfo Dirzo. 'Biological annihilation via the ongoing sixth mass extinction signaled by vertebrate population losses and declines'. *Proceedings of the National Academy of Sciences of the United States of America* 114, no. 30 (2017): E6089–E6096. https://doi.org/10.1073/pnas.1704949114.

Chambers, Robert. 'Participatory rural appraisal (PRA): analysis of experience'. *World Development* 22, no. 9 (1994): 1253–68.

Cross, Lucienne. 'Climate anxiety: is hopelessness preventing us from confronting our biggest challenge?' *Inhabitat*, 24 July 2019. https://inhabitat.com/climate-anxiety-is-hopelessness-preventing-us-from-confronting-our-biggest-challenge.

Curry, George. 'Moving beyond postdevelopment: facilitating indigenous alternatives for "development"'. *Economic Geography* 79, no. 4 (2003): 405–23.

Escobar, Arturo. *Encountering Development: The Making and Unmaking of the Third World*. Princeton, NJ: Princeton University Press, 1995.

Escobar, Arturo. 'Imagining a post-development era'. In *The Power of Development*, edited by Jonathan Crush, 205–21. London: Routledge, 1995.

Escobar, Arturo. 'Reflections on "development": grassroots approaches and alternative politics in the Third World'. *Futures* 24, no. 5 (1992): 411–36.

Esteva, Gustavo, Salvatore Babones and Philipp Babcicky. *The Future of Development: A Radical Manifesto*. Chicago: Policy Press, 2013.

Fileborn, Bianca. 'Acting on gender-based violence must be a priority for the next federal government'. *The Conversation*, 7 March 2019. https://theconversation.com/acting-on-gender-based-violence-must-be-a-priority-for-the-next-federal-government-110765.

Funnell, Antony. 'Why we see the past through rose-coloured glasses, but not the future'. *ABC News*, 29 August 2019. https://www.abc.net.au/news/2019-08-29/humans-pessimistic-by-nature-but-future-not-all-bad/11452114.

Ghosh, Amitav. *The Great Derangement: Climate Change and the Unthinkable*. Chicago: University of Chicago Press, 2016.

Hisham, Idura N., Giles Townsend, Steve Gillard, Brishti Debnath and Jacqueline Sin. 'COVID-19: the perfect vector for a mental health epidemic'. *BJPsych Bulletin* 45, no. 6 (2021): 332–38.

How To Academy. 'Slavoj Žižek vs Will Self in Dangerous Ideas'. Filmed 18 May 2017 in London. Video, 1:17:33. https://www.youtube.com/watch?v=CId1iOWQUuo.

Jackson, Michael. *Existential Anthropology: Events, Exigencies and Effects*. New York: Berghahn Books, 2005.

Jackson, Michael. 'Introduction: phenomenology, radical empiricism, and anthropological critique'. In *Things as They Are: New Directions in Phenomenological Anthropology*, edited by Michael Jackson, 1–50. Bloomington, IN: Indiana University Press, 1996.

Jackson, Michael. *The Politics of Storytelling: Violence, Transgression and Intersubjectivity*. Copenhagen: Museum Tusculanum Press, 2002.

Jones, Jonathan. 'Why we can't help but see the whale in the forest as an omen'. *The Guardian*, 27 February 2019. https://www.theguardian.com/environment/shortcuts/2019/feb/26/why-we-cant-help-but-see-the-whale-in-the-forest-as-an-omen.

Kofman, Fred, and Peter Senge. 'Communities of commitment: the heart of learning organizations'. *Organizational Dynamics* 22, no. 2 (1993): 5–23.

Lang, Claudia. 'A convenient lie'. *Here Be Dragons* 6 (2019): 7–10.

Manne, Robert. 'Diabolical: why have we failed to address climate change?' *The Monthly* (December 2015–January 2016): 24–34.

Nederveen Pieterse, Jan. *Development Theory*. London: Sage, 2000.

O'Barr, William. 'Culture and causality: non-western systems of explanation'. *Law and Contemporary Problems* 64, no. 4 (2001): 317–23.

Perkins, Miki. '"We can't let this happen": how ordinary people handle climate distress'. *The Age*, 11 August 2021. https://www.theage.com.au/national/we-can-t-let-this-happen-how-ordinary-people-handle-climate-distress-20210811-p58hpw.html.

Phillips, Lynn. *Flirting with Danger: Young Women's Reflections on Sexuality and Domination*. New York: New York University Press, 2000.

Radio Tamazuj. 'Cattle keepers, farmers commit to peaceful co-existence in W. Bahr el-Ghazal'. 23 May 2021. https://radiotamazuj.org/en/news/article/cattle-keepers-farmers-commit-to-peaceful-co-existence-in-w-bahr-el-ghazal.

Sachs, Wolfgang. *The Development Dictionary: A Guide to Knowledge as Power*. London: Zed Books, 1992.

Sarchet, Penny. 'Stressed about climate change? Eight tips for managing eco-anxiety'. *New Scientist*, 21 October 2019. https://www.newscientist.com/article/2220561-stressed-about-climate-change-eight-tips-for-managing-eco-anxiety/.

Schutz, Alfred. *Alfred Schutz on Phenomenology and Social Relations: Selected Writings*, edited by Helmut R. Wagner. Chicago: University of Chicago Press, 1970.

Self, Will. 'The Courage of Hopelessness by Slavoj Žižek review – how the big hairy Marxist would change the world'. *The Guardian*, 28 April 2017. https://www.theguardian.com/books/2017/apr/28/courage-of-hopelessness-slavoj-zizek-review.

Talwalker, Clare. 'Fixing poverty'. In *Encountering Poverty: Thinking and Acting in an Unequal World*, edited by Ananya Roy, Genevieve Negrón-Gonzales, Kweku Opoku-Agyemang and Clare Talwalker, 121–48. Oakland, CA: University of California Press, 2016.

Thunberg, Greta. *No One Is Too Small to Make a Difference*. London: Penguin, 2019.

Tsjeng, Zing. 'The climate change paper so depressing it's sending people to therapy'. *Vice*, 27 February 2019. https://www.vice.com/en_au/article/vbwpdb/the-climate-change-paper-so-depressing-its-sending-people-to-therapy.

UCD. 'Will Self | Q&A with UCD Clinton Institute for American Studies'. Filmed 31 March 2017 at the Royal Irish Academy, Dublin. Video, 22:18. https://www.youtube.com/watch?v=qOP4XV7iQgw.

UN Women. 'The shadow pandemic: violence against women during COVID-19'. 2020. https://www.unwomen.org/en/news/in-focus/in-focus-gender-equality-in-covid-19-response/violence-against-women-during-covid-19.

World Bank. 'Poverty: overview/context'. 7 October 2020. https://www.worldbank.org/en/topic/poverty/overview#1.

Yarrow, Thomas, and Soumhya Venkatesan. 'Anthropology and development: critical framings'. In *Differentiating Development: Beyond an Anthropology of Critique*, edited by Soumhya Venkatesan and Thomas Yarrow, 1–20. New York: Berghahn Books, 2012.

Žižek, Slavoj. *The Courage of Hopelessness: Chronicles of a Year of Acting Dangerously*. London: Penguin Books, 2018 (2017).

Chapter 4: 'Will there be a day that I say I am an equal human being?' Living With the Compounding Precarity of Seeking Asylum in Australia (Salem Askari and Caroline Fleay)

Australian Human Rights Commission. 'Indigenous deaths in custody 1989–1996: a report prepared by the Office of the Aboriginal and Torres Strait Islander Social Justice Commissioner for the Aboriginal and Torres Strait Islander Commission'. Australia: AHRC, 1996. https://humanrights.gov.au/our-work/indigenous-deaths-custody.

Australian Human Rights Commission. 'Lives on hold: refugees and asylum seekers in the "Legacy caseload" (2019)'. Sydney, NSW: AHRC, 2019. https://www. humanrights.gov.au/our-work/asylum-seekers-and-refugees/publications/lives-hold-refugees-and-asylum-seekers-legacy.

Australian Human Rights Commission. 'Sharing the stories of Australian Muslims report (2021)'. Sydney, NSW: AHRC, 2021. https://humanrights.gov.au/our-work/race-discrimination/publications/sharing-stories-australian-muslims-2021.

Butler, Judith. 'Precarious life, vulnerability, and the ethics of cohabitation'. *Journal of Speculative Philosophy* 26, no. 2 (2012): 134–51.

Campbell, Iain, and Robin Price. 'Precarious work and precarious workers: towards an improved conceptualisation'. *The Economic and Labour Relations Review* 27, no. 3 (2016): 314–32.

Colic-Peisker, Val. 'The "visibly different" refugees in the Australian labour market: settlement policies and employment realities'. In *Refugees, Recent Migrants and Employment: Challenging Barriers and Exploring Pathways*, edited by Sonia McKay, 67–83. New York: Routledge, 2009.

Colic-Peisker, Val, and Farida Tilbury. 'Employment niches for recent refugees: segmented labour market in twenty-first century Australia'. *Journal of Refugee Studies* 19, no. 2 (2006): 203–29.

Department of Home Affairs, Australian Government. 'Australia's Offshore Humanitarian Program: 2019–20'. 2020. https://www.homeaffairs.gov.au/research-and-stats/files/australia-offshore-humanitarian-program-2019-20.pdf.

Fleay, Caroline. *Australia and Human Rights: Situating the Howard Government*. Newcastle upon Tyne: Cambridge Scholars Publishing, 2010.

Fleay, Caroline, Lisa Hartley and Mary Anne Kenny. 'Refugees and asylum seekers living in the Australian community: the importance of work rights and employment support'. *Australian Journal of Social Issues* 48, no. 4 (2013): 473–93.

Fleay, Caroline, Mary Anne Kenny, Atefeh Andaveh, Salem Askari, Rohullah Hassani, Kate Leaney and Teresa Lee. '"Doing something for the future": building relationships and hope through refugee and asylum seeker advocacy in Australia'. In *Handbook of Migration and Global Justice*, edited by Leanne Weber and Claudia Tazreiter, 279–95. Cheltenham: Edward Elgar Publishing, 2021.

Hartley, Lisa, Caroline Fleay, Sally Baker, Rachel Burke and Rebecca Field. *People Seeking Asylum in Australia: Access and Support in Higher Education*. Perth, WA: Curtin University, 2018. https://www.ncsehe.edu.au/wp-content/uploads/2018/11/Hartley_PeopleSeekingAsylum.pdf.

Kenny, Mary Anne, Carol Grech and Nicholas Procter. 'A trauma informed response to COVID-19 and the deteriorating mental health of refugees and asylum seekers with insecure status in Australia'. *International Journal of Mental Health Nursing* 31, no. 1 (2022): 62–69.

Lobo, Michele. 'Living on the edge: precarity and freedom in Darwin, Australia'. *Journal of Ethnic and Migration Studies* 47, no. 20 (2021): 4615–30.

Manne, Robert. 'How we came to be so cruel to asylum seekers'. *The Conversation*, 26 October 2016. https://theconversation.com/robert-manne-how-we-came-to-be-so-cruel-to-asylum-seekers-67542.

McAdam, Jane, and Fiona Chong. *Refugee Rights and Policy Wrongs*. Sydney, NSW: University of New South Wales Press, 2019.

McAllister, Ian. 'Border protection, the 2001 Australian election and the coalition victory'. *Australian Journal of Political Science* 38, no. 3 (2003): 445–63.

National Museum of Australia. 'White Australia policy'. Last modified 31 August 2021. https://www.nma.gov.au/defining-moments/resources/white-australia-policy.

Newman, Louise, and Sarah Mares. 'Mental health and wellbeing implications of family separation for children and adults seeking asylum'. In *Together in Safety: A Report on the Australian Government's Separation of Families Seeking Safety*. Melbourne, VIC: Human Law Rights Centre, 2021. https://www.hrlc.org.au/reports/2021/9/1/together-in-safety-report.

Newnham, Elizabeth, April Pearman, Stephanie Olinga-Shannon and Angela Nickerson. 'The mental health effects of visa insecurity for refugees and people seeking asylum: a latent class analysis'. *International Journal of Public Health* 64, no. 5 (2019): 763–72.

Procter, Nicholas, Mary Anne Kenny, Heather Eaton and Carol Grech. 'Lethal hopelessness: understanding and responding to asylum seeker distress and mental deterioration'. *International Journal of Mental Health Nursing* 27, no. 1 (2018): 448–54.

RMIT ABC Fact Check. 'Alex Hawke says Australia's resettlement of refugees ranks third-highest globally. Is that correct?' *ABC News*, 14 September 2021. https://www.abc.net.au/news/2021-09-14/fact-check-does-australia-s-resettlement-of-refugees-rank-third/100436334.

Sidoti, Chris. 'Foreword'. In Don McMaster, *Asylum Seekers: Australia's Responses to Refugees*, v–vii. Melbourne, VIC: Melbourne University Press, 2001.

United Nations High Commissioner for Refugees. *Global Trends: Forced Displacement in 2020*. Copenhagen: UNHRC, 2021. https://www.unhcr.org/flagship-reports/globaltrends/.

United Nations High Commissioner for Refugees. 'Refugee data finder'. 2021. https://www.unhcr.org/refugee-statistics/.

van Kooy, John, and Dina Bowman. '"Surrounded with so much uncertainty": asylum seekers and manufactured precarity in Australia'. *Journal of Ethnic and Migration Studies* 45, no. 5 (2019): 693–710.

Waite, Louise. 'A place and space for a critical geography of precarity?' *Geography Compass* 3, no. 1 (2009): 412–33.

Part Two: Precarious Spaces

Chapter 5: Haunted Futures: (Making) Home in the Ghost City of Ordos Kangbashi (Christina Lee)

Albrecht, Glenn. 'Solastalgia'. *Alternatives Journal* 32, no. 4/5 (2006): 34–36.

Baker, Phil. 'Secret city: psychogeography and the end of London'. In *London: From Punk to Blair*, 2nd edition, edited by Joe Kerr and Andrew Gibson, 277–91. London: Reaktion Books, 2012.

Blunt, Alison, and Robyn Dowling. *Home*. London: Routledge, 2006.

Bochner, Arthur. 'Putting meanings into motion: autoethnography's existential calling'. In *Handbook of Autoethnography*, edited by Stacy Holman Jones, Tony Adams and Carolyn Ellis, 50–56. Walnut Creek, CA: Left Coast Press, 2013.

Brickell, Katherine. '"Mapping" and "doing" critical geographies of home'. *Progress in Human Geography* 36, no. 2 (2012): 225–44.

Brown, Michael Christopher. 'Ordos, China: a modern ghost town'. *Time* (n.d.). http://content.time.com/time/photogallery/0,29307,1975397_2094492,00.html.

Chambers, Iain. 'Cities without maps'. In *Mapping the Futures: Local Cultures, Global Change*, edited by Jon Bird, Barry Curtis, Tim Putnam, George Robertson and Lisa Tickner, 188–98. London: Routledge, 1993.

Chan, Melissa. 'China's empty city'. *Al Jazeera*, 10 November 2009. http://www.aljazeera.com/news/asia-pacific/2009/11/2009111061722672521.html.

Coverley, Merlin. *Psychogeography*. Harpenden: Pocket Essentials, 2006.

Crampton, Jeremy. *Mapping: A Critical Introduction to Cartography and GIS*. Chichester: Wiley-Blackwell, 2010.

de Certeau, Michel. *The Practice of Everyday Life*. Translated by Steven Rendall. Berkeley, CA: University of California Press, 1984.

Dobraszczyk, Paul. 'Petrified ruin: Chernobyl, Pripyat and the death of the city'. *City* 14, no. 4 (2010): 370–89.

Ellis, Carolyn. 'Preface: Carrying the torch for autoethnography'. In *Handbook of Autoethnography*, edited by Stacy Holman Jones, Tony Adams and Carolyn Ellis, 9–12. Walnut Creek, CA: Left Coast Press, 2013.

Kim, Annette. 'Critical cartography 2.0: from "participatory mapping" to authored visualizations of power and people'. *Landscape and Urban Planning* 142 (2015): 215–25.

Kochan, Dror. 'Home is where I lay down my hat? The complexities and functions of home for internal migrants in contemporary China'. *Geoforum* 71 (2016): 21–32.

Lee, Christina. 'Building the new urban ruin: the ghost city of Ordos Kangbashi, Inner Mongolia'. In *The New Urban Ruins: Vacancy, Urban Politics and International Experiments in the Post-Crisis City*, edited by Cian O'Callaghan and Cesare Di Feliciantonio, 73–88. Bristol: Policy Press, 2021.

Lee, Christina. 'Home is where the hearth *was*: remembering and place-making a vanished town'. In *Spectral Spaces and Hauntings: The Affects of Absence*, edited by Christina Lee, 51–69. New York: Routledge, 2017.

Robinson, Melia. 'Surreal photos of China's failed "city of the future"'. *Tech Insider*, 30 January 2016. https://www.businessinsider.com/chinese-ghost-town-2016-1.

Rosen, Jody. 'The colossal strangeness of China's most excellent tourist city'. *The New York Times*, 6 March 2015. https://www.nytimes.com/2015/03/06/t-magazine/ordos-china-tourist-city.html.

Shepard, Wade. 'An update on China's largest ghost city – what Ordos Kangbashi is like today'. *Forbes*, 19 April 2016. http://www.forbes.com/sites/wadeshepard/2016/04/19/an-update-on-chinas-largest-ghost-city-what-ordos-kangbashi-is-like-today/.

Shepard, Wade. *Ghost Cities of China*. London: Zed Books, 2015.

Sorace, Christian, and William Hurst. 'China's phantom urbanisation and the pathology of ghost cities'. *Journal of Contemporary Asia* 46, no. 2 (2016): 304–22.

Woodworth, Max. 'Frontier boomtown urbanism in Ordos, Inner Mongolia Autonomous Region'. *Cross-Currents: East Asian History and Culture Review* 1, no. 1 (2012): 74–101.

Woodworth, Max. 'Picturing urban China in ruin: "ghost city" photography and speculative urbanization'. *GeoHumanities* 6, no. 2 (2020): 233–51.

Woodworth, Max, and Jeremy Wallace. 'Seeing ghosts: parsing China's "ghost city" controversy'. *Urban Geography* 38, no. 8 (2017): 1270–81.

Xinhuanet. 'Across China: from ghost town to boomtown – the new look of boomtown'. 29 June 2017. http://www.xinhuanet.com/english/2017-06/29/c_136402110.htm.

Yin, Duo, Junxi Qian and Hong Zhu. 'Living in the "ghost city": media discourses and the negotiation of home in Ordos, Inner Mongolia, China'. *Sustainability* 9, no. 11 (2017): 1–14.

Chapter 6: Upgrading Downsizing: Tiny Houses as a Response to Precarity (Madeleine Esch)

Bach, Trevor. 'A Detroit project's spin on helping the homeless: homeownership'. *The Washington Post*, 26 October 2018. https://www.washingtonpost.com/graphics/2018/national/tiny-houses/#detroit.

Dale, Joshua Paul, Joyce Goggin, Julia Leyda, Anthony McIntyre and Diane Negra. 'The aesthetics and affects of cuteness'. In *The Aesthetics and Affects of Cuteness*, edited by Joshua Paul Dale, Joyce Goggin, Julia Leyda, Anthony McIntyre and Diane Negra, 1–34. New York: Routledge, 2016.

Dallas, Kelsey. 'Can a tiny house play a role in helping the homeless?' *Deseret News*, 30 April 2017. https://www.statesboroherald.com/churches/faith/can-a-tiny-house-play-a-role-in-helping-the-homeless/.

Dirksen, Kirsten, dir. *We the Tiny House People*. USA: faircompanies, 2012. Documentary, 81 min.

Edwards, Tennessee, exec. prod. *Tiny House Nation*. Season 4, episode 4, '325 sq. ft Texan's take tiny house'. Aired 28 January 2017 on FYI.

Esch, Madeleine. 'Renovating TV, remodeling gender: home improvement television and gendered domesticities, 1990–2005'. PhD diss., University of Colorado, 2009.

Etzioni, Amitai. 'Introduction: voluntary simplicity – psychological implications, societal consequences'. In *Voluntary Simplicity: Responding to Consumer Culture*, edited by Daniel Doherty and Amitai Etzioni, 1–25. Lanham, MD: Rowman and Littlefield, 2003.

Fry, Richard. 'Amid a pandemic and a recession, Americans go on a near-record homebuying spree'. Pew Research Center, 8 March 2021. https://www.pewresearch. org/fact-tank/2021/03/08/amid-a-pandemic-and-a-recession-americans-go-on-a-near-record-homebuying-spree/.

Gay, Roxane. '"Tiny House hunters" and the shrinking American dream'. *Curbed*, 25 October 2017. https://archive.curbed.com/2017/10/25/16526872/tiny-house-hunters-roxane-gay.

Gupta, Raveesha, Andrea Hasler, Annamaria Lusardi and Noemi Oggero. 'Financial fragility in the US: evidence and implications'. National Endowment for Financial Education, 16 April 2018. https://www.nefe.org/research/research-projects/completed-research/2018/financial-fragility-in-the-us-evidence-and-implications. aspx.

Joint Center for Housing Studies of Harvard University. 'The state of the nation's housing 2019'. President and Fellows of Harvard College, Boston. 2020. https://www. jchs.harvard.edu/state-nations-housing-2019.

Kahn, Eve M. 'A roof of one's own, with or without the gingerbread'. *The New York Times*, 3 October 2019. https://www.nytimes.com/2019/10/01/style/tiny-houses. html.

Kiviat, Barbara. 'The case against home ownership'. *Time International (Atlantic Edition)* 176, no. 13 (2010): 39–44.

Littlejohn, Donna. '"Doghouses" for homeless create uproar in Los Angeles'. *The Mercury News*, 12 August 2015. https://www.mercurynews.com/2015/08/12/doghouses-for-homeless-create-uproar-in-los-angeles/.

Littlejohn, Donna. 'Tiny houses for homeless rejected by Los Angeles lawmakers; "only legal use … is for dogs"'. *The Mercury News*, 25 August 2015. https://www. mercurynews.com/2015/08/25/tiny-houses-for-homeless-rejected-by-los-angeles-lawmakers-only-legal-use-is-for-dogs/.

Lowrey, Annie. 'The great affordability crisis breaking America'. *The Atlantic*, 7 February 2020. https://www.theatlantic.com/ideas/archive/2020/02/great-affordability-crisis-breaking-america/606046/.

McElroy, Ruth. 'Mediating home in an age of austerity: the values of British property television'. *European Journal of Cultural Studies* 20, no. 5 (2017): 525–42.

Mueller, Merete, and Christopher Smith, dir. *TINY: A Story about Living Small*. New York: First Run Features, 2013. Documentary, 61 min.

Nir, Sarah Maslin. 'Thinking outside the box by moving into one'. *The New York Times*, 13 October 2015. https://www.nytimes.com/2015/10/14/us/live-in-boxes-in-oakland-redefine-housing-squeeze.html.

Palmer, Gareth. 'Introduction – the habit of scrutiny'. In *Exposing Lifestyle Television: The Big Reveal*, edited by Gareth Palmer, 1–13. Aldershot: Ashgate, 2008.

Pew Research Center. 'Even as housing values sink, there's comfort in homeownership'. 19 February 2009. https://www.pewresearch.org/social-trends/2009/02/19/even-as-housing-values-sink-theres-comfort-in-homeownership/.

Plunkett, Mike. 'Tiny houses multiply amid big issues as communities tackle homelessness'. *The Washington Post*, 26 October 2018. https://www.washingtonpost.com/graphics/2018/national/tiny-houses/.

Schor, Juliet. 'The problem of over-consumption: why economists don't get it'. In *Voluntary Simplicity: Responding to Consumer Culture*, edited by Daniel Doherty and Amitai Etzioni, 65–82. Lanham, MD: Rowman and Littlefield, 2003.

Shimpach, Shawn. 'Realty reality: HGTV and the subprime crisis'. *American Quarterly* 64, no. 3 (2012): 515–42.

Spoto, Cara. 'Tiny houses for homeless vets – nonprofit envisions veterans village'. *The Journal Times*, 4 April 2016. https://journaltimes.com/news/local/tiny-houses-for-homeless-vets-nonprofit-envisions-veterans-village/article_77fb1f12-2d7b-509b-b942-a760e8d031a9.html.

Standing, Guy. *The Precariat: The New Dangerous Class*. London: Bloomsbury Academic, 2011.

Sullivan, Esther. 'America's most invisible communities – mobile home parks'. Filmed 7 July 2017 at Ellie Caulkins Opera House, Denver. Video, 14:35. https://www.ted.com/talks/esther_sullivan_america_s_most_invisible_communities_mobile_home_parks.

Sullivan, Esther. *Manufactured Insecurity: Mobile Home Parks and Americans' Tenuous Right to Place*. Oakland, CA: University of California Press, 2018.

Sullivan, Jenny. 'Is the McMansion dead?' *Builder: The Magazine of the National Association of Home Builders* 32, no. 11 (2009): 46–50.

Terruso, Julia. 'Could tiny houses help solve Philly's big homelessness problem?' *The Philadelphia Inquirer*, 13 December 2018. https://www.inquirer.com/news/tiny-houses-homelessness-stephanie-sena-seattle-frankford-poverty-affordable-housing-20181213.html.

Thompson, Derek. '"We wish like hell we had never bought": voices from the housing crisis'. *The Atlantic*, 2 March 2012. https://www.theatlantic.com/business/archive/2012/03/we-wish-like-hell-we-had-never-bought-voices-from-the-housing-crisis/253888/.

Thoreau, Henry David. *Walden: 150th Anniversary Edition*. Princeton, NJ: Princeton University Press, 2004.

US Census Bureau. 'Characteristics of new housing'. 1 June 2020. https://www.census.gov/construction/chars/.

US Interagency Council on Homelessness, 'HUD releases 2020 annual homeless assessment report. Part 1', 18 March 2021. https://www.usich.gov/news/hud-releases-2020-annual-homeless-assessment-report-part-1/.

White, Mimi. 'Gender territories: house hunting on American real estate TV'. *Television and New Media* 14, no. 3 (2012): 228–43.

White, Mimi. 'A house divided'. *European Journal of Cultural Studies* 20, no. 5 (2017): 575–91.

Wilkens, John. 'Homeless in Seattle: tent encampments seem to be working'. *The San Diego Union-Tribune*, 15 October 2017. https://www.sandiegouniontribune.com/news/homelessness/sd-me-tents-seattle-20171013-story.html.

Wilson, Jim. 'Tiny houses: affordable living for hipsters and homeless alike'. *The New York Times*, 13 October 2015. https://cn.nytimes.com/slideshow/20151016/t16containers-ss/en-us/#1.

Witt, Shawn, exec. prod. *Tiny House Hunting*. Season 1, episode 6, 'Going tiny in the Tetons'. Aired 5 January 2015 on FYI.

Chapter 7: Thinking Climate Through Precarity (Ben Beitler)

Agarwal, Anil, and Sunita Narain. 'Global warming in an unequal world'. In *India in a Warming World*, edited by Navroz K. Dubash, 81–91. Oxford: Oxford University Press, 2019.

Barnett, Joshua Trey. 'Thinking ecologically with Judith Butler'. *Culture, Theory and Critique* 59, no. 1 (2018): 20–39.

Berlant, Lauren. *Cruel Optimism*. Durham, NC: Duke University Press, 2011.

Butler, Judith. *Precarious Life: The Powers of Mourning and Violence*. New York: Verso, 2004.

Crockford, Susan J. 'Attenborough's tragedy porn of walruses plunging to their deaths because of climate change is contrived nonsense'. *Polar Bear Science*, 7 April 2019. https://polarbearscience.com/2019/04/07/attenboroughs-tragedy-porn-of-walruses-plunging-to-their-deaths-because-of-climate-change-is-contrived-nonsense/.

Crockford, Susan J. 'Netflix is lying about those falling walruses. It's another "tragedy porn" climate hoax'. *Financial Post*, 24 April 2019. https://financialpost.com/opinion/netflix-is-lying-about-those-falling-walruses-its-another-tragedy-porn-climate-hoax.

Ferdinand, Malcom. *Decolonial Ecology: Thinking from the Caribbean World*. Translated by Anthony Paul Smith. Cambridge: Polity Press, 2022.

Fothergill, Alastair, and Keith Scholey, prod. *Our Planet*. UK: Silverback Films, 2019. Documentary series.

Ghosh, Amitav. *The Great Derangement: Climate Change and the Unthinkable*. Chicago: University of Chicago Press, 2016.

Ghosh, Amitav. *The Hungry Tide*. Boston: Mariner Books, 2006.

Guha, Ramachandra, and Juan Martinez-Alier. *Varieties of Environmentalism: Essays North and South*. London: Earthscan, 1997.

Haraway, Donna J. *Staying with the Trouble: Making Kin in the Chthulucene*. Durham, NC: Duke University Press, 2016.

Homewood, Paul. 'Why Attenborough's walrus claims are fake'. *Not A Lot of People Know That*, 14 April 2019. https://notalotofpeopleknowthat.wordpress.com/2019/04/14/why-attenboroughs-walrus-claims-are-fake/.

IPCC. 'Summary for Policymakers'. In *Climate Change 2022: Impacts, Adaptation and Vulnerability. Contribution of Working Group II to the Sixth Assessment Report of the Intergovernmental Panel on Climate Change*, edited by H.-O. Pörtner, D.C. Roberts, E.S. Poloczanska, K. Mintenbeck, M. Tignor, A. Alegría, M. Craig, S. Langsdorf, S. Löschke, V. Möller, A. Okem and B. Rama. Cambridge: Cambridge University Press, in press. https://www.ipcc.ch/report/sixth-assessment-report-working-group-ii/.

Latour, Bruno. *Down to Earth: Politics in the New Climatic Regime*. Translated by Catherine Porter. Cambridge: Polity Press, 2018.

Latour, Bruno. *Facing Gaia: Eight Lectures on the New Climatic Regime*. Translated by Catherine Porter. Cambridge: Polity Press, 2017.

Malm, Andreas. *Fossil Capital: The Rise of Steam Power and the Roots of Global Warming*. New York: Verso, 2016.

Montford, Andrew. 'Has Netflix's *Our Planet* hidden the real cause of walrus deaths?' *The Spectator*, 9 April 2019. https://www.spectator.co.uk/article/has-netflix-s-our-planet-hidden-the-real-cause-of-walrus-deaths.

OED. 'precarious, adj.' 2021. www.oed.com/view/Entry/149548.

Popovich, Nadja, and Brad Plumer. 'Who has the most historical responsibility for climate change?' *The New York Times*, 12 November 2021. www.nytimes.com/interactive/2021/11/12/climate/cop26-emissions-compensation.html.

Puar, Jasbir. 'Precarity talk: a virtual roundtable with Lauren Berlant, Judith Butler, Bojana Cvejić, Isabell Lorey, Jasbir Puar, and Ana Vujanović'. *The Drama Review* 56, no. 4 (2012): 163–77.

Sen, Malcolm. 'Spatial justice: the ecological imperative and postcolonial development'. *Journal of Postcolonial Writing* 45, no. 4 (2009): 365–77.

Trexler, Adam. 'Mediating climate change: ecocriticism, science studies, and *The Hungry Tide*'. In *The Oxford Handbook of Ecocriticism*, edited by Greg Garrard, 205–24. Oxford: Oxford University Press, 2014.

Tsing, Anna Lowenhaupt. *The Mushroom at the End of the World: On the Possibility of Life in Capitalist Ruins*. Princeton, NJ: Princeton University Press, 2015.

White, Laura A. 'Novel vision: seeing the Sunderbans through Amitav Ghosh's *The Hungry Tide*'. *ISLE: Interdisciplinary Studies in Literature and Environment* 20, no. 3 (2013): 513–31.

Yong, Ed. 'Netflix's *Our Planet* says what other nature series have omitted'. *The Atlantic*, 1 April 2019. www.theatlantic.com/science/archive/2019/04/wildlife-series-finally-addresses-elephant-room/586066/.

Yong, Ed. 'The disturbing walrus scene in *Our Planet*'. *The Atlantic*, 8 April 2019. https://www.theatlantic.com/science/archive/2019/04/why-are-walruses-walking-off-cliffs/586510/.

Chapter 8: Precarity in a Time of Fire and Pandemic (Julie Macken and Sonia M. Tascón)

Brown, Wendy. *Edgework: Critical Essays on Knowledge and Politics*. Princeton, NJ: Princeton University Press, 2005.

Brown, Wendy. *Undoing the Demos: Neoliberalism's Stealth Revolution*. New York: Zone Books, 2015.

BT Insights. 'How has COVID-19 changed Australian consumer spending habits?' 22 July 2020. https://www.bt.com.au/insights/perspectives/2020/australian-consumer-spending-changes.html.

Butler, Judith. *Precarious Life: The Powers of Mourning and Violence*. New York: Verso, 2004.

Channel Nine. 'Interview by Leila McKinnon, *A Current Affair*'. Transcript, 7 January 2020. https://ministers.treasury.gov.au/ministers/josh-frydenberg-2018/transcripts/interview-leila-mckinnon-current-affair-channel-9.

Connolly, Anne. 'Coronavirus is devastating the aged care sector, and it all feels shockingly familiar'. *ABC News*, 25 August 2020. https://www.abc.net.au/news/2020-08-25/coronavirus-aged-care-australia-crisis-feels-shockingly-familiar/12592178.

Costin, Luke. 'Pop-up mall for bushfire-ravaged town Mogo'. *The Leader*, 15 February 2020. https://www.theleader.com.au/story/6632084/pop-up-mall-for-bushfire-ravaged-town-mogo/.

Cull, Michelle. 'Value beyond money: Australia's special dependence on volunteer firefighters'. *Australian Emergency Services Magazine*, 4 February 2020. https://ausemergencyservices.com.au/emergency-disaster-management/value-beyond-money-australias-special-dependence-on-volunteer-firefighters/.

Denniss, Richard. 'Dead right: how neoliberalism ate itself and what comes next'. *Quarterly Essay* 70 (2018): 1–79.

'Former fire chiefs "tried to warn Scott Morrison" to bring in more water-bombers ahead of horror bushfire season'. *ABC News*, 14 November 2019. https://www.abc.net.au/news/2019-11-14/former-fire-chief-calls-out-pm-over-refusal-of-meeting/11705330.

Hamann, Trent. 'Neoliberalism, governmentality, and ethics'. *Foucault Studies* 6 (2009): 37–59.

Harvey, David. *A Brief History of Neoliberalism*. Oxford: Oxford University Press, 2005.

Hayek, Friedrich. 'The fatal conceit'. In *The Collected Works of Friedrich August Hayek: Volume 1*, edited by W.W. Bartley III, 66–88. London: Routledge, 1988.

International Labour Office. 'ILO highlights global challenge to trade unions'. Press release, 1997. https://www.ilo.org/global/about-the-ilo/newsroom/news/WCMS_008032.

Jackson, James, Martin Weiss, Andres Schwarzenberg, Rebecca Nelson, Karen Sutter and Michael Sutherland. 'Global economic effects of COVID-19'. Congressional Research Service. Last modified 9 July 2020. https://crsreports.congress.gov/product/pdf/R/R46270.

Lowe, Philip. 'Statement by Philip Lowe, Governor: monetary policy decision (number 2020–17)'. Reserve Bank of Australia press release, 7 July 2020. https://www.rba.gov.au/media-releases/2020/mr-20-17.html.

Merle, Renae. 'A guide to the financial crisis – 10 years later'. *The Washington Post*, 10 September 2018. https://www.washingtonpost.com/business/economy/a-guide-to-the-financial-crisis–10-years-later/2018/09/10/114b76ba-af10-11e8-a20b-5f4f84429666_story.html.

Morrison, Scott. 'Press conference – Australian Parliament House, ACT'. Transcript, 14 August 2020. https://pmtranscripts.pmc.gov.au/release/transcript-42975.

Read, Paul, and Richard Denniss. 'With costs approaching $100 billion, the fires are Australia's costliest natural disaster'. *The Conversation*, 17 January 2020. https://theconversation.com/with-costs-approaching-100-billion-the-fires-are-australias-costliest-natural-disaster-129433.

RMIT ABC Fact Check. 'COVID-19 has put jobs in danger. How many workers don't have leave entitlements?' *ABC News*, 30 March 2020. https://www.abc.net.au/news/2020-03-30/fact-file-casual-employment-paid-leave-entitlements/12089056.

Rose, Nikolas. *Powers of Freedom: Reframing Political Thought*. Cambridge: Cambridge University Press, 1999.

Rotondaro, Vinnie. 'The "precariat": stressed out, insecure, alienated and angry'. *National Catholic Reporter*, 19 August 2015. https://www.ncronline.org/blogs/ncr-today/precariat-stressed-out-insecure-alienated-and-angry.

Russell, Sarah. 'Passing the buck: why Victoria's Covid is raging in private aged care homes'. *Michael West Media*, 24 July 2020. https://www.michaelwest.com.au/passing-the-buck-why-victorias-covid-is-raging-in-private-aged-care-homes.

Schneiders, Ben. 'How hotel quarantine let COVID-19 out of the bag in Victoria'. *The Age*, 3 July 2020. https://www.theage.com.au/national/victoria/how-hotel-quarantine-let-covid-19-out-of-the-bag-in-victoria-20200703-p558og.html.

Standing, Guy. *A Precariat Charter: From Denizens to Citizens*. London: Bloomsbury, 2014.

Standing, Guy. *Plunder of the Commons: A Manifesto for Sharing Public Wealth*. London: Pelican Books, 2019.

Standing, Guy. 'The precariat and class struggle'. *RCCS Annual Review* 7, no. 7 (2015): 3–16.

Standing, Guy. 'Who are "the precariat" and why do they threaten our society?' *Euronews*, 2 May 2018. https://www.euronews.com/2018/05/01/who-are-the-precariat-and-why-they-threaten-our-society-view.

Stratton, Jon. *Uncertain Lives: Culture, Race and Neoliberalism in Australia*. Newcastle upon Tyne: Cambridge Scholars Publishing, 2011.

Tobin, Grace, and Alex McDonald. 'Coronavirus quarantine guards in Melbourne hotels were recruited via WhatsApp, then "told to bring their own masks"'. *ABC Online*, 21 July 2020. https://www.abc.net.au/news/2020-07-21/coronavirus-quarantine-hotel-security-guards-recruited-whatsapp/12476574.

Part Three: Precarious Bodies

Chapter 10: Grieve-able Lives: Precarity in Residential Aged Care (Helen Fordham)

Angus, Jocelyn, and Patricia Reeve. 'Ageism: a threat to "aging well" in the 21st century'. *The Journal of Applied Gerontology* 25, no. 2 (2006): 137–52.

Australian Institute of Health and Welfare. 'People leaving aged care'. Last modified 22 June 2021. https://www.gen-agedcaredata.gov.au/Topics/People-leaving-aged-care.

Bai, Xue. 'Images of ageing in society: a literature review'. *Journal of Population Ageing* 7, no. 3 (2014): 231–53.

Butler, Judith. 'Performativity, precarity and sexual politics'. *Revista de Antropología Iberoamericana* 4, no. 3 (2009): i–xiii.

Butler, Judith. *Precarious Life: The Powers of Mourning and Violence*. London: Verso, 2004.

Butler, Judith. 'Precarious life, vulnerability, and the ethics of cohabitation'. *Journal of Speculative Philosophy* 26, no. 2 (2012): 134–51.

Butler, Judith. 'Violence, mourning, politics'. *Studies in Gender and Sexuality* 4, no. 1 (2003): 9–37.

Department of Health, Australian Government. '2020 Aged Care Workforce Census Report'. 2 September 2021. https://www.health.gov.au/.

Fedele, Robert. 'Aged care workers underpaid, undervalued and short-staffed, Royal Commission told'. *Australian Nursing and Midwifery Journal*, 16 October 2019. https://anmj.org.au/aged-care-workers-underpaid-undervalued-and-short-staffed-royal-commission-told/.

Foucault, Michel. *Ethics, Subjectivity and Truth: Essential Works of Foucault 1954–1984*, edited by Paul Rabinow. Translated by Robert Hurley. New York: New Press, 1997.

'The future of aged care'. *Amana Living*, 28 May 2021. https://www.amanaliving.com.au/about-us/news-and-events/the-future-of-aged-care.

Grenier, Amanda, Liz Lloyd and Chris Phillipson. 'Precarity in late life: rethinking dementia as a "frailed" old age'. In *Ageing, Dementia and the Social Mind*, 2nd edition, edited by Paul Higgs and Chris Gilleard, 142–54. Hoboken, NJ: Wiley-Blackwell, 2017.

Long, Benjamin. 'Collaboration and continuity key to good medical support in aged care'. University of Wollongong Australia (news), 15 April 2021. https://www.uow.edu.au/media/?year=2021#stories.

Martin, Sarah. 'Australia's aged care sector may not be financially sustainable, Senate committee hears'. *The Guardian*, 23 October 2019. https://www.theguardian.com/australia-news/2019/oct/23/australias-aged-care-sector-may-not-be-financially-sustainable-senate-committee-hears.

Portacolone, Elena, Robert Rubinstein, Kenneth Covinsky, Jodi Halpern and Julene Johnson. 'The precarity of older adults living alone with cognitive impairment'. *The Gerontologist* 59, no. 2 (2019): 271–80.

Royal Commission into Aged Care Quality and Safety. 'Final Report – Volume 1: Summary and Recommendations'. Commonwealth of Australia (report), 1 March 2021. https://agedcare.royalcommission.gov.au/publications/final-report-volume-1.

Royal Commission into Aged Care Quality and Safety. 'Interim Report: Neglect'. Commonwealth of Australia (report), 31 October 2019. https://agedcare. royalcommission.gov.au/publications/interim-report.

Royal Commission into Aged Care Quality and Safety. 'Report on the profitability and viability of the Australian aged care industry: research paper 12'. Commonwealth of Australia (paper), 9 September 2020. https://agedcare.royalcommission.gov.au/publications/research-paper-12-report-profitability-and-viability-australian-aged-care-industry.

Royal Commission into Aged Care Quality and Safety. 'What Australians think of ageing and aged care: research paper 4'. Commonwealth of Australia (paper), 13 July 2020. https://agedcare.royalcommission.gov.au/publications/research-paper-4-what-australians-think-ageing-and-aged-care.

Savy, Pauline, and Suzanne Hodgkin. 'Australian rural community aged care services: precarity and capacity'. *Australian Journal of Public Administration* 80, no. 2 (2021): 324–39.

Smith, K-lynn. 'Why greater private sector participation has not improved aged care performance'. *Health System Sustainability*, 28 October 2021. https://healthsystemsustainability.com.au/.

Swift, Hannah, and Ben Steeden. 'Exploring representations of old age and ageing: literature review'. London: Centre for Ageing Better, 2020.

Wright, Shane. 'Debt, deficit and grey haired: COVID-19 upends economic future'. *The Sydney Morning Herald*, 27 June 2021. https://www.smh.com.au/politics/federal/debt-deficit-and-grey-haired-covid-19-upends-economic-future-20210627-p584n3.html.

Chapter 11: The Precarious Lives of Slavery Survivors (Alicia Rana and Kevin Bales)

Al-Dayel, Nadia, Andrew Mumford and Kevin Bales. 'Not yet dead: the establishment and regulation of slavery by the Islamic State'. *Studies in Conflict and Terrorism* 45, no. 11 (2022): 929–52. https://doi.org/10.1080/1057610X.2020.1711590.

Bales, Kevin. *Blood and Earth: Modern Slavery, Ecocide, and the Secret to Saving the World*. New York: Spiegel and Grau, 2016.

Bales, Kevin. 'The social psychology of modern slavery'. *Scientific American* 286, no. 4 (2002): 80–88.

Bales, Kevin. 'Unlocking the statistics of slavery'. *Chance (Journal of the American Statistical Association): The Best of Chance* 32, no. 1 (2019): 18–26.

Bales, Kevin, and Jody Sarich. 'The paradox of women, children, and slavery'. In *Trafficking in Slavery's Wake: Law and the Experience of Women and Children in*

Africa, edited by Benjamin N. Lawrance and Richard L. Roberts, 241–53. Ohio: Ohio University Press, 2012.

Bales, Kevin, and Ron Soodalter. *The Slave Next Door: Human Trafficking and Slavery in America Today*. Berkeley, CA: University of California Press, 2009.

Dang, Minh. 'Confronting the paradoxes of higher education'. In *Building the Field of Higher Education Engagement: Foundational Ideas and Future Directions*, edited by Lorilee Sandmann and Diann Jones, 232–34. Sterling, VA: Stylus Publishing, 2019.

Dang, Minh. 'The paradox of survivor leadership'. In *Wicked Problems: The Ethics of Action for Peace, Rights, and Justice*, edited by Austin Choi-Fitzpatrick, Douglas Irvin-Erickson and Ernesto Verdeja, 87–96. Oxford: Oxford University Press, 2022.

Dang, Minh. 'Strategic priorities 2021–2023'. *Survivor Alliance* (n.d.). https://www.survivoralliance.org/about.

Dang, Minh. 'Survivors are speaking. Are we listening?' *Walk Free Foundation*, 2018. https://www.globalslaveryindex.org/resources/essays/survivors-are-speaking-are-we-listening.

Dang, Minh, Monica Anderson, Kimberly Forbess, Ummra Hang, Catie Hart, Amy Rahe, Celia Roberts, Genèvieve Tiangco and alix lutnick. 'Achieving health in freedom: what are we aiming for?' Paper presented at the Institute of Mental Health, Nottingham, UK (March 2018).

Dang, Minh, Ummra Hang and alix lutnick. 'Forging partnerships between the researcher and the researched: a community based anti-trafficking response'. Paper presented at Society of Social Work and Research Conference, Washington, DC (January 2018).

Global Slavery Index. 'Global slavery index, 2016'. *Walk Free Foundation*, 2018. https://www.globalslaveryindex.org/.

Hayes, Rebecca, Katherine Lorenz and Kristin Bell. 'Victim blaming others: rape myth acceptance and the just world belief'. *Feminist Criminology* 8, no. 3 (2013): 202–22.

Lockyer, Sue. 'Beyond inclusion: survivor-leader voice in anti-human trafficking organizations'. *Journal of Human Trafficking* 8, no. 2 (2020): 135–56.

Nicholson, Andrea, Minh Dang and Zoe Trodd. 'A full freedom: contemporary survivors' definitions of slavery'. *Human Rights Law Review* 18, no. 4 (2018): 689–704.

OED. 'precarious (adj.)'. 2001–2022. https://www.etymonline.com/search?q=precarious.

Patterson, Orlando. *Slavery and Social Death: A Comparative Study*. Cambridge, MA: Harvard University Press, 1982.

Schwarz, Katarina, and Jean Allain. *Antislavery in Domestic Legislation: An Empirical Analysis of National Prohibition Globally*. Nottingham: University of Nottingham, 2020. https://antislaverylaw.ac.uk/resources/summary-of-findings/.

Seelinger, Kim Thuy, Helene Silverberg and Robin Mejia. *The Investigation and Prosecution of Sexual Violence: A Working Paper of the Sexual Violence and Accountability Project*. Berkeley, CA: University of California Press, 2011. https://www.usip.org/sites/default/files/missing-peace/seelinger-the-investigation.pdf.

Universities and Colleges Admissions Service. 'UK university scholarships for refugees and asylum seekers' (blog post). Last modified 28 June 2021. https://www.ucas.com/connect/blogs/uk-university-scholarships-refugees-and-asylum-seekers.

Chapter 12: *216 Westbound*: A Topography of Latent Fear (Shona Illingworth, John Tulloch and Caterina Albano)

Albano, Caterina. *Memory, Forgetting and the Moving Image*. Basingstoke: Palgrave Macmillan, 2016.

Hirst, William, Alexandru Cuc and Dana Wohl. 'Of sins and virtues: memory and collective identity'. In *Understanding Autobiographical Memory: Theories and Approaches*, edited by Dorthe Berntsen and David C. Rubin, 141–59. Cambridge: Cambridge University Press, 2012.

Hoskins, Andrew. '7/7 and connective memory: interactional trajectories of remembering in post-scarcity culture'. *Memory Studies* 4, no. 3 (2011): 269–80.

Illingworth, Shona. *The Watch Man Balnakiel*. London: Film and Video Umbrella, 2011.

Latour, Bruno. 'Air'. In *Sensorium: Embodied Experience, Technology, and Contemporary Art*, edited by Caroline A. Jones, 104–107. Cambridge, MA: MIT Press, 2006.

London Assembly. 'Report of the 7 July Review Committee'. Greater London Authority (report), June 2006. https://www.london.gov.uk.

Pastötter, Bernhard, and Karl-Heinz T. Bäuml. 'Retrieval inhibition in autobiographical memory'. In *The Act of Remembering: Toward an Understanding of How We Recall the Past*, edited by John H. Mace, 202–27. Oxford: Wiley-Blackwell, 2010.

Quicke, Audrey, and Ebony Bennett. 'Climate of the Nation 2020'. The Australian Institute (report), 27 October 2020. https://australiainstitute.org.au/report/climate-of-the-nation-climate-change-concern-hits-82/.

Rancière, Jacques. *The Emancipated Spectator*. Translated by Gregory Elliott. London: Verso, 2009.

Serres, Michel, and Bruno Latour. *Conversations on Science, Culture, and Time*. Translated by Roxanne Lapidus. Ann Arbor, MI: University of Michigan Press, 1995.

Slezak, Michael. 'Climate change worrying more Australians than ever before, Australia Institute report reveals'. *ABC News*, 27 October 2020. https://www.abc.net.au/news/2020-10-28/australia-institute-2020-climate-change-report-concern-growing/12764874.

Stengers, Isabelle. *Cosmopolitics I*. Translated by Robert Bononno. Minneapolis, MN: University of Minnesota Press, 2010.

Tulloch, John. *One Day in July: Experiencing 7/7*. London: Little, Brown, 2006.

Tulloch, John, and Warwick Blood. *Icons of War and Terror: Media Images in an Age of International Risk*. London: Routledge, 2012.

Chapter 13: Precarious States: Small Explosions in the Time of COVID-19 (Alexandra Halkias)

Agamben, Giorgio. *Homo Sacer: Sovereign Power and Bare Life*. Stanford, CA: Stanford University Press, 1998.

Ahmed, Sara. *Living a Feminist Life*. Durham, NC: Duke University Press, 2017.

Allen-Collinson, Jacquelyn. 'Autoethnography as the engagement of self/other, self/culture, self/politics, and self/futures'. In *Handbook of Autoethnography*, edited by Stacy Holman Jones, Tony Adams and Carolyn Ellis, 281–99. Walnut Creek, CA: Left Coast Press, 2013.

Allison, Anne. *Precarious Japan*. Durham, NC: Duke University Press, 2013.

Allison, Anne. 'Precarity: commentary from Anne Allison'. *Cultural Anthropology*, Curated Collection on Precarity (2016). https://journal.culanth.org/index.php/ca/precarity-commentary-by-anne-allison.

Butler, Judith. *Frames of War: When is Life Grievable?* London: Verso, 2009.

Butler, Judith. *Precarious Life: The Powers of Mourning and Violence*. London: Verso, 2004.

'Coronavirus: New York mass graves operations ramp up amid virus'. *BBC*, 10 April 2020.

Ellis, Carolyn. *Revision: Autoethnographic Reflections on Life and Work*. Walnut Creek, CA: Left Coast Press, 2009.

Ettman, Catherine, Salma Abdalla, Gregory Cohen, Laura Sampson, Patrick Vivier and Sandro Galea. 'Prevalence of depression symptoms in US adults before and during the Covid-19 pandemic'. *JAMA Network Open* 3, no. 9 (2020): e2019686. https://doi.org/10.1001/jamanetworkopen.2020.19686.

'From the American dream to the American nightmare'. *To Vema*, 12 April 2020.

Foucault, Michel. *The History of Sexuality Vol. 1: The Will to Knowledge*. London: Penguin, 1990.

Halkias, Alexandra. *The Empty Cradle of Democracy: Sex, Abortion and Nationalism in Modern Greece*. Durham, NC: Duke University Press, 2004.

'Mitsotakis on 25 March: our enemy now is the pandemic'. *I Efimerida*, 25 March 2020.

Mitsotakis, Kyriakos. 'Address to the nation about the SARS-CoV-2'. Hellenic Republic: Prime Minister, 11 March 2020. https://primeminister.gr/en/the-prime-minister/the-office.

Papakonstandinou, Petros. 'The week of passions in New York'. *Kathimerini*, 5 April 2020.

Povinelli, Elizabeth. *Economies of Abandonment: Social Belonging and Endurance in Late Liberalism*. Durham, NC: Duke University Press, 2011.

Povinelli, Elizabeth. 'Routes/worlds'. *e-flux Journal* 27 (2011). https://www.e-flux.com/journal/27/67991/routes-worlds/.

Safi, Michael, Angela Giuffrida and Martin Farrer. 'Coronavirus: Italy bans any movement inside country as toll nears 5500'. *The Guardian*, 23 March 2020.

Shaw, Jennifer, and Darren Byler. 'Precarity: interview with the authors'. *Cultural Anthropology*, Curated Collection on Precarity (2016). https://journal.culanth.org/index.php/ca/precarity-interview-with-the-authors.

Stewart, Kathleen. 'Precarity's forms'. *Cultural Anthropology* 27, no. 3 (2012): 518–25.

Tsing, Anna Lowenhaupt. *The Mushroom at the End of the World: On the Possibility of Life in Capitalist Ruins*. Princeton, NJ: Princeton University Press, 2015.

Wall, Sarah. 'Easier said than done: writing an autoethnography'. *International Journal of Qualitative Methods* 7, no. 1 (2008): 38–53.

Index

Entries in *italics* denote figures.

www.ingramcontent.com/pod-product-compliance
Lightning Source LLC
Chambersburg PA
CBHW070239290326
41929CB00046B/2065